THE FOG OF GETTYSBURG

Anne
Thanks for your
interest + good luck on
holding back the man cave.
Ken ___
Gettysburg 2010

D0802039

THE FOG OF GETTYSBURG

THE Myths AND Mysteries OF THE BATTLE

Ken Allers Jr.

CUMBERLAND HOUSE

AN IMPRINT OF SOURCEBOOKS, INC.

THE FOG OF GETTYSBURG: THE MYTHS AND MYSTERIES OF THE BATTLE
PUBLISHED BY CUMBERLAND HOUSE PUBLISHING, AN IMPRINT OF SOURCEBOOKS, INC.
P.O. Box 4410
Naperville, Illinois 60567-4410
www.sourcebooks.com

Copyright © 2008 by Ken Allers Jr.

All rights reserved. No part of this book may be reproduced or transmitted in any form or by any means, electronic or mechanical, including photocopying and recording, or by any information storage and retrieval system, without permission in writing from the publisher, except for brief quotations in critical reviews and articles.

Cover design by Gore Studio Inc., Nashville, Tennessee

Library of Congress Cataloging-in-Publication Data
   Allers, Ken
     The fog of Gettysburg : the myths and mysteries of the battle / Ken Allers, Jr.
       p.   cm.
     Includes bibliographical references and index.
     1. Gettysburg, Battle of, Gettysburg, Pa., 1863—Miscellanea. I. Title.
   E475.53.A43 2008
   973.7'349—dc22   2008031149

Printed in the United States of America

VP 10 9 8 7 6 5 4 3

To my father, one of the many heroes of World War II,

T/Sgt. Kenneth L. Allers

37th Squadron, 316th Troop Carrier Group, 9th Army Air Force
A man who experienced the "fog" of war

Contents

Foreword

$\mathcal{J}$ULY 3, 1863, 3:30 p.m., Col. Joseph Mayo and his men, the Third Virginia Infantry Regiment, had just reached a snake-rail fence along the Emmitsburg Road, within clear sight of their main objective, when enemy fire began to tear them apart. They had marched nearly twenty minutes over open ground to reach this point, suffering random blasts of enemy artillery most of the entire way. Their journey was nearly at its end. Only a few more paces to a low stone wall situated behind a clump of trees, where they would supposedly find a thin line of Union troops.

Rapidly Mayo's command began to fall apart, scythed down by red-hot bullets, thousands of them. Companies of comrades, so very alive only moments before, were breathing their last as stinging bullets from their right and front pierced their bodies and shattered their bones. To Mayo, "Everything was a wild kaleidoscopic whirl . . . a hissing sound, like the hooded cobra's whisper of death, a deafening explosion, a sharp pang of pain somewhere, a momentary blank, and when I got to my feet again there were splinters of bone and lumps of flesh sticking to my clothes."

So reigns the fog of war, that boundless netherworld where the deafening tempest of unknowns bewilders the senses. Witnesses are conscious only of their immediate surroundings and nothing more.

In the professional field of history, we are blessed with convenient hindsight. We can wade deeply into the mist of the aftermath when there is no danger, take our time to look around, and piece together what happened. But we who reside more than a century away from Mayo and his doomed men must also contend with the whirlwind. Any given moment in time is subject to incomplete recording. Perceptions are blurred, recollections are lost or never written down, agendas arise that alter the truth.

Of all that is lost to history, worse are the myths and legends that attach themselves to the facts. Misconceptions are painfully tenacious, and the more popular they are, the harder it is to dislodge their firm grip on the public psyche. But we historians must charge into the powder smoke of assumptions and slam against the stone walls of apocrypha.

This is the purpose of Ken Allers's *Fog of Gettysburg*: to bring his encyclopedic knowledge and diligent research of the campaign to bear. To be sure, his task is not small. Gettysburg holds considerable weight in the American mind, in part because so many myths, unending questions, and what-ifs have piled upon it. He is the right man for the job. It is an understatement to say that Allers is an authority on the battle. An associate member of the Association of Gettysburg Battlefield Guides, and my coauthor on *The History Buff's Guide to Gettysburg,* he has studied that pivotal time and place for decades. He knows those hallowed grounds well, they are like a second home to him, and he has thoroughly entrenched himself in the thicket of its records and legacy. To follow his lead into the whirlwind is a wise decision for anyone who desires to seek out the reality, to truly know the great battle that echoes still.

Thomas R. Flagel
December 2007

Prologue

$\mathscr{A}$ VETERAN OF GETTYSBURG allegedly said, "A bunch of us went to Gettysburg. Some of us didn't come back. If you weren't there, you will never understand." Despite the veracity of this statement, historians have struggled to understand what happened during those fateful days of July 1863, days that witnessed the largest and deadliest battle of the American Civil War. Gettysburg, with more than 150,000 soldiers, was the quintessential battle of the war, and this would seemingly produce a wealth of information about the battle. An incalculable number of officers and soldiers left reports, accounts, letters, or diaries of their experiences. Hundreds of civilians witnessed the battle from embattled farms and homes in the town. Thousands of people came to the battlefield immediately afterward to help the wounded or to sightsee.

Officers in both armies compiled their official reports after the battle. But there is no shortage of firsthand accounts. Not limited to official reports, officers and enlisted men forwarded information to newspapers, those in power in the government, families, loved ones, and anyone who would listen. Newspaper correspondents traveled with the army to give testimony to the events. Letters to loved ones at home described and reflected on the sights and sounds of army life, the locales of camps, and the emotion of battle. Often erroneous, it would take weeks, months, and years to resolve the confusion. One newspaper falsely reported the Confederates pushing back the Union line five miles before failing during Pickett's Charge.[1] The tremendous task of differentiating reality from fiction began during the battle and has never ended.

We are left with myriad myths, misconceptions, mysteries, and misunderstandings. These "fogs" of Gettysburg range from the subtle to the obvious, from the anecdotal to the critical actions that determined the course of the battle. Peering into these fogs, one knows there is a reality to be found rather than a mystery to preserve. Who said or saw what, when or where, and differing opinions about answers to those questions often leave us with more of the mystery. The question remains, however: there were so many at Gettysburg, how can their accounts be so divergent? Yet the more the information is scrutinized, the more problems are revealed. These problems are rife among the recounts of the battle by veterans, observers, and their interpreters.

The battlefield itself does not present an unending panorama of the battle. Soldiers could only see what was in front of them. Hills, ridges, trees, farm buildings, and crops obscured the battlefield, and the mass of men who fought here had to limit their vision to what was happening directly in front of them. Buildings in town masked not only troop movements but also obstructed the field of vision for civilians as well as soldiers. For men in uniform, powder smoke generated a dense white fog. Common are the stories of men lying down to shoot at targets that could only be seen by peering under the smoke. Noise was deafening to the point that officers shouted into the ears of subordinates or stood in front of their men to demonstrate the action needed.

To soldiers on the battlefield, the mental heat of combat can make time stand still or pass faster. Thirteen days after the battle, Union Lt. Frank Haskell wrote a thirty-thousand-word letter home that is rich with detail and descriptions. Participating in the repulse of Pickett's Charge at the Angle, his narrative falters as to time required to repulse the charge. Haskell observed, "Seconds seemed minutes, minutes seemed hours. . . . I have no knowledge and little notion of how long a time elapsed from the moment the fire of the infantry commenced, until the enemy was entirely repulsed, in this his grand assault. I judge, from the amount of fighting and the changes of position that occurred, that probably the fight was of nearly an hour's duration, but I cannot tell, and I have seen none who knew. The time seemed but a very few minutes, when the battle was over."[2] This account is one that historians love to read, but how much of the letter can we trust if we know the timing is wrong?

Perhaps no one said it better when the adjutant of the 10th Massachusetts said after the battle at the Copse of Trees, "Well, of course, you know it is very difficult to form an idea as to the time occupied in any Battle, but I should say it was not over fifteen minutes, although I have never found any two men who will agree to the exact lapse of time on an occasion like that."[3] The problem is what all veterans of combat face. Without looking at a clock or watch, time loses all sense of proportion to the events.

Warriors rarely describe adequately the sensations and overwhelming emotions or lack of emotions during a battle. My father was a combat veteran of World War II. We talked countless times about his experiences, but he could never find the words to describe the feelings he experienced under fire. A friend, a Vietnam veteran, similarly cannot describe his emotions during combat. If the raw and unrelenting power of battle can have such affect on soldiers, what effect does it have on their memories or their recall of time passing during an engagement? A memory may perfectly recall events or distort them, but others will never know with certainty on the basis of a single eyewitness account.

Understanding that combat can disorient one's senses and even fashion an event that does not fit properly with a serene moment, it follows that human frailty drives one to make sense of what does not conform to reason. The mind finds ways to fill in the holes where facts, evidence, or reasons are missing. The more an act seems unexplainable, the greater the urges of our thought processes to offer explanations. Credible assumptions are made. Is that enough to allow remembrances to be trusted? In 1916 a Union veteran wrote, "Sight and impressions are not always correct."[4] Combat can certainly skewer one's memories and impressions.

But more than just the jamming and congestion of the senses caused the fogs of Gettysburg to emerge. Author Troy Harmon reminded us of this phenomena when he referred to the writings of historian Carl Becker and wrote, "In summary, Becker implied here that the 'ephemeral event,' which literally means 'short lived,' is the event as it actually occurred, but it is fleeting and disappears soon after the event ceases. This is where the 'affirmed event' takes over which becomes the event, which everyone agrees upon."[5]

How could a Confederate soldier on the right flank of Pickett's Charge know what was happening on the left flank? A momentary glance from an advantageous position might impress upon that soldier an idea of what was happening. He saw only a fraction of the ephemeral event. What that soldier saw and conceived as the truth became, in his mind, an affirmed event.

On the other end of the Confederate line, another soldier would look at a different time and see different actions. His affirmed event could differ from the first soldier. A third soldier on the Union side would see the same ephemeral event from the opposite view, and the affirmed event for the Union soldier could conflict with the first two soldiers. We are left with three affirmed events that may or may not reflect the ephemeral event.

Students of the battle are frustrated by Union and Confederate field officers, ranking from regimental commanders on up, who submitted official reports of the battle that were either rich in detail and the consequences of actions or short to the point of being meaningless. Some accounts are filled with pointless details. The egos of officers took control, and their reports are either self-laudatory, critical of other units, or both. More disappointing, official reports are missing, including the critical report of Maj. Gen. George E. Pickett. Worse, participants from the battle seeking glory or to lay off blame would fit their memories to their benefit. For example, Union 3rd Corps commander, Maj. Gen. Daniel E. Sickles was first rate in his public relations after the event, working hard to blame others and credit himself with the Union victory.

Not all of the soldiers wrote of the battle, however. The dead could no longer speak. Those wounded in body or spirit would find it difficult to write of their traumatic experiences. Post-traumatic stress affected soldiers then as now. Painful memories were more than some veterans could overcome. If one-tenth of the participants wrote of the battle, we would have 15,000 accounts, a seeming bonanza of information. On the flip side, it means we are missing 135,000 accounts. Suddenly the bonanza seems more like a meager offering, a teasing collection of partial recall. Adding to our frustration, diaries, letters, and newspapers have been lost over time. Today, a single discovery of an unknown written description can send shock waves through the historical community.

Writing about the battle continued for decades, and the fog became thicker with the passing years and bruised egos. Agreement was not always a common object. Such was the case when John Dineen of the 33rd Massachusetts wrote to the editor of the *National Tribune* in 1909. In response to an article submitted by J. L. Dickelman of the 4th Ohio on the repulse of Harry Hays's Louisiana Brigade on East Cemetery Hill during the evening of July 2, Dineen wrote: "I think he is a little off when he said that the Louisiana Tigers broke our line on Cemetery Ridge. He also said that [Samuel S.] Carroll's Brigade charged up the hill, drove the Tigers off the hill, thru the cemetery, down and over the stone wall, they (the brigade) never stopping until they came to the stone wall when they began firing at the Tigers, as they (the Tigers) retreated thru the wheat field. . . . I want to ask the comrade where the hill was."[6]

The victors did not always agree. The losers did not always agree. The victors and the losers did not always agree. Where there was agreement, students of the battle rejoiced. Where there was no agreement, a fog of the battle falls, and we must look deeper into the mist to search out the truth. As a result, we are left with more than a few pieces of the puzzle that do not fit neatly together. Several pieces may never be found, leaving holes in the tapestry of the battle. Over time, many have conjectured about the missing pieces and drawn conclusions from related pieces; incomplete or incorrect conclusions came to be accepted as fact.

Thousands of books, articles, journals, diaries, and histories on Gettysburg have been published. But has any single book offered an unerring account of the battle? Not yet. Perhaps, as Frank Haskell wrote, "A full account of the battle *as it was* will never, can never, be made."[7] How many of the authors and writers of these thousands of Gettysburg books merely allude to or pass over the various fogs of the battle? How many have agendas that taint the answers we seek.

As a result of these fogs, can the place of the battle of Gettysburg in military history and our nation's soul be positioned in its correct hole or does it resemble a square peg looking for a round hole. Much like oil on water, we can see it, but we cannot grasp it. Historian Carol Reardon identified this dilemma when she wrote, "Pickett's Charge holds a secure place in our national imagination, but it rests on the double foundation of both history and memory. The two forces have blended together so seamlessly over the years that we cannot separate them now. . . . Over the years, Pickett's Charge has roamed restlessly through both the world of history and the world of myth. It finds an entirely comfortable place in neither realm."[8]

Reardon misses the larger implication of her statement. Substituting the word *Gettysburg* for *Pickett's Charge* creates a better conception of the battle and the subsequent study of the battle. Indeed, over the years, Gettysburg has roamed restlessly through both the world of history and the world of myth. Separating history and myth is all that we are left with when serious study of the battle is commenced.

It is this roaming between history and myth, referred to by Reardon, that generated my personal frustration with the myths and mysteries and led to this book. A number of the fogs of the battle are cleared in this book. Others may become even denser—because the evidence just does not exist. But either way, the reader will achieve an understanding of the battle as neither black nor white. Much of it is gray. The fog of battle for the soldier is as dense as the fog for the student of the battle.

The writing of a book while holding full-time employment requires the support and encouragement of many. I thank my wife, Deb, who tolerated the many hours I was in front of a computer or with my head in a book. My children, Matt and Amy, who teased me on my interest in Gettysburg yet cheered my efforts. Thomas Flagel, my coauthor on the first book, continues to be an inspiration and model to emulate. Thanks to the great people at Cumberland House for the opportunity to continue my writing. Talented songwriter and musician Bob Welch deserves thanks for the use of his lyrics to "The Ballad of Jennie Wade." The McElwains—Norm, Carolyn, and Maureen—always deserve my thanks for their support and presence at Gettysburg. The wonderful owners of the Brickhouse Inn, Tessa Bardo and Brian Duncan, have always made my stays at Gettysburg a pleasant excursion. Licensed battlefield guides Howie Frankenfield and Tim Smith have provided invaluable insight into the battle. A special thank-you to Dave Lang for the offer of information incorporated herein. Others who offered their assistance and deserve my thanks are Noel Harman, Lucille Lettow, Dick Pohorsky, Roberta Sniffin, and every member of the Civil War Round Table of Cedar Rapids, Iowa. Finally, but not least, my parents, Ken and Lorna Allers, deserve my undying appreciation for introducing me to Gettysburg.

THE FOG OF GETTYSBURG

Part 1

Storm Clouds Gather

1

Gettysburg and Slavery

ANYWAY YOU ADD UP the numbers, the total is huge: 151,000 soldiers, 2,500 townspeople, hundreds of farm residents, tens of thousands of visitors after the battle. Of this last group, people came to give aid to the wounded. Many came to find a wounded or dead family member. Others came to gawk at the debris of the battle. A few came looking to make a fast buck. Their stories are legion and varied. Choosing one over another to exemplify an aspect of the battle of Gettysburg is no easy task. And yet Mag Palm is one such person.

She has never been recognized as, nor did she claim to be, a hero of the battle. Instead, Mag Palm represents the substantial number of African Americans living in and around Gettysburg at the time of the battle. Stories of civilians during the battle rarely mention African Americans, and thus their stories surprise many visitors to the town and battlefield when they are suddenly learn of African Americans living in the area at the time of the fighting. But there was a substantial African American presence in Gettysburg; almost two hundred of the twenty-five hundred townspeople were of African heritage. More lived outside of town.

African Americans in Gettysburg and Adams County have a long history. The first slave may have been in Adams County as early as 1749, and the last registered slaveholder did so in 1841.[1] At one time, Adams County had the highest percentage of slaves in the state of Pennsylvania.[2] The names of early slaveholders in Gettysburg are recognizable. They include

the founder of the town, James Gettys, and his son, Samuel. The Reverend
Alexander Dobbin built a home here in 1776, and he was a slaveholder. His
former residence is now a popular restaurant and tavern in the town.[3]

Denied membership in the local Methodist church because of their
heritage, black churchgoers founded the St. Paul's African Methodist Epis-
copal Church in 1838 to minister to black families in the area. The church
still carries on that mission today.

Racism colored the 1867 founding of the town's Lincoln Cemetery.
Local African Americans proposed to inter here black soldiers who had died
in the war but were denied access to national cemeteries. The cemetery
grew in 1906 when many locals were reburied in this cemetery when the
former "colored cemetery" was forced to move to make way for a housing
development.

Business ownership was not a possibility for many blacks in America.
While most African American men worked on farms in the area and maintained small plots for their families, black women worked for white families, cleaning homes and washing clothes. Even though the twin specters of
racial injustice and discrimination were omnipresent, Gettysburg's black
residents were free and not owned by anyone. Yet a climate of fear over-
shadowed their lives here in the mid-1800s. Subject to the 1850 Fugitive
Slave Law and being only seven miles from the border with the slave state
of Maryland, African Americans daily risked being kidnapped, taken south,
and being sold into slavery. Mag Palm herself fought off such an attempt in
1858.[4] When the war broke out and the Confederate army coming very
close, the danger of being captured and enslaved was too real to be ignored
by the black residents of southern Pennsylvania.

By mid-1863, 8 percent of Gettysburg's population consisted of
African Americans. These 191 people have 191 stories, but they are rarely
told. Why? The answer is simple. When the Confederate army approached
in late June, most anticipated the advice of yet-to-be Western movies "to
get out of town before sundown." Thus, in late June 1863, the white population witnessed the sudden exodus of African Americans from these
precincts. One woman, known as Liz, allegedly hid in the cupola of Gettysburg's Christ Lutheran Church. She stayed there until the Confederates departed after the first occupation of the town on June 26–27.[5]

Mag Palm, her violent husband Alf, and daughter Josephine lived in a rented home to the south of town,[6] on the land of Abraham Brian (some sources spell the last name as Bryan). In addition to her work as a laundress and maid, Mag also worked as a "conductor" on the Underground Railroad, safeguarding runaway slaves as they sought freedom in the North. In this capacity, she garnered the nickname "Maggie Bluecoat" for the 1812 military coat she wore while offering aid and comfort to those who were fleeing toward a new life.[7]

Mag's landlord used his savings in 1857 to purchase fifteen acres of land with a barn and two small houses. Acquiring the small farm was a remarkable accomplishment for an African American in the nineteenth century, as landownership was not common among blacks. Abraham Brian also had experienced the worst nightmare of African Americans when a slave catcher in 1845 kidnapped his second wife. She never returned to freedom,[8] and he was left with five children to rear. He married a third time. On his farm he raised wheat, barley, and hay.

When the advance elements of Confederate cavalry under Albert Jenkins approached the Gettysburg area, Mag Palm and Abraham Brian and his family escaped with their lives and little else. Brian's property would not be so fortunate. It lay directly in the path of Pickett's Charge, which was to occur with the week.[9] When Brian returned, he found the house all but destroyed and some of his pastureland turned into a graveyard. He rebuilt his home and his farm as best he could. Brian farmed the land until 1869 and then moved to town and worked in a hotel. Years later the government allowed people to seek payment for property destroyed during the war. Brian submitted a claim for $1,028; he received $15, which is more than many people received. He died in 1875.[10]

Another African American to suffer from the war and especially the battle at Gettysburg was the longtime custodian of the college, John "Jack" Hopkins. From the beginning of his working for the college in 1847 until his death in 1868, Hopkins was a mainstay on the campus. At the time of the battle, he took his family farther north, perhaps to Yellow Hill, nine miles north of Gettysburg, near Biglersville. Yellow Hill was a prewar African American and Quaker settlement. The deep wooded areas of the vicinity offered people excellent refuge from roving Confederate soldiers.

When Hopkins returned to Gettysburg after the battle, he found his home had been ransacked but his job was waiting for him. His twenty-one-year-old son joined the 25th U.S. Colored Troops in 1864, but diseases ravaged his body, and he returned home weak and disabled.[11]

Among the stories of African Americans at Gettysburg is that of a Georgia slave who was brought to the battlefield by his master. On the first day of battle, Lt. Col. William L. McLeod of the 38th Georgia was mortally wounded during the afternoon fighting north of town. The Jacob Kime family found McLeod's manservant Moses grieving while he tried to comfort the Confederate officer until he died that evening. After he helped to bury McLeod, Moses remained with Gordon's brigade and then returned to Virginia en route to Georgia to tell the family of their loss.[12] How Moses made it to Georgia on his own is a mystery that has no answer.

After the war, Moses, now a free man, agreed to return to Gettysburg with members of the McLeod family to retrieve the remains of the twenty-one-year-old Confederate officer.[13] After William's body was brought home, his mother refused to allow him to be buried alone in the empty family cemetery. So the body remained in an oak casket in state in the home until a brother-in-law died in 1872, and the two men were buried together.[14]

The story of the Civil War often founders with the stereotypical image of plantation slaves anxiously awaiting "Uncle Abraham" and his army of white soldiers to free them. This fog needs to lift. The stories of African Americans—both free and slave—are woven deeply into the tapestry of the war.

2

George Sandoe

First or a Side Note?

"Americans love a winner," said George C. Scott in his role as George S. Patton in the epic file *Patton*. The statement is borne out by Americans' love of "firsts." Who was first to cross the Atlantic in a single-engine plane? Who was the first native-born American president? Who was the first person to reach the North Pole? The list is endless. Normally, we equate our firsts with winners and those whose accomplishments are special, particularly in sports categories. But there are firsts awarded to honorees who would rather decline the honor.

Firsts at Gettysburg were and still are subject to discussion. On the Chambersburg Road west of Gettysburg stands a monument on Herr Ridge. It marks the position of Lt. Marcellus Jones of the 8th Illinois Cavalry, who borrowed the carbine of Sgt. Levi Shaffer and fired the first shot toward the oncoming men of James J. Archer's Confederate brigade at 7:30 a.m. on July 1.[1] Histories of the battle often give credit for various firsts at Gettysburg, including the first infantry regiment to fire a shot in anger or the first battery to fire a round at the enemy.

A fog surrounds the monument marking the death of George Sandoe of Gettysburg. Who was Sandoe, and how did he come to be associated with the battle? Was his death the first of the battle, or was he a footnote to the Gettysburg campaign? Suffice it to say that, either way, Sandoe would have preferred not to have either distinction.

He was a native of Adams County and had volunteered for duty. During his stay in Harrisburg, the Confederate invasion motivated the Pennsylvania state government to form militias. Sandoe was assigned to Company B of the 21st Pennsylvania Cavalry. After moving to the Gettysburg area on June 25, this company of troopers was on the Baltimore Pike (now called Baltimore Road) near McAllister's field. The men failed to spot the approaching pickets of the 35th Virginia Cavalry Battalion. When ordered to surrender by the Confederate horsemen, the Union men spurred their horses. Sandoe's horse stumbled, and in his late bid to escape, he was shot dead after firing at the Confederates.[2] The other militiamen escaped. The Confederates were part of Jubal Early's Division prior to its occupation of the town on June 26 (see "The Second Occupation of Gettysburg").

Two monuments for Company B, 21st Pennsylvania are set in the area near where George Sandoe met his untimely death. On the Baltimore Road one and a quarter miles from the entrance to Evergreen Cemetery, the first of these is topped with a granite ball and the relief of a horse head on the front. The inscription reads:

> Near this spot on June 25th, 1863, fell
> Private George W. Sandoe
> an advance scout of a company of volunteer cavalry
> afterwards Co. B. 21st Pennsylvania Cavalry
> the first Union soldier killed at Gettysburg.

Technically correct, the monument does not claim that Sandoe was the first Union soldier killed at the battle of Gettysburg. Although many locals regard Sandoe as the first casualty of the battle, not all historians accept this as proper. Between Sandoe's death on June 25 and the battle that began on July 1, four and a half days elapsed without bloodshed in the vicinity. If Sandoe was the first casualty of the battle of Gettysburg, how does Marcellus Jones fire the first shot west of town on July 1? Would this mean the first shots of the battle occurred on June 25?

The larger question is, when did the battle begin? Historically, most regard the morning of July 1 as the start of the battle as it instituted and sustained the fierce combat for three days while the two armies attempted to outmaneuver and outfight each other. In Sandoe's case, Confederate pickets and Union advance scouts came too close to each other and a couple of shots were fired. There was no further attempt at combat after the incident on the Baltimore Pike. It is hard to tie Sandoe's death directly to the three-day battle.

If we accept Sandoe's death as part of the battle of Gettysburg or, better named, the Gettysburg campaign, then we must take notice of a death on June 22 near Greencastle, Pennsylvania. The town is directly north of Martinsburg, West Virginia, and thirty miles southwest of Gettysburg. On the day in question, the 1st New York Cavalry was shadowing Robert E. Lee's northward-moving army and looking for an opportunity to obtain intelligence. Near the Fleming and Kiessecker farms, Confederate cavalry commander Brig. Gen. Albert G. Jenkins had laid a trap for the Union horsemen. Approaching the Fleming farm, the Union commander, Capt. William H. Boyd, sensed not all was right and halted his men. But two Union troopers advanced from behind the Fleming house, and dismounted Confederate troopers fired at them. One, Sgt. Milton Cafferty, was wounded, and the other, Cpl. William Rihl, was instantly killed when he was struck in the head.[3] Rihl was buried at Greencastle near the Fleming farm, where a monument was also erected in his honor.

With Rihl, we have a Union soldier's death earlier in the campaign than Sandoe's demise. When and where does the campaign begin? Lee's journey to Gettysburg started on June 3 in Virginia. The battle of Brandy Station was fought on June 9 and is considered part of the campaign. The battle of Second Winchester was fought on June 14–15. Were the casualties of those battles considered a part of the Gettysburg campaign? To answer these questions, two things must be defined. First, we need definitions to distinguish the campaign from the battle. Second, a time period for the campaign and the battle of Gettysburg must be agreed upon. Then we can determine the first casualty of the campaign or battle. The Gettysburg campaign contained more than just one battle; it began on June 3 and ended when Lee's army recrossed the Potomac on July 14. During the interval, there were numerous battles, skirmishes, and military activities. Soldiers were wounded and died throughout this time. The battle of Gettysburg, however, occurred from July 1 to July 3 and does not include any activity on June 30 or July 4. On these three days, the two armies attempted to destroy each other.

Where does this leave George Sandoe? First, his is another tragic story in the bloody legacy of the Civil War. Loved ones were left to mourn a young life ended all too soon. It is too difficult to tie his death directly to the battle, and he certainly was not the first to die in the campaign. Perhaps Sandoe's legacy in his short military career is best stated by the monument on the Baltimore Road southeast of Gettysburg—the first Union soldier killed at Gettysburg. Sandoe was indeed the first Union soldier to be killed by Confederate fire at Gettysburg, nothing more, nothing less. It matters not whether he died during the battle or the campaign. It only matters that he died in the service of his country. His memory should not be enveloped by a fog.

3

The Second Occupation of Gettysburg

I F ANY TOWN IN America had more problems in the Civil War than Winchester, Virginia, it mysteriously failed to garner any attention. Winchester had its share of problems, with the town changing hands no less than seventy times.[1] One can only wonder if any residents, for self-preservation, kept two flags in their homes, one Union and one Confederate. Battles fought nearby include the First Winchester (1862), First Kernstown (1862), Second Winchester (1863), Third Winchester (1864), Second Kernstown (1864), and Cool Springs (1864). Despite the hardships, at least Winchester escaped the largest battle of the war.

For the people of Gettysburg, one battle was enough. Early on the morning of July 1, many of them awoke and felt anxious about the unfolding events ahead. A few brave, or foolish, townspeople ventured west, onto roofs, or to Cemetery Hill to watch the fighting to the west of the town.[2] By evening, they were merely trying to survive while their homes were being commandeered as hospitals. Food and animals were confiscated. Windows shattered and walls shook as shells burst and bullets pinged around them.

At dawn on July 1, the Union army held the town; by dusk, the Confederates occupied the same precincts. North of Middle Street, the townspeople kept a watchful eye on the Confederates patrolling their streets and buildings. South of Middle Street, the residents were wary of both Union and Confederate soldiers, as the area could be more appropriately called a no-man's-land. Trapped between the two armies, civilians risked their lives simply showing themselves outside, standing in a doorway, or looking out a window. Despite some claims made by tours in Gettysburg today, there was no clearly marked line separating the two armies. By July 4, Lee pulled his soldiers out of town to Seminary Ridge, west of town. Union forces slowly reclaimed the town. The danger was not over, since the town was within range of the Confederate guns to the west. Unlike Winchester, the occupation of Gettysburg lasted just over two days. Yet the stress and constant danger was indelibly scorched into the minds and memories of the townspeople long after the armies departed.

A study of the three-day battle, however, often misses or fails to mention this was the second occupation of Gettysburg by the Confederates. With a point on the battlefield labeled as the High Water Mark of the Confederacy, there is an impression that the Army of Northern Virginia moved no farther north than Gettysburg. But a review of the days prior to the battle quickly clears this fog.

Lee launched the Gettysburg campaign by moving his army northeast through the Shenandoah Valley, with the mountains to the east providing security and ensuring secrecy. At the head of the valley, his army spread out, advanced across Maryland and eventually threatened the prominent Pennsylvania towns of Carlisle, Harrisburg, and York. After Lee's Confederates occupied Chambersburg, they were spread out like an umbrella over Gettysburg from the west to the north and east. Union forces were farther south, thus little resistance was offered other than hastily arranged militias that could do little to obstruct the Confederate advance.

On the morning of July 26, Confederate Maj. Gen. Jubal A. Early's division broke camp at Chambersburg and moved east toward Gettysburg. After hearing of a force near the town, Early divided his division as he approached the area. One part would continue on the main road to Gettysburg and the other swung north toward Mummasburg. This maneuver would allow Early to strike the flank of any force he encountered west of Gettysburg.[3] None of this was necessary, though, as the force facing the Confederates was a recently mustered group, the 26th Pennsylvania Militia. This unit had been together only four days and had no military training.[4] When they confronted Early's combat-hardened veterans, the Union militia wisely retreated. Still, 175 of these men were captured.[5]

John B. Gordon's brigade first entered Gettysburg around 3 p.m.[6] A Confederate band assembled at the city diamond and played Southern tunes.[7] At 4 p.m., Early submitted demands to the town leaders for twelve hundred pounds of sugar, six hundred pounds of coffee, sixty barrels of flour, one thousand pounds of salt, seven thousand pounds of bacon, ten barrels of whiskey, ten barrels of onions, one thousand pairs of shoes, and five hundred hats—or five thousand dollars.[8] He probably suspected that the townspeople would not be able to gather such supplies. His men searched homes and businesses, gathering whatever they could find.[9] Afterward, Early was satisfied his men could find nothing more and allowed his soldiers to rest before marching on York the next day.[10]

The arrival of the Rebels had taken most of the citizens by surprise. A few daring souls fled the area. Telegraph operator Hugh Scott had heard rumors that the Confederates would "draft" all telegraph operators.[11] As the Confederates approached, Scott sent a warning to Hanover that the enemy had made it to Gettysburg. He then fled on his horse to York.[12] Another resident who fled was thirty-three-year-old William King. A member of the local militia, he was resting at home after having been thrown from his horse. His wife's alerts were all that he needed to mount his horse and head east on York Road, the Confederates hard on his heels.[13] Others fled to prevent their horses from being taken by the Rebels.

One of the questions plaguing historians about the genesis of the battle is, did Early's knowledge of the scarcity of supplies at Gettysburg find its way to Lt. Gen. A. P. Hill? If it did, would Hill have allowed Henry Heth's division to move toward Gettysburg on July 1 in search of supplies? As Early's division was in Richard S. Ewell's Corps, and not Hill's, it seems unlikely the information made it to Hill or his staff. Was Hill even aware of Early's short occupation of the town? It seems unlikely. The *Official Reports* are silent on the matter, and we will never know for certain.

4

Lee and Ewell

ROBERT E. LEE AND Richard S. Ewell garnered the admiration of officers and men in the ranks in the Confederate army. By the war's end, Lee came to epitomize the Southern soldier and gentleman and was perceived as a symbol of the Confederate nation. His name is one of the few recognized by most Americans. A synopsis of his career can and has occupied books, including the four-volume biography by Douglas Southall Freeman.

Ewell was the 2nd Corps commander for Lee at Gettysburg. He was forty-six at the time of the battle and had been a soldier all his life. Ewell suffered from chronic indigestion, and when he spoke, he had an odd habit of tilting his head to one side. With a bald head, bugging eyes, and a ribald vocabulary, Ewell was the opposite image of the Southern gentleman.[1] Ewell did not support secession, but when Virginia seceded, he resigned from the U.S. Army and accepted a commission in the Confederate service. By the time of the battle of First Manassas (Bull Run), he was a brigadier general. By January 1862, he had gained the rank of major general and divisional command under the legendary Thomas J. "Stonewall" Jackson. Critically wounded in the campaign of Second Manassas (Bull Run), Ewell did not return to the army until May 1863 to command one of the three corps formed by Lee after Jackson's death.[2]

The relationship between Lee and Ewell was foggy, a fact not often noticed. The relationship between the two men may have played a role in the harsh criticism Ewell received after his performance at Gettysburg. Before the battle, Ewell was already under Jackson's long shadow. When analysis began of the Confederate collapse at Gettysburg, Ewell's failure to push the attack on the first day and his late start on the second day secured his position as a timeless scapegoat of the battle. The criticisms of Ewell fail to mention his actions and results from June 3 to July 1 with good reason: prior to July 1, Ewell's performance as a corps commander was textbook. Even Lee's strongest defender, Douglas Southall Freeman, admits, "His [Ewell's] first operations as a corps commander seemed to duplicate, if not to outdo, the cherished accomplishments of the dead 'Stonewall.'"[3]

So what happened on the first day of the battle? The reasons are varied and discussed elsewhere in this book (see "The Long Shadow of Stonewall"). Overriding all discussion is the order from Lee to Ewell to capture Cemetery and Culp's hills "if practicable."[4] Were Lee's orders too vague? Ewell comes under criticism, but should an accusing finger also be aimed at Lee? To answer this question we have to momentarily move into the 1960s, when Ken Blanchard and Paul Hersey developed a model of situational leadership. In this model, leaders change their leadership style to meet the situation. Circumstances, personnel, goals, and strategies change. The leader needs to react to keep moving forward. The concept is not a new idea; it has been in use for centuries. Blanchard and Hersey placed the concept into model form in order to study it.[5] They defined the goal of situational leadership: "By adopting the right style to suit the follower's development level, work gets done, relationships are built up, and most importantly, the follower's development level will rise to D4 (the highest level), to everyone's benefit."[6]

The relationship between Robert E. Lee, Stonewall Jackson, and James Longstreet was strong and almost unspoken. Lee would merely suggest a plan and leave the details to Jackson and Longstreet. But at Gettysburg, Lee had three corps, and two of his corps commanders were new to their position. Was it acceptable for Lee to continue his previous leadership style in the face of a new situation? Ewell performed well during the advance, but Lee never met with Ewell from June 3 until July 1.[7] How did Lee view his role in guiding and leading Ewell and Hill? Lee did not approach Ewell until darkness was setting in on July 1. By that time, it was too late to launch an attack, and discussions turned to the strategy for the next day.[8] Would Lee's activities fulfill the model of situational leadership?

If Lee had strongly desired that Ewell attack on July 1 instead of July 2, should he have gone directly to Ewell? Gettysburg was Ewell's first action as a corps commander with the entire Army of Northern Virginia coming to grips with the Army of the Potomac. How could Lee be sure his order would be obeyed or even understood? This was the time for Lee to assess his role as leader and be more active until he developed the same rapport with his new corps commanders that he previously had with Jackson and Longstreet. It was time to employ the model of situational leadership. One of Lee's superb qualities was his ability to assess quickly a combat situation and to react to it. He needed to ensure that his lieutenants understood his strategies and goals.

Under the situational leadership model, the words "if practicable" should not have been used in an order to a first-time corps commander. Perhaps a face-to-face meeting with Ewell would have been a better idea. Conversely, Ewell perhaps should have sought out Lee to clarify his position for the commanding general, pointing out what he could or could not accomplish on the first day of the battle. This fog of communication was due to leadership deficiencies that plagued the Confederate army throughout its three days at Gettysburg.

5

Words Between Lee and Stuart

OPEN A DICTIONARY TO the word *controversy* and you may find a photo of Maj. Gen. Jeb Stuart, the Confederate cavalry commander of the Gettysburg campaign. After the Confederates lost the battle, blame had to fall on someone, and both James Longstreet and Stuart received their share of criticism. If Stuart had survived the war, veterans and historians would have been riveted on any words he would have written or spoken. His mortal wound in May 1864, however, forever sealed his lips, and history has never known his thoughts or reflections on the subject of Gettysburg. True, Stuart left a lengthy official report in August 1863,[1] but the report is short on details during the first days of July, the days when Lee most needed Stuart.

With only a quarter moon to light the way, three brigades of Stuart's cavalry began their historic and controversial ride at 1 a.m. on July 25.[2] Traveling for seven days without wagons, Stuart and his men were of no use to Lee since they were out of touch with the main body of Confederates and unable to force the Union army to make a mistake. Blocked by the Army of the Potomac's northward movement in pursuit of the Army of Northern Virginia, Stuart would not come under Lee's gaze until July 2, too late to be of use to the Confederate commander in the days leading up to the battle and the first two days of fighting. The debate about Stuart is not whether his absence impaired Lee's ability—it did—but should Lee or Stuart or anyone else be blamed for Stuart's absence? The question has been fertile fodder in all the debates about what happened at Gettysburg.

Stuart's absence and that of his three best and most experienced cavalry brigades were not the result of sudden intervention by the Union army or other misfortune. The idea of a ride around the Union army was a not a spur-of-the-moment decision by Stuart. Rather, Stuart limited his options when he made the decision to change course after encountering the Union 5th Corps at Haymarket.[3] There was a plan before June 25, but with this deviation the plan had gone awry.

The basis of the Stuart controversy is a series of messages sent between Lee, Stuart, and Longstreet prior to June 25. On June 22, with his army protected by the mountains, Lee sent a message to Stuart: "If you find he [the enemy] is moving northward, and that two brigades can guard the Blue Ridge and take care of your rear, you can move with the other three into Maryland and take position on General Ewell's right, place yourself in communication with him, guard his flank, keep him informed of the enemy's movements, and collect all the supplies you can for the use of the army."[4]

Lee also sent a message to Ewell regard his instructions to Stuart: "I also directed General Stuart, should the enemy have so far retired from his front as to permit of the departure of a portion of the cavalry, to march with three brigades across the Potomac, and place himself on your right and in communication with you, keep you advised of the movements of the enemy, and assist in collection supplies for the army."[5]

On the basis of these communications, Lee certainly approved the idea of Stuart's crossing the Blue Ridge Mountains and proceeding northward to Ewell. The idea of both the mountain range and Stuart screening his advance would have pleased Lee.

But a message from Longstreet to Stuart on the evening of June 22 raises questions. Longstreet mentions, "The suggestion that he [Stuart] pass by the enemy's rear if he thinks that he may get through." The note raises the specter of other correspondence between Lee and Stuart about such a maneuver. Unfortunately, no one has found these notes, and we are left in the first fog of the Stuart controversy.[6] Who first broached the subject? Was there an outright order from Lee?

A final message from Lee to Stuart came on June 25. It reveals that Lee assumed the Union army had not moved:

This 1893 drawing of three of the most beloved Confederate commanders includes Thomas J. "Stonewall" Jackson, Robert E. Lee, and Jeb Stuart, but not James Longstreet.

If General [Joseph] Hooker's army remains inactive you can leave two brigades to watch him and withdraw with the three others, but should he not appear to be moving northward, I think you had better withdraw this side of the mountain tomorrow night, cross at Shepherdstown next day, and move over to Fredericktown.

You will, however, be able to judge whether you can pass around their army without hindrance, doing them all the damage you can, and cross the river east of the mountains. In either case, after crossing the river, you must move on and feel the right of Ewell's troops, collecting information, provisions, & c.[7]

It was official and from no one less than Lee: Stuart would be the one to decide if he could pass around the Union army. For a man as determined as Stuart, such authority would be a delight. Although this second note is often quoted by Stuart supporters, there is a caveat. At the end of the message, Lee writes, "But I think the sooner you cross into Maryland, after tomorrow, the better."[8] The pace of Lee's advance was still a key element in the commander's mind.

Thus the plan was simple: Stuart would proceed east of the Bull Run

Mountains to Centreville, turn northeast and cross the Potomac River into Maryland at Dranesville, and then proceed north to meet the lead elements of the army under Ewell. Those were the general intentions, but should an opportunity arise to harass the Union army or collect supplies, then do so. But as with all military plans, events go askew as soon as a campaign begins. For Stuart, the plan came apart on the first day. Near Haymarket, the Union 5th Corps was spotted on the march northward in pursuit of Lee. A courier was sent to Lee with this information, but the rider never reached the commander, and Lee remained ignorant of the Union army's activity.[9]

With the Union army blocking his route, June 25 was a day of reckoning and inactivity for Stuart. His two options were to either wait for the men in blue to pass or to head farther south and then east. Lee's timetable for Stuart had evaporated in the first hours of the first day of the ride.[10] Stuart's decision was to head southeast and then turn north. By June 26 his horsemen were at Wolf Run Shoals, a full eighteen miles south of Dranesville, where Stuart had planned to cross the Potomac River. Turning northward, Stuart would be at Fairfax Court House, Virginia, on June 27; Rockville, Maryland, on June 28; Westminster, Maryland, on June 29; Hanover, Pennsylvania, on June 30; Carlisle, Pennsylvania, on July 1; and Gettysburg on July 2.[11]

The route of Stuart's cavalry was long and hard. Added to the weight against Lee were numerous encounters with Union cavalry. Battles at Westminster and Hanover only served to delay Stuart even more. The capture of 125 fully loaded Union supply wagons on June 28 also further delayed Stuart's returning to Lee's army.[12]

The arguments have been made, modified, and argued again. For anyone who studies the battle, it is almost impossible to stay neutral as to whether Lee or Stuart was to blame for Stuart's absence. Were Lee's orders too discretionary and vague? Did Stuart's ego block his logic? Should Lee have made better use of the three brigades of cavalry still with his army? If any question on the controversy has not been asked, it is hard to know what it might be.

Reading the considerable amount of literature on the debate, certain points have been agreed upon. First, the 125 captured wagons were a hindrance to Stuart and were of little benefit to Lee in comparison to Stuart's returning sooner to Lee. The Army of Northern Virginia could always use supplies, but not at the cost of Stuart's absence. Second, Lee missed Stuart as much if not more than Stuart's men. With Thomas J. "Stonewall" Jackson gone, James Longstreet in a mood, and two new corps commanders in A. P. Hill and Richard S. Ewell, Stuart's analysis could have been a great benefit to Lee's planning. Third, Stuart's absence cost Lee and his lieutenants valuable information that was critical to the battle. Stuart lost sight of his primary duty: to be Lee's eyes and ears.

Despite the agreement, no final answer has been made about placing blame. Erick Wittenburg and J. David Petruzzi's book *Plenty of Blame to Go Around: Jeb Stuart's Controversial Ride to Gettysburg* contains a superb chapter summarizing the various viewpoints of the historians of the battle.[13] Wittenburg and Petruzzi's analysis contains yet another point commonly overlooked. Rather than placing blame, perhaps credit should be given to someone for the delays encountered by Stuart, namely, the Union cavalry.[14] Stuart's ride was no Sunday picnic. Every time the Confederate cavalrymen had to stop and deploy for a skirmish or a battle, time was lost. Fatigue became a factor, and horses and material were lost. Wittenburg and Petruzzi are to be congratulated for the emphasis on this element of Stuart's excursion for it corrects a misstep that leads in the wrong direction. After the war, the South was consumed with placing blame. Very little effort was made to credit the victorious side for being lead well and doing what it took to produce a victory. The result was an overabundance of accusations and fault finding and insufficient recognition of creditable action by their opponents.

This fog of Stuart and Lee is as thick now as it was after the war. Despite the recent well-written additions of analysis, the fog will not dissipate. Students of the battle should be well prepared for the miasma.

6

Harrison

The Mystery Man

*M*YSTERY, AS AN ELEMENT of literature, music, art, or pop culture always attracts interest. During the golden age of radio, shows bore titles to entice the listener to the story—*The Shadow, The Man Called X, Inner Sanctum Mysteries*. In the 1960s a pop group called itself "? [Question Mark] and the Mysterians." The passage of time fails to dim interest in historical mysteries. Witness the ongoing searches for the Holy Grail, the Lost Dutchman mine, Amelia Earhart, and the gunman on the grassy knoll in Dallas. Tapping into the eternal spring of mystery virtually grants anyone the legacy of everlasting contemplation of his or her deeds by succeeding generations.

A study of the battle of Gettysburg finds no shortage of mysteries. One mystery was highlighted in the 1993 theatrical film *Gettysburg*. Simply called Harrison, the man was a scout, a spy, a member of the nineteenth-century military intelligence community. Described as "dirt stained, travel worn, and very much broken down," Harrison carefully approached the Confederate lines on the evening of June 28, and by 10 p.m. he was presented to James Longstreet's staff. Awakened to news of Harrison's arrival and critical intelligence, Longstreet promptly sent the man to Lee. Harrison, rather than Jeb Stuart, presented the news to Lee that the Army of the Potomac was on the move and closer than Lee realized. Additionally, Harrison informed Lee that Joseph Hooker was the latest to be ousted from the position of commander of the Union army. Lee learned from Harrison that Maj. Gen. George G. Meade was the fifth commander of the Army of the

Potomac.[1] Without the benefit of Stuart and half his cavalry, Lee had little choice but to accept the information from Harrison. He could not be caught in Pennsylvania with his forces spread over the countryside.

Little is known about Harrison except that he was somehow in Long-street's employ.[2] Several historians refer to Harrison as an actor by profession.[3] The movie *Gettysburg* emphasizes a connection to the theater with two scenes that tie him to alleged past roles as a Shakespearian thespian.

By 1986 the mysterious spy began to emerge from the shadows. Research by James O. Hall and Bernie Becker, a descendant of Harrison, cast new light on the mystery man, and acting was not in his résumé. His full name was Henry T. Harrison, and he was born in Nashville, Tennessee, in April 1832. With the outbreak of the war, he volunteered and served with the 12th Mississippi Infantry. By November 1861, he received a medical discharge.[4] At this point, Harrison commenced a career as a spy. His travels took him far and wide, from Mississippi to North Carolina to Pennsylvania. Harrison did not work solely for Longstreet but was employed by other Confederate commanders. Once, he was captured near New Berne, but he was released when no evidence could be found to charge him.[5]

The portrayal of Harrison as an actor can be, according to Becker, traced to John Bakeless, a historian who confused Henry Harrison with the actor James Harrison. Becker points out that Harrison was onstage once, in September 1863, as the result of a fifty-dollar bet. Henry T. Harrison led an "out of the ordinary" life during and after the Civil War. He traveled from Mexico to Montana to New York. Fame and fortune eluded him, though. He died in 1923 in Covington, Kentucky, with few if any assets. Despite his connection to the early tactics of Lee at Gettysburg, Harrison remained obscured in fog for decades after the war.

7

The Shoes, Always the Shoes

*T*HE BATTLE OF GETTYSBURG was fought because of shoes, or so the legend goes. On the evening of June 30, Confederate division commander Harry Heth asked his corps commander, Maj. Gen. A. P. Hill, "If there is no objection, I will take my division tomorrow to go to Gettysburg and get those shoes." Hill had no objection.[1] From this alleged conversation developed one of the most persistent myths of the battle—that the battle was fought over a chance meeting between Confederate soldiers looking for shoes at Gettysburg and the Union army. (See chapter 9, "What Was Heth Thinking?") This simplistic myth overlooks the numerous reasons as to why the battle was fought at Gettysburg. Historian Thomas Flagel addresses this myth with a simple answer: "Lee's campaign was not a shopping trip gone bad."[2]

The campaign was the result of discussions between Lee and the highest levels of the Confederate government.[3] Despite a string of successes by Lee, including the battles of Fredericksburg and Chancellorsville, there were still problems enough for Jefferson Davis's administration. The South was being severely pressed militarily, economically, and politically. Military supplies were at a premium and desperately needed. Northern Virginia was becoming a land barren of crops and food.[4] Looking at a map in May 1863, Confederate officials could see many threatening developments. Union forces held many points along the coasts of North Carolina and South Carolina. Charleston Harbor was blockaded. The fighting in Tennessee was at a stalemate. Port Hudson in Mississippi, not far from Vicksburg, was under siege.[5]

Foremost, however, was the problem on the Mississippi River, more than one thousand miles away. Maj. Gen. Ulysses S. Grant's army and naval auxiliary began a siege of Vicksburg on May 26. President Davis described Vicksburg as the nail that held the Confederacy together; but Union forces now threatened to capture the city and gain total control of the critical Mississippi River. No great insight was needed to see that the Confederacy could ill afford to lose close contact with the states of Arkansas, Louisiana, and Texas. Men and materiel from these states were needed badly. Coordination of military activity between the separated states would be almost impossible. Furthermore, the loss of Vicksburg would signal to Europe that the Confederacy was losing the war and further endanger sorely needed recognition by the European powers.

At a meeting in Richmond, the leaders discussed ways in which to relieve the Confederate garrison at Vicksburg. One suggestion was to send reinforcements from Lee's army. This would be no easy task, as westbound troops would have a long and difficult journey. Southern railroads were not interconnected, nor were they of the same gauge. Each railroad would have to furnish enough cars to transport substantial numbers of soldiers, artillery, and supplies to Mississippi. The route would meander through the Deep South, because Kentucky and Tennessee held too many Union soldiers to allow the reinforcements easy passage.[6] Lee, however, was not in favor of weakening his army; he saw such a move as a portent for disaster for the Confederacy. Instead, Lee made another suggestion: He would take his army into the North via Maryland and Pennsylvania. There he could threaten the cities of Harrisburg, Philadelphia, Baltimore, and Washington.[7]

He elaborated on several benefits of a campaign into southern Pennsylvania. First, the Union would have to reinforce Hooker, and this would drain troops from the Vicksburg siege, thus relieving the town's dire situation. Additionally, the nightmare of transporting thousands of men and their equipment could be avoided.[8] Second, a major victory by Lee over the Army of the Potomac in the North would have a crippling blow to Union morale and it would undermine support for war in the North.[9] Third, the war in the East had devastated northern Virginia. Crops and animals were used up. To the north lay the ripe fields and farms of the North, containing a smorgasbord for the sorely underequipped and underfed Army of Northern Virginia.[10] It would allow time for northern Virginia to recover. With the blessing of the Davis administration, then, the Gettysburg campaign began on June 4 as Lee's army snaked its way northward through the Shenandoah Valley.

The myth that the battle began over shoes is an answer hiding the real purpose of Lee's campaign. The Confederates were always looking for shoes, but they were always looking for shoes, horses, clothing, food, or anything of value to the army's well-being. True, neither Lee nor Meade planned to do battle at Gettysburg. The many roads to Gettysburg simply drew the armies to each other as they looked for an opportunity to deliver a knockout blow to the enemy. The fog of the shoes is lifted.

Part 2

July 1

Incomplete Victory

8

What Is the Pipe Creek Line?

$\mathcal{T}$HE MORE ONE READS about the battle, the more one reads of the Pipe Creek line and its role in the debates and disagreements after the battle. For critics of George G. Meade, the general's written contingency plan of early July 1 was what they needed to belittle his effort and trumpet the reputations of others. The circular did not directly affect the fighting at Gettysburg, but it lay open like a bear trap, ready to spring and mangle Meade's reputation. Its existence can and has been used to create a fog regarding Meade's intentions on those first few days of July.

Early on the morning of July 1, the circular on the Pipe Creek line was issued by Asst. Adj. Gen. Seth Williams at Meade's request. Meade was at Taneytown, just ten miles southeast of Gettysburg. If Meade was to protect Washington and Baltimore, and if the Confederates were in the Chambersburg-Gettysburg area, Union engineers had to find a defensible position from which the army could resist Lee's attacks. His staff found such a position in an area they dubbed the Pipe Creek line. Fifteen miles north of Westminster, Maryland, Pipe Creek flows southwest, past Union Mills. South of Taneytown, the line turns westward, passes Middleburg, and curves southward. On the south side of the creek are a number of hills and ridges that could provide a line of excellent defensive positions. The area was approximately twenty miles southeast of Gettysburg.[1]

Several factors should be kept in mind whenever one comes across a reference to the Pipe Creek circular. First, the information was circulated very early on July 1, prior to the initial reports of fighting at Gettysburg. Second, the circular created a quandary for 3rd Corps commander Daniel E. Sickles. He received the circular after he had received messages from Gen. John F. Reynolds urging him to move his corps to Gettysburg. This was a crucial command moment for Sickles. So much depended on where he would move his corps. Third, Meade had to protect both Washington and Baltimore, and the positions around Pipe Creek were a perfect fit for defense. Fourth, to use the line, Meade had to entice Lee into battle at Pipe Creek. Fifth, the Pipe Creek plan employed defensive tactics, the same tactics Meade employed at Gettysburg. Finally, the difference between Pipe Creek and Gettysburg was that, at Gettysburg, Meade advanced his army and engaged Lee on good defensive ground rather than simply digging into a position and waiting for an attack.[2] Historian Stephen Sears points out Meade's brief disclaimer amid the highly detailed directions on how and where the army should move: "Developments may cause the commanding general to assume the offensive from his present position." Sears also notes the Pipe Creek circular consisted of twenty paragraphs on defensive measures and one paragraph regarding the offensive opportunity.[3] Mindful of these points, those who study the battle will not lose time wading into uncharted territory that can be of little use in comprehending the battle that was fought.

The text of the circular can be found in the *Official Reports*,[4] although finding it is no easy task as it is not listed under Meade's report or correspondence, but rather under the papers of his assistant adjutant general, Seth Williams. The circular reads as follows:[5]

Headquarters Army of the Potomac, Taneytown, July 1, 1863.

From information received, the commanding general is satisfied that the object of the movement of the army in this direction has been accomplished, via, the relief of Harrisburg, and the prevention of the enemy's intended invasion of Philadelphia, &c., beyond the Susquehanna.

It is no longer his intention to assume the offensive until the enemy's movements or position should render such an operation certain of success. If the enemy assume the offensive, and attack, it is his intention, after holding them in check sufficiently long, to withdraw the trains and other impedimenta; to Withdraw the army from its present position, and form line of battle with the left resting in the neighborhood of Middleburg, and the right at Manchester, the general direction being that of Pipe Creek.

For this purpose, General [John F.] Reynolds, in command of the left, will withdraw the force at present at Gettysburg, two corps by the road to Taneytown and Westminster, and, after crossing Pipe Creek, deploy toward Middleburg. The corps at Emmitsburg will be withdrawn, via Mechanics-ville, to Middleburg, or, if a more direct route can be found leaving Taney-town to their left, to withdraw direct to Middleburg.

General [Henry W.] Slocum will assume command of the two corps at Hanover and Two Taverns, and withdraw them, via Union Mills, deploying one to the right and one to the left, after crossing Pipe Creek, connecting on the left with General Reynolds, and communicating his right to General [John] Sedgwick at Manchester, who will connect with him and form the right.

The time for falling back can only be developed by circumstances. Whenever such circumstances arise as would seem to indicate the necessity for falling back and assuming this general line indicated, notice of such movement will be at once communicated to these headquarters and to all adjoining corps commanders.

The Second Corps now at Taneytown will be held in reserve in the vicin-ity of Uniontown and Frizellburg, to be thrown to the point of strongest at-tack, should the enemy make it. In the event of these movements being necessary, the trains and impedimenta will all be sent to the rear of West-minster. Corps commanders, with their officers commanding artillery and the divisions, should make themselves thoroughly familiar with the country indicated, all the roads and positions, so that no possible confusion can ensue, and that the movement, if made, be done with good order, precision, and care, without loss or any detriment to the morale of the troops.

The commanders of corps are requested to communicate at once the na-ture of their present positions, and their ability to hold them in case of any sudden attack at any point by the enemy.

This order is communicated, that a general plan, perfectly understood by all, may be had for receiving attack, if made in strong force, upon any por-tion of our present position.

Developments may cause the commanding general to assume the offensive from his present positions.

The Artillery Reserve will, in the event of the general movement indicated, move to the rear of Frizellburg, and be placed in position, or sent to corps, as circumstances may require, under the general supervision of the chief of artillery.

The chief quartermaster will, in case of the general movement indicated, give directions for the orderly and proper position of the trains in rear of Westminster. All the trains will keep well to the right of the road in moving, and, in case of any accident requiring a halt, the team must be hauled out of the line, and not delay the movements.

The trains ordered to Union Bridge in these events will be sent to Westminster.

General headquarters will be, in case of this movement, at Frizellburg.

General Slocum as near Union Mills as the line will render best for him.

General Reynolds at or near the road from Taneytown to Frizellburg.

The chief of artillery will examine the line, and select positions for artillery. The cavalry will be held on the right and left flanks after the movement is completed. Previous to its completion, it will, as now directed, cover the front and exterior lines, well out.

The commands must be prepared for a movement, and, in the event of the enemy attacking us on the ground indicated herein, to follow up any repulse.

The chief signal officer will examine the line thoroughly, and at once, upon the commencement of this movement, extend telegraphic communication from each of the following points to general headquarters near Frizellburg, viz, Manchester, Union Mills, Middleburg, and the Taneytown road.

All true Union people should be advised to harass and annoy the enemy in every way, to send in information, and taught how to do it; giving regiments by number of colors, number of guns, generals' names, &c. All their supplies brought to us will be paid for, and not fall into the enemy's hands.

Roads and ways to move to the right or left of the general line should be studied and thoroughly understood. All movements of troops should be concealed, and our dispositions kept from the enemy. Their knowledge of these dispositions would be fatal to our success, and the greatest care must be taken to prevent such an occurrence.

By command of Major-General Meade: S. Williams, Assistant Adjutant-General.

Headquarters Army of the Potomac, July 1, 1863.

So much of the instructions contained in the circular of this date, just sent to you, as relates to the withdrawal of the corps at Emmitsburg should read as follows:

The corps at Emmitsburg should be withdrawn, via Mechanicstown, to Middleburg, or, if a more direct route can be found leaving Taneytown to the left, to withdraw direct to Middleburg. Please correct the circular accordingly.

By command of Major-General Meade: S. Williams, Assistant Adjutant-General.

9

What Was
Heth Thinking?

$\mathcal{C}$ONFEDERATE MAJ. GEN. Henry "Harry" Heth was not dull or unintelligent. Nor did he fail to understand his own weaknesses. As a commander of a seventy-four-hundred-man division in the Army of Northern Virginia he bore much responsibility and did not shirk from it. Still, after his division initiated the fighting at Gettysburg on the morning of July 1 with John Buford's cavalry and then against the Union 1st Corps, three fogs drifted into the history of the battle: confusion over the shoes, confusion over his division's alignment on the road to Gettysburg, and confusion over the continued fighting on the first day.

Heth was a career military man with connections. After graduating dead last in his class at West Point in 1847, he served in the army for fourteen years with a record that was markedly improved over his class ranking. After the outbreak of the Civil War, Heth served on Robert E. Lee's first staff. The two men formed a close friendship that was exemplified by Heth's being the only officer whom Lee addressed by his first name. Heth advanced quickly with minimal combat experience. After his first service under Lee, he left for a brief stint in western Virginia and eastern Tennessee. Returning east in March 1863, Heth rejoined Lee's command. At the May 1863 battle of Chancellorsville, he was the senior brigadier general in A. P. Hill's Light Division. During the southern army's reorganization after Stonewall Jackson's death, Heth was given command of a new division in

Hill's 3rd Corps despite an ordinary performance at Chancellorsville.[1] This was an amazing promotion for a soldier who had not seen significant combat, let alone successful combat leadership. Heth's relationship with Lee was of immense benefit.

*   *   *

Learning the true disposition of the Union army on the evening of June 28, Lee ordered his forces to assemble in the Cashtown-Gettysburg area.[2] Already in the region, Heth's division encamped a scant seven miles west of Gettysburg, near Cashtown, on June 29.[3] On the morning of June 30, Heth ordered Brig. Gen. J. Johnston Pettigrew's brigade to Gettysburg in search of supplies. As a precaution, Pettigrew was forbidden to initiate hostilities with any force from the Army of Potomac or any other force capable of combat.[4] Evidently, the local militia was to be ignored or brushed away. Near Gettysburg, however, Pettigrew encountered Union troopers from Gen. John Buford's division. Mindful of his order not to press any such contact toward combat, Pettigrew withdrew his brigade to Cashtown and reported what he had found to Heth. For unknown reasons, Heth did not believe Pettigrew. Corps commander A. P. Hill arrived, and Pettigrew repeated his report. Hill also discounted Pettigrew's perceptions of the Union military force at Gettysburg. Lt. Louis Young, an aide to Pettigrew, joined the group and corroborated Pettigrew's reading of the Union soldiers they had seen that morning. Neither Hill nor Heth was convinced that Union cavalry was in the area. In his memoirs, Heth claims that he asked Hill's permission to go to Gettysburg the next day "to get those shoes." Hill had no objection.[5] The story of the shoes was born.

The lack of concern demonstrated by Heth and Hill is remarkable. Louis Young described their reactions as a "spirit of disbelief."[6] Hill knew that Stuart was missing. Heth knew he had no cavalry to assist him in reconnaissance of Gettysburg. Both Hill and Heth agree that Heth was ordered to move toward Gettysburg on the morning of July 1.[7] After the battle Pettigrew could shed no further light on his conversation with Hill and Heth; he was fatally wounded two weeks later at Falling Waters. The story of the shoes did not emerge until 1877, for neither Heth nor Hill mention the search for shoes in their reports. Why did Heth wait fourteen years to explain his purpose for going to Gettysburg with the story on the shoes? What was Heth thinking when he wrote of the shoes? Is that what he believed, or was he covering up perceived errors in judgment? The first fog for Heth rolls in on the soles of these alleged shoes.

*   *   *

On July 1, shortly after dawn, Heth's division began its momentous march to Gettysburg. Awaiting them was Buford's cavalry division, aligned to retard a potential Confederate advance and buy time for Union reinforcements to arrive. Knowing he had no cavalry to screen his advance and knowing Pettigrew's report of Union cavalry in the area, Heth made an odd decision to allow William J. Pegram's five artillery batteries to lead the march to Gettysburg.[8] Heth never explained this arrangement, but he claimed in his official report that he was ignorant of what forces lay in front of him: "On nearing Gettysburg, it was evident that the enemy was in the vicinity of the town in some force. It may not be improper to remark that at this time—9 o'clock on the morning of July 1—I was ignorant of what force was at or near Gettysburg, and supposed it consisted of cavalry, most probably supported by a brigade or two of infantry."[9]

Fourteen years later Heth indicated that his deployment of batteries initiated the first contact of battle, and this action provided valuable information for Lee:

> On July 1st I moved my division from Cashtown in the direction of Gettysburg, reaching the heights, a mile (more or less) from the town, about 9 o'clock A.M. No opposition had been made and no enemy discovered. While the division was coming up I placed several batteries in position and shelled the woods to the right and left of the town. No reply was made. Two brigades were then deployed to the right and left of the railroad leading into Gettysburg, and, with the railroad as a point of direction, were ordered to advance and occupy Gettysburg. These brigades, on moving forward, soon struck the enemy, which proved to be [John F.] Reynolds' corps of the Federal army, and were driven back with some loss. This was the first intimation

that General Lee had that the enemy had moved from the point he supposed him to occupy, possibly thirty miles distant.[10]

In 1913, a Union veteran of the early morning fight wrote that Heth had told him that his arrangement was due to overconfidence and that he thought his division would be facing only militia.[11] Because the statement was made after Heth's death, the general had no response.

What was Heth thinking? Inconsistencies in his comments and explanations leave us in a second fog as to why he had artillery (without cavalry) lead his troops into unknown territory. Did he give no thought to the alignment of his men? Did he mismanage the march to Gettysburg? We are left with questions that have no answers.

*   *   *

The fighting on the morning of July 1 brings the historian to the last fog. Why did Heth persist in the fight when Lee had ordered that a general engagement should be avoided until the entire army had recombined?[12] Heth's commander, A. P. Hill, acknowledged such orders and confirmed to Lee that he had advised Heth not to force an engagement.[13] But Heth forced the engagement by bringing his entire division into the line of battle, and by the end of the day, two Confederate corps were engaged against two Union corps. The fighting could only be considered a battle, not a skirmish.

Although soundly defeated on the first day, the Union forces held the high ground after a general retreat. With four more corps arriving at Gettysburg, the Northerners now held the advantage. The next two days of battle brought suffering and defeat for the Confederates. Perhaps the defeat is the reason that Heth never offered a sound reason for allowing the engagement to escalate into a full battle. Did Heth understand that he had forced a battle on Lee; one Lee was not prepared for that day? Historian Edwin B. Coddington suggested that perhaps Buford and his troopers "fooled Heth into thinking that he had not fought cavalry and instead had engaged a relatively weak infantry force."[14] According to the previous quotes from Heth in 1863 and 1877, the fight with Buford did or did not happen. Whatever the reason was, Heth never explained his decision to continue the fight. His multiple conflicting explanations created the final fog for which we have no answer.

By the end of July 1, Heth's division had been severely damaged. Sadly, his men were also chosen to participate in Pickett's Charge, reducing their numbers further. On July 1, Heth himself suffered a wound on McPherson's Ridge when a spent bullet struck him in the head and knocked him unconscious. Folded paper inside the headband of his hat saved him from a more serous injury. Johnston Pettigrew took command for the last two days of the battle. Heth did not return to command until July 7.[15] The paper in his headband had saved Heth from death, but it could not save Heth from the criticism that his actions brought Lee to battle in a location and time not of Lee's choosing. The fog of Gettysburg would forever envelop him.

10

John Reynolds
So Little Time, So Many Mysteries

$\mathcal{H}$E ARRIVED IN GETTYSBURG at 8:30 a.m.; he was dead by 10:30 a.m. The time spent by forty-two-year-old Maj. Gen John F. Reynolds at Gettysburg was short—very short. Yet within a few days and into the years that followed layers of fog encircled the man and a woman known as Kate. The mysteries cover the time before, during, and after the battle.

The first murkiness came on June 2, 1863, a month before the battle. Reynolds was a West Point graduate and held the respect of all who knew him and fought with him. The Federal debacle at Chancellorsville had left doubt in the minds of many as to the competence of the commander of the army, Maj. Gen. Joseph Hooker. On May 31, almost a month after that battle and less than a month before the Gettysburg battle, Reynolds was summoned to Washington for a conference with Abraham Lincoln. Purportedly, Lincoln offered Reynolds command of the Army of the Potomac. But Reynolds stipulated that he would accept the position only if the president guaranteed that he would have no political interference in commanding the army—a condition Lincoln could not grant—and thus the proffered position was withdrawn. Reynolds returned to his command, the 1st Corps.[1]

If the story is true, Reynolds was a first-class choice to lead the Army of the Potomac: he was a soldier of the regular army but knew the ins and outs of handling volunteer soldiers. The 1st Corps consisted of all volunteers and was regarded as one of the toughest units on the field.[2] At the same time, Reynolds had liabilities: he was a Democrat, and he was not the senior officer in the army. As a prior supporter of the deposed George B. McClellan, Reynolds would not be able to curry favor from Republicans in Washington.[3] No records were kept of Reynolds's meeting with Lincoln, but it seems likely the offer was indeed made. There would be little other reason to summon Reynolds to Washington, D.C. Unfortunately, without a written record of the meeting and with the sudden death of Reynolds on July 1, we can never be certain.

So great was the esteem for Reynolds's abilities that when George Meade was given command on June 28, Meade delegated Reynolds to command of the Left Wing, which consisted of the 1st, 3rd, and 11th Corps—more than thirty-five thousand men. The appointment was not official, but it demonstrated Meade's confidence in Reynolds.

While Buford's troopers were at Gettysburg on June 30, Reynolds spent the last night of his life at the Moritz Tavern, six miles south of the town. An aide awakened him at 4 a.m. with dispatches from Meade, ordering the 1st and 11th Corps to Gettysburg and the 3rd Corps to Emmitsburg. Setting all in motion, Reynolds was aware of Buford's sighting of Confederates at Gettysburg on June 30.[4] Heading north on the Emmitsburg Road, Reynolds arrived just south of the town at 8:30 a.m.[5] Heading toward the northwest, he arrived at the west side of town and met with Buford to assess the situation.

Placement of Lysander Cutler's brigade and James A. Hall's battery were Reynolds and Buford's top priority as Confederate infantry was fast approaching the McPherson farm and ridge west of Gettysburg.[6] As Solomon Meredith's Iron Brigade arrived to exchange blows with the Rebels, Reynolds began to urge them forward. A single bullet struck him low in the back of his head as he turned in his saddle. According to his aide, Sgt. Charles Veil, Reynolds slowly sank and some men caught him and gently lowered him to the ground. He was unconscious and not in pain. Reynolds most probably died while he was being carried from McPherson's Ridge toward Seminary Ridge.[7] His body was eventually transported to his home at Lancaster, about fifty-five miles from Gettysburg.

After the battle, the site of Reynolds's mortal wounding became an uncertainty. In 1886 a monument was erected in McPherson (Herbst) Woods south of the McPherson farm. Today, visitors gather at the site to photograph the block of granite and to stand on the ground where Reynolds fell. But are they?

John F. Reynolds

In 1995 William Frassanito's *Early Photography at Gettysburg* demonstrated the confusion over the site. Various trees had been marked with signs and the capital letter *R*, all to mark the site of Reynolds's mortal wounding. Yet there is uncertainty and conflict between the various photographs. Which tree is the proper one? Where was Reynolds shot? Frassanito attempted to sort out the truth, but despite his amazing, fascinating research, he could not pinpoint the position. It could be anywhere in the area, possibly in the same region as the 151st Pennsylvania Infantry marker.[8] Visitors to the battlefield should understand that the Reynolds monument is an "area marker" and may not be the exact spot of the general's passing.

Of equal debate is the number of Confederates who claimed to have shot Reynolds. In no particular order, the following men professed to be the shooter or with a group that shot Reynolds: Sharpshooter Sgt. Ben Thorpe, 55th North Carolina; Pvt. John Hendrix, Co. F, 13th Alabama; Sharpshooter Frank Wood, 55th North Carolina (Claimed Unit); Samuel J. Duke, Co. B, 7th Tennessee (made by his major); a captain named Simpson and some soldiers of Co. F, 13th Alabama; Maj. Felix Buchanan and a group of soldiers from the 1st Tennessee; and an unknown sharpshooter in the trees directly overhead—as claimed by Reynolds's aide, Capt. Joseph G. Rosengarten. Even gunners from artillery batteries claimed to be responsible.[9] Study of these individuals' claims finds them to be unsubstantiated or impossible. For example, Frank Wood claimed to be the shooter, but an examination of the records show that he is not listed on the roster of the 55th North Carolina.[10]

It has been suggested that Reynolds was killed by "friendly fire."[11] But such an act would require Reynolds to be in front of the 2nd Wisconsin, not behind the firing line.

The likeliest scenario is that Reynolds was hit by fire from James J.

Archer's brigade as an unknown soldier fired on the Union soldiers in front of Reynolds. Disregarding the general's personal endangerment by his actions, Reynolds was simply in the wrong place at the wrong time. Perhaps a Confederate saw an officer on a horse, took aim, and fired his rifle. That soldier may have never made a claim to be the shooter because he also became a casualty during the fighting. But as with the monument marking the site, no one will ever know for sure who pulled the trigger on that fateful shot.

A romantic mystery developed after the general's death. Reynolds's body was taken from Gettysburg to his sister's home in Philadelphia. There, as the family looked through his personal effects, a tale of love emerged of a close relationship with a woman named Kate who was previously unknown to the family. This mystery was short-lived, though, when Catharine "Kate" Hewitt came to the house to view the remains of her life's love. While the family embraced her then, the relationship was short. Devastated by the general's death, Kate did not attend the funeral. She eventually joined the order of the Daughters of Charity in Emmitsburg, Maryland—about thirteen miles south of Gettysburg.[12]

Kate Hewitt and John Reynolds met during a voyage from San Francisco to Philadelphia. Love took root but never blossomed into marriage. At the time, Reynolds was commandant at West Point, and after the Civil War began, he found himself a combat officer in the field. Any exchange of vows would have to wait. Perhaps the nineteenth-century disapproval of Catholic-Protestant marriages required the secrecy and the delay.[13] Kate Hewitt died in 1902, having never married.[14] A mystery to the Reynolds family, her quiet, unassuming life after the general's death kept her a mystery to all but probing historians.

Finally, a mystery and debate

One of several trees claimed to be the site of Reynolds's mortal wounding.

erupted after the war concerning the tactics of the first day's fighting at Gettysburg. These questions arose in the natural course of the study of the battle. Had Reynolds lived, would he have maintained the Union line west of town and allowed the 11th Corps to head north of town? With perfect hindsight, historians acknowledge the Union position on the first day was risky. Would Reynolds have perceived these risks and moved the Union line back to Cemetery Hill, Cemetery Ridge, and Culp's Hill? Did Reynolds's successor as 1st Corps leader, Maj. Gen. Abner Doubleday, recognize the deficiencies of his position? Did he fear to counter Reynolds's orders more than he feared the Confederate army? These are the questions that have tantalized historians since the last wisps of powder smoke dissipated from the battlefield.

No one was on the field of battle for such a short period of time and left such a plethora of points to ponder. John F. Reynolds's legacy carries on, muddled in an abundance of fogs.

11

The World of John Burns

Have you heard the story that gossips tell
Of Burns of Gettysburg?—No? Ah, well:
Brief is the glory that hero earns,
Briefer the story of poor John Burns.
He was the fellow who won renown,—
The only man who didn't back down
When the rebels rode through his native town;
But held his own in the fight next day,
When all his townsfolk ran away.
            —*John Burns of Gettysburg*
            Francis Bret Harte

A TRIBUTE IN VERSE is a grand and glorious means to pay homage to a war hero. Seventy-year-old John Burns of Gettysburg found himself in such a position after news spread of his actions on the first day of the battle at Gettysburg. His status as a hero was further enlarged when he was mentioned and given credit in Maj. Gen. Abner Doubleday's official report.[1] Finally, John Burns's claim to be a hero was cemented into place in 1903 with a monument on the McPherson farm. Even without the poem and the monument, the mere thought of a seventy-year-old grabbing an antique musket and placing himself in harm's way would still inspire all who hear the story. Sadly, a closer examination of Burns's life finds a story of a solemn person with problems. Hailed as a hero after the battle, Burns did not necessarily receive the accolades or respect of the citizens of Gettysburg either before or after the battle.

Around noon on July 1 he rushed to the Union line at McPherson's farm and volunteered his services. Burns appeared for duty dressed in his best suit; historian Harry Pfanz described his appearance as "though Rip Van Winkle had come down from South Mountain."[2] To the first officer he encountered, Burns reported that he was a noncombat veteran of the War of 1812.[3] Not able to turn down any offer of assistance, Col. Langhorne Wister of the 150th Pennsylvania Infantry directed him toward McPherson's Woods for protection from the sun and some cover from the bullets.[4] At the woods, Lt. Col. John B. Callis of the 7th Wisconsin doubted that Burns would add anything to his regiment and possibly pose a detriment. One version of the story gives a hint into Burns's personality; he allegedly told Callis, "There are three hundred cowards back in that town who ought to come out of their cellars and fight, and I will show you that there is one man in Gettysburg who is not afraid."[5] As the tale is told, Burns demonstrated his ability by firing on and hitting a mounted Confederate officer.

Burns fought with the 7th Wisconsin for a time. Later, after the Union battle lines were adjusted, he was with the 24th Michigan.[6] As the remnants

of the Iron Brigade began a slow and orderly retreat under fire to the grounds of the Lutheran Seminary, Burns became a casualty with three wounds. After receiving treatment from the assistant surgeon of the 24th Michigan, Burns lay on the ground with wounds in an arm, a leg, and his chest.[7] When Confederates later occupied this area, an officer questioned Burns; the elderly

Civilian John Burns joined the fighting on July 1 and was wounded for his efforts.

man convinced his captors he was an innocent casualty, wounded while seeking help for his wife.[8]

In the days after the battle, visitors to the battlefield eagerly sought out Burns. His home at the western end of Chambersburg Street was easy to find. The house still stands today, although its features are modified from its wartime days. When photographers came to town, Burns boldly charged five dollars to pose for them. In November, when Abraham Lincoln arrived for the dedication of the national cemetery, the president expressed an interest in meeting the "hero of the battle." Together, Lincoln and Burns attended a church service after the cemetery dedication ceremony.

Despite his popularity, there were several skeletons in John Burns's closet. A longtime resident of the area, Burns was known for his strong personality. Biographer Timothy Smith noted about Burns: "Humble, modest, and unassuming he was not." Rev. Leonard Marsden Gardner described Burns as "stern, gruff, and decided in his manners, he was a man who was strong in his prejudices and equally so in devotion to any cause or person whom he liked."[9] Such a personality is prone to have many controversies in life.

Taking advantage of his serious and humorless demeanor, Burns was the subject of innumerable practical jokes prior to the war.[10] He was an easy target. As the town constable for four and a half years, Burns was involved in the disputes of the town, including some of his own choosing.[11] Despite this public service, Burns was not likely regarded as a leading citizen of the town before the battle.

His strong personality emerged after the battle, when he encouraged the perception that he was the only civilian hero of the battle.[12] To the contrary, two other townsmen joined in the fighting. James Watson approached the 9th New York Cavalry and asked to fight. The New Yorkers took him up on his offer and outfitted him with a carbine and a saber. The other resident's story began on June 30, near Emmitsburg, when fifteen-year-old J. W. Wheatley asked to join the 12th Massachusetts Infantry as the unit moved toward Gettysburg. The Bay Staters allowed him to do so, expecting him to tire of military life in a few hours. Instead he was drawn into combat on July 1 and wounded twice, in the left hand and in the left thigh, when a bullet struck and shattered his rifle. The last the regiment saw of Wheatley, he was in a field hospital crying for his mother and family.[13]

A statue of Burns was erected in 1903 on
Stone Avenue on McPherson Ridge.

Another townsperson to achieve
fame was Jennie Wade (see chapter
30, "One More Needless Death").
Following her place in history as the
only civilian killed during the battle,
she too obtained the honor of being
the subject of a poem. This did not
meet with John Burns's approval, and
he did much to discredit her status as
a heroine of the battle. Biographer
Timothy Smith described Burns's
motivation as a "hatred" of Wade. In a letter that chided an author's attempt
to write of Jennie Wade, Burns wrote, "Charity to her reputation forbids
any further remarks. . . . I called her a she-rebel."[14] In her account of the
story of Jennie Wade, Cindy Small examines Burns's attitude toward Wade.
She could find no reason for his disdain.

Was John Burns a veteran of the War of 1812? In the years after the
battle, numerous claims of his prior combat experience were woven into
the accounts of his story. Timothy Smith examined the evidence and concluded that he possibly served for a short time, but not in combat.[15]

Burns freely took advantage of his status to the detriment of the other
townspeople, creating much ill feeling in the community. Some citizens
and battlefield guides flatly denied Burns's involvement in the combat of
July 1. Burns had not been popular before the war, and he did nothing to
improve his relationships with his neighbors after the battle.

The story of John Burns and Gettysburg is intriguing and can be easily
overlooked by the short version of his efforts in combat. Despite being a
hero of the battle, his life before and after were those of a seemingly different man. Timothy Smith's *John Burns: The Hero of Gettysburg* disperses any
fog encircling the oldest Gettysburg combatant.

12

The Long Shadow of Stonewall Jackson

*T*HE WEATHER WAS WARM. Four thousand civilians, soldiers, and government officials had gathered in Lexington, Virginia, to say their final farewell to thirty-nine-year-old Thomas Jonathan Jackson. Tears flowed freely from battled-hardened veterans. Equally great was the oratory over the loss of one of the South's most illustrious commanders. Mortally wounded at the battle of Chancellorsville by friendly fire on May 2, 1863, he died eight days later of pneumonia. After lying in state in Richmond, his body was taken to his hometown for burial on Friday, May 15. The huge funeral procession left the Presbyterian church and traveled to the cemetery for a short graveside service. The procession included the VMI cadet battalion, four pieces of artillery, a company from the Stonewall Brigade, convalescing veterans, a squadron of cavalry, and the governor of Virginia.[1]

The shadow of Stonewall Jackson would never again see the earth as a casket bearing the simple inscription "Lieutenant General T.J. Jackson. Born January 21st 1824; died May 10th 1863" was lowered into the ground next to the graves of his first wife, Ellie, a stillborn son, and a daughter.[2] The immense shock of Jackson's loss was felt immediately throughout the Confederacy. Typical of the deep feelings for Jackson was the reaction of former VMI cadet Abram Fulkerson: "The intelligence of the death of Gen. Jackson came upon us like a shock. We feel that his death is a national calamity. The poorest soldiers among us appreciated his worth—loved the man, and mourn his loss."[3]

For the Confederate leadership the loss was more than just mourning. How would the army cope? Who would take Jackson's place? Robert E. Lee lamented: "I know not how to replace him. God's will be done. I trust He will raise up someone in his place."[4] Maj. Jedediah Hotchkiss, a member of Stonewall's staff, summed up the fears for the future in a letter to his wife: "He is gone and sleeps in the Valley he loved so much. We miss him all the time & a void is made here which time can hardly fill."[5] For the Confederacy, the time would come in less than two months at a crossroads in Pennsylvania.

After relying on Jackson and James Longstreet as his two corps commanders, and without an ideal candidate to replace Jackson, Lee fundamentally reshaped his army by making three corps out of two corps. They would be smaller units commanded by Longstreet (1st Corps), Lt. Gen. Richard S. Ewell (2nd Corps), and Lt. General A. P. Hill (3rd Corps), with Ewell and Hill being new to corps command. At Chancellorsville, Lee had the luxury of having two experienced corps commanders. The approaching campaign would find two-thirds of his men under new commanders. More foreboding was the lower command structure in Ewell's 2nd Corps. Of the seventeen brigade commanders, only three were in place six months prior to the battle of Gettysburg. In Hill's 3rd Corps, five of the thirteen brigadiers were new.[6] This inexperience among his corps and brigade commanders was a pressing question for Lee. Despite the uncertainties surrounding his army, the Gettysburg campaign began on June 3.

Jackson was gone, but his legend hovered over Ewell and Hill during this invasion of the North. Both men would be judged by Stonewall's standards.

The campaign and movement into Pennsylvania went well in the opening days, and both men performed well. Victorious after the first day's fighting at Gettysburg, Ewell had flanked the Union 11th Corps and chased the defeated Federal troops through the town toward Cemetery Hill. Jackson's shadow receded slightly, but that began to change as the sun set on the first day at Gettysburg. Ewell chose not to pursue the defeated Union soldiers, and this inactivity firmly cemented Stonewall's shadow over Ewell at Gettysburg.

The crux of the dispute over Ewell's inaction is based on Lee's verbal order to Ewell as reported by aide Col. Walter M. Taylor. He recounted that the army commander had said "that it was only necessary to press 'those people' in order to secure possession of the heights, and that, if possible, he wished him to do this."[7] The "heights" Taylor referred to was East Cemetery Hill, where Union soldiers were attempting to rally. The hill dominated the town and the surrounding area to the north and northwest. Lee knew the high ground was key to any defense the Union could construct against Confederate attacks. In contrast to Taylor's recall, Lee, in his official report,

Richard S. Ewell

wrote that he ordered Ewell to take the heights "if practicable, but to avoid a general engagement until the arrival of the other divisions of the army, which were ordered to hasten forward."[8] But was it "practicable"? The debate over this phrase has raged without pause since the question was first asked as to how the battle of Gettysburg was lost.

When Ewell entered Gettysburg late in the afternoon of July 1, he found two of his three division commanders—Robert E. Rodes and Jubal A. Early—in agreement to continue the attack.[9] To the dismay of the Confederates, however, each passing minute brought more dour news for continuing the attack. The information caused Rodes to change his mind; he felt further attacks would be of no benefit.[10] Of Ewell's three divisions, Edward Johnson's was not yet at Gettysburg. Early was missing two of his four brigades (William Smith's and John B. Gordon's). Both had been sent east of Gettysburg along the York Road to guard the flank. Jeb Stuart's absent cavalry continued to plague the Confederate command as to information about any threats on the flanks. A third brigade, Harry T. Hays's, was snarled in the town, pursuing Union stragglers. With his brigades in Gettysburg and only one available to maintain the pursuit, Rodes no longer favored continuing the attack.[11]

Two other factors plagued Ewell. First, the town itself was an obstacle to his moving forward. The buildings and streets earlier had hampered the Union retreat and now worked against the Confederates.[12] Second, his staff reported that there were few favorable artillery positions.[13] As the information was digested, Rodes and Early's enthusiasm diminished for further attacks. Ewell also decided that he could not press the attack under these circumstances.

Would Jackson have acted otherwise? Would he perform like the aggressive commander of the Shenandoah Valley and Chancellorsville or like the less impressive leader of the Seven Days' battles? Would Stuart's absence have made Stonewall more conservative or, despite the obstacles cataloged by Ewell, would he have spied an opportunity that had to be grabbed? Would the battle even be fought at Gettysburg if Jackson had been in the advance? Such questions, of course, have no answers. We are left with only conjecture. In reality, Ewell did not attack, and forever after he has been a scapegoat for the Gettysburg loss. Stonewall's shadow would cast an eternal shadow on Richard S. Ewell.

This is a discouraging postscript to what many deemed the first successful step toward a Confederate victory. Instead, Ewell wrote its epitaph—and for his reputation and career as well—when he reported, "Day was now breaking, and it is too late for any change of place." Ewell's corps would stay where it was, and the Confederates would have to fight futilely for the hills in their front.[14]

13

Getting Slocum to Move

$\mathcal{O}$N A PAR WITH the question of what Jackson might have done at Gettysburg is the question of what might have happened had Union Maj. Gen. Henry W. Slocum's 12th Corps arrived on the scene earlier than it did. In the late morning on July 1, his corps was less than five miles from Gettysburg, but these men did not arrive on the battlefield until the late afternoon, after the Union line had broken. What might his 10,700 men have accomplished on the first day of the battle if they had joined their comrades before the line was broken?

At age thirty-six, Slocum was the highest-ranking Union general on the field at Gettysburg, even senior to Meade, the army commander. His rise in rank and responsibilities during the war had been dazzling. In command of a regiment at the battle of First Bull Run in July 1861, he was promoted to command of the 12th Corps in October 1862.[1] A West Pointer with great ability, Slocum achieved success through his handling of troops and not by political connections.

As the Army of the Potomac felt its way northward in late June 1863, the 12th Corps approached Gettysburg from the southeast via the Baltimore Pike. This position represented the right flank of the Union army on the night of June 30. During the first day of the battle, Slocum moved his corps seven miles from Littlestown to Two Taverns. Arriving there by 11:00 a.m., his ten thousand troops were less than five miles from Gettysburg.[2]

Henry W. Slocum

But the 12th Corps did not reach Gettysburg until after the fighting on the first day of the battle had ended. Why?

Their march to Gettysburg was not severe. Most regimental commanders mention marches of two to four miles from Two Taverns to Gettysburg before being deployed. The lack of any comments about a difficult or taxing advance is a continuous theme throughout the reports of the regimental commanders of the 12th Corps.[3] Thoughts of overwhelming needs to rest their troops could not have been a reason for the lateness of their arrival.

As to Slocum's activity or inactivity, two debates have developed. First, did Slocum fail to understand the signs of battle? Upon reaching Two Taverns, he should have been aware of the sound of artillery fire coming from Gettysburg. Both Lt. Col. Charles Morse of the 2nd Massachusetts and Col. William Packer of the 5th Connecticut noted the sounds of fighting in their official reports.[4] E. R. Brown of the 27th Indiana never understood why the corps was not rushed toward the sound of battle.[5] Slocum sent no one forward to investigate the situation until a civilian told him of the conflict at Gettysburg. After the death of John F. Reynolds on the morning of July 1, the burden of command passed to Maj. Gen. Oliver O. Howard of the 11th Corps. He sent two messages to Slocum—at 1:00 p.m. and 3:00 p.m. Slocum did not advance his corps until he received the second message.[6] No explanation was offered as to why Slocum was not more aggressive in determining what was happening in front of him.

The second debate over Slocum's inaction follows the conflicting orders addressed to the 12th Corps. Key to this controversy is the Pipe Creek circular. George Meade's command staff had reconnoitered a defensive line along Pipe Creek, which was near Slocum's position. This contingency plan would be at the center of its own controversy after the battle (see chapter 8, "What Is the Pipe Creek Line?"). Yet Slocum knew he was on the right flank of the army and had to protect against any movement toward his position.[7] In addition, Slocum knew that Reynolds was to his west and in charge of three of the Union's six infantry corps. Did he assume the three corps were adequate to handle the situation or was he simply waiting for Meade's orders?

We are left to ponder what would have happened had the 12th Corps moved to Gettysburg by noon or 1:00 p.m. Slocum submitted his official report in August and made no comment concerning the time required for his corps to reach Gettysburg.[8] In December 1863 he sent an additional report to Meade to correct what Slocum believed were errors and injustices to divisions and brigades of his corps. In neither of the two reports does he comment on his movement to Gettysburg on the first day of the battle.[9]

When he learned of Reynolds's death on July 1, Meade sent 2nd Corps commander Maj. Gen. Winfield Scott Hancock to take control of the Gettysburg front. Upon his arrival on the scene, Slocum explained to one of Hancock's staff that his reluctant approach to Gettysburg was caused by his encountering refugees from the 11th Corps. Fearing that Gettysburg had become another Chancellorsville, he was cautious to avoid a rout.[10]

Initially, disapproval of Slocum's actions was confined within the army after the battle.[11] Public discussion began in 1875 with the publication of Samuel P. Bates's *The Battle of Gettysburg*.[12] David Martin's *Gettysburg—July 1* finds three reasons for the lack of controversy after the battle. First, since the Union won the battle, no one needed to be blamed. Second, Slocum did not violate orders. If anything, he misinterpreted the intensity of the battle. Third, Slocum had a strong reputation as a combat leader and no political enemies.[13] Had Gettysburg been a disaster for the Union army, Slocum's lack of action would have been an issue demanding correction.

Could the 12th Corps have saved the Union line on the first day? If the army had not held Cemetery Hill or Culp's Hill, would the 12th Corps have been in position to threaten the left flank of the Confederate army? Slocum could have been the hero of the battle or the scapegoat. In the face of speculation, we are left in a fog that will never clear.

14

In a Pigsty

$\mathscr{T}$HE MAY 1863 BATTLE of Chancellorsville left the Union 11th Corps with a tarnished reputation. Let down by its commanding officers, Maj. Gen. Oliver O. Howard and his subordinates, the corps' unsupported right wing bore the brunt of Stonewall Jackson's textbook flank attack. Additionally, most of the ninety-eight hundred men in the corps were German immigrants, thereafter derided as "Flying Dutchmen" and "Howard's Cowards" by soldiers in the other corps. Most of the officers were also immigrants: Wladimir Krzyzanowski, Alexander Schimmelfennig, Leopold von Gilsa, and Adolph Wilhelm August Friedrich von Steinwehr. So deep was the distrust of the foreign-born soldiers that negative perceptions were held by most non-German soldiers in the corps.[1] After being assigned to command a division in the 11th Corps after the Chancellorsville debacle, Brig. Gen. Francis C. Barlow was not sure of the combat worthiness of his men.[2] So he drilled them endlessly, and they considered him a "petty tyrant."[3]

The 11th Corps was the smallest of the six Union corps to fight at Gettysburg, but it was the second corps to reach Gettysburg on July 1. Despite the weeks of taunting and the lack of respect, the soldiers of the 11th Corps were eager to prove themselves. Unfortunately, they never had the opportunity to do that. Their field commanders again faltered under fire, most notably Barlow, who failed to anchor the corps' right flank and left it open to a flank attack. By moving his division without orders or sufficient

Alexander Schimmelfennig

men to cover the ground, he subjected the corps to attack from the Harrisburg Road to the north. Jubal Early's division approached the battlefield via that road, and the Confederates struck Barlow here with devastating effects.

As they had done at Chancellorsville, the 11th Corps was forced to retreat. They fell back to the south, through the town, toward the only area with reinforcements: Cemetery Hill. The reputation of the corps never recovered from this final hammering. Few officers' reputations were spared, but none was more damaged than Brig. Gen. Alexander Schimmelfennig. Besides placing his brigade in an untenable position, one of its units, the 157th New York, was almost destroyed when it made a charge against the enemy. By late afternoon, while the regiments were heading south toward Cemetery Hill, many men became lost and trapped in unfamiliar streets, alleys, and backyards. With Confederates closing in on all sides, choices for the retiring Union soldiers were limited, and seeds for a myth were sown. After the battle, a story was told of Schimmelfennig's taking refuge in a pigsty during the pull back—and he stayed there for three days.

While his brigade was withdrawing, Schimmelfennig wound up in an alley and found no avenue of escape. When his horse was shot out from underneath him, he jumped over a fence at Anna Garlach's home and headed to Baltimore Street. That option closed for him when he found the street occupied by Confederates. Fortunately for the harried general, the Garlach home had a small drainage ditch covered by wooden planks. Schimmelfennig crawled into this culvert to avoid capture. After dark, he moved to an area between a stack of firewood and a swill barrel. Making himself a shelter with the wood, he avoided being seen by Confederates.[4]

That evening, he surprised Anna Garlach in that position while she was going to the stables to feed the animals. On July 2, she provided bread and water for the fugitive general, but fear of detection by Confederates overtook her, and she did not go out to check on Schimmelfennig again until

July 4. By that time, the Confederates had moved out of the town, and Schimmelfennig had left his refuge for a joyous reunion with his men.[5]

Through the years, the story submerged into a fog that alleged Schimmelfennig had hidden in a pigsty. Conjuring up images of lying in a wet pen strewn with manure, the indignity of the story seemed to follow Schimmelfennig just as the 11th Corps was never able to shake its reputation of the flying Dutchmen. Just as the corps was allowed opportunities to better its standing in the army, the unfortunate general deserves better too. True, a swill barrel made up part of this cover, but he was not found to be lying with the hogs or in their filth. The whole affair could be considered a miracle that he was not discovered by Confederates looking for fuel from woodpiles or fences while they occupied the town.

Nevertheless, the words *Schimmelfennig* and *pigsty* have been closely aligned since the battle. The humor of the story overshadows his actions. The fog of Schimmelfennig's refuge from capture has been cleared and should not prevent an examination of his actions on July 1.

Part 3

July 2

A Sea of Blood

15

Someone Blundered

IN HIS WARTIME MEMOIRS, James Longstreet wrote of the defeat at Gettysburg: "Weird spirits keep midnight watch about the great boulders, while unknown comrades stalk in ghostly ranks through the blank fastness of Devil's Den, wailing the lament, 'Some one blundered at Gettysburg! Woe is me, whose duty was to die.'"[1]

Did someone blunder at Gettysburg? Who? Attempts to place responsibility on a person or event are a common reaction for any losing side in a war. A victorious nation is more forgiving of its political and military leaders. Had the Confederacy won its independence, Gettysburg might have been regarded as but three bad days for the army, a low point in the war the army overcame to go on to achieve brilliant victory. As it was, their war was lost, and the Confederacy reacted no differently than any losing side.[2] Recriminations and blame as to what went wrong and who failed to do something reverberated across the South.

One explanation came with the emergence of the "Lost Cause," which gravitated to a few central themes. First and foremost was the inculpability of Robert E. Lee. If Lee was not responsible, then someone else or some other act must shoulder the blame. Two essential components of the Lost Cause are the misfortunes of war and accusation. In this case, the misfortune was the loss of Jackson in May 1863, and the accusation was made against James Longstreet for a failure to perform well at Gettysburg.[3]

James Longstreet

Critical to understanding the criticism of Longstreet is the death of Lee in 1870; the first accusations against Longstreet came in 1872, when Jubal Early accused him of not acting quickly on July 2 and for not overseeing Pickett's Charge on July 3. A year later, the former artillery chief of the Army of Northern Virginia, William Pendleton, concurred with Early's allegations and added that Longstreet had failed to execute Lee's order for a "sunrise attack" on the morning of July 2.[4] This nebulous and imaginative sunrise attack order provided an uncomplicated explanation for the failure at Gettysburg. It not only provided a scapegoat for Lee but also exonerated others who had failed at Gettysburg—including Early and Pendleton. Over the years a number of historians have debunked this myth.[5] Yet in the nineteenth century, the sunrise attack order was a problematic charge Longstreet was forced to face.

When Lee came to Gettysburg, he needed Longstreet as much as he needed Jeb Stuart. Jackson was gone. A. P. Hill and Richard S. Ewell were in their first campaign as corps commanders. And the army was in hostile territory.

Longstreet on the second and third days of the battle has been described as sullen and argumentative; two uncommon characteristics for him in previous campaigns. What explanation could be found for the attitude of Lee's "Old War Horse"? Could depression over the loss of his children affect his mood? The Longstreets had six children and had already lost two when, in January 1862, the four surviving children came down with scarlet fever. In short order, three died.[6] Twenty-first-century medicine and current understandings of depression allow for treatment long after such a traumatic event, but there was no such perspective or treatment in the nineteenth century. Had something just prior to the campaign triggered Longstreet's depression in ways that affected his mood during the battle of Gettysburg? Whatever the reason, the fact that he behaved differently than he had in any other campaign was more than

enough evidence for his enemies to blame
him for the loss at Gettysburg.

Longstreet's actions and statements during the battle did much to contribute to his
scapegoat-ness in the eyes of many Southerners. Although Longstreet's corps did not
participate in the first day's battle, he was on
the scene ahead of his corps and was with Lee
when the two studied the positions to which
the Union army was falling back at the end of
the first day. At around 5:00 p.m. on July 1,
Longstreet made his first attempt to sway Lee

Robert E. Lee

into swinging around the Union army. If the Confederates occupied a defensive position, the Union army would be forced to destroy itself against
the dug-in Confederates. This had been, after all, Longstreet's understanding of the type of campaign the army would be waging in Pennsylvania.[7] Re-
buffed by Lee, Longstreet did not press the issue further that evening. Still,
he was in a dour mood throughout the evening.[8]

Shortly after dawn on July 2, at an informal gathering, Longstreet again
pressed his argument to Lee in front of Generals A. P. Hill, Henry Heth,
and John Bell Hood. Again Lee rejected his argument. Hill failed to en-
dorse Longstreet's position and, rather, approved Lee's plan of attack as long
as it did not occur too late in the day.[9] The rejection of Longstreet's proposed plan did little to improve his mood for the day. After Lee's aide,
Capt. Samuel R. Johnston, had returned from an early morning reconnaissance, Longstreet's attitude continued to sour, and he remained contrary to
the others. He would not let Lafayette McLaws leave his division for a reconnaissance, and he was corrected by Lee on the position of McLaws's
troops for the pending attack.[10] When he finally resumed a more support-
ive attitude, Longstreet ordered his artillery chief to prepare for the attack.[11]
Yet Longstreet's aide described the general's manners for the rest of the
morning as "apparent apathy" and "lacked the fire and point of his usual
bearing on the battlefield."[12]

Around 9:00 a.m., Lee rode to his left flank to visit with Ewell. Critics
claim that upon Lee's return, he inquired as to the status of Longstreet and

was dismayed that the 1st Corps had not yet attacked. This seems implausible, as Lee would not have ordered the attack until after his visit with Ewell.[13] Again, however, Longstreet provided more ammunition to his critics when he failed to expedite the movement of his corps in Lee's absence.[14]

It was almost 1:00 p.m. before Longstreet's corps began to move to the assigned position for the attack. Any thoughts Lee had of an attack as early as possible on July 2 were fading. To further complicate matters, the route of the lead division—McLaws's—came to a ridge in full view of the Union lines. Unable to cross the ridge, fearing he would lose the element of surprise, McLaws halted his division. Hood made matters worse by running into the back of McLaws's division, creating a military traffic jam. When Longstreet arrived, everyone's sense of humor was long gone. A countermarch was necessary, and McLaws insisted that he should lead it. Although Hood and Longstreet thought it would be more expeditious if Hood made the first move, McLaws would not be dissuaded. Longstreet lost a golden opportunity to reassert his authority when he allowed McLaws to have his way.[15] The sad part of the event was the refusal of McLaws, Hood, and Longstreet to accept the advice of Col. E. Porter Alexander, the corps' artillery chief. Alexander had found a way across the field after encountering the same ridge earlier. No one has ever explained why Alexander's advice was rejected.[16]

Longstreet's troubling attitude showed once more before the day was over. His corps (minus Pickett's division) had reached the jumping-off point, and Hood's division was to launch the attack. At this critical moment, Hood protested his route and urged Longstreet to modify the plan and sweep around the Round Tops to attack the Union line. But Longstreet would have none of it, clearly using Lee orders as an inflexible command that was to be followed. Twice Hood objected and twice Longstreet turned him down.[17] Longstreet's behavior improved remarkably as the attack proceeded. He stayed in contact with his subordinates and helped time the attacks of various brigades in the en echelon attack.

On the morning of July 3 Longstreet surveyed the damage to his corps. Two divisions—Hood's and McLaws's—had been badly used up in some of the toughest fighting in the war. Pickett's division arrived, adding six thousand men to the fight. The morning also found Longstreet again at odds with Lee over the plan for the day. Early on July 3 the Union launched an attack on the Confederate left flank, leaving those troops unable to support what was to come in the afternoon. As Lee's plan for Pickett's Charge emerged, Longstreet appeared to have little faith in it.

Three particulars support this lack of enthusiasm. First, as the person in charge, Longstreet never made arrangements for support.[18] Would a second wave of troops provide the necessary manpower to make the charge a success? Brig. Gen. Ambrose Wright's brigade made it to the crest of Cemetery Ridge on July 2. In conversing with Alexander before the afternoon cannonade on July 3, Wright said to the young artillery chief: "Well, Alexander, it's mostly a question of supports. It is not as hard to get there as it looks. I was there yesterday with my brigade. The real difficulty is to stay there after you get there—for the whole infernal Yankee army is up there in a bunch."[19] As it turned out, the men in Pickett's Charge made it to the crest, but they could not stay there. Belated efforts by Longstreet made no difference in the outcome.

Second, Longstreet attempted to shift responsibility for the timing of the charge to Porter Alexander. He was to advise Longstreet when the Union guns had pulled back so that the infantry could be sent forward. Such action by Longstreet is unfathomable; Alexander was not an infantry commander and never had been.[20] There was simply too much at stake. Two days of fierce combat had not produced a victory. The Confederates were in enemy country. Far from home, their supplies and ammunition continued to dwindle. Much of the artillery was involved in the cannonade, but the gunners had a limited amount of precious ammunition. The only fresh infantry division was to be used. There were no reserves to plug into the line. All had to go as planned—and go well. Yet Longstreet deemed it appropriate to let an artillerist decide when the foot soldiers should advance. If Longstreet had been next to Alexander, watching and discussing the effects of the cannonade, little criticism could be leveled at Longstreet, for that would have been a proper place for a commanding general to be.

Third, a painful and often overlooked moment demonstrates Longstreet's frame of mind—or better, his emotional state. When Alexander thought the Union guns were gone, he sent two notes for the infantry to advance.[21] When asked if the attack should proceed, Longstreet merely nodded his head.[22] Clearly, he thought the attack would be futile. His emotions were in control of his actions. When he foresaw the dismal results of the effort, despair seemed to overwhelm him. One cannot fault Longstreet for such feelings. But as the commander of the charge, Longstreet had a duty to control his emotions or turn them into action to better prepare for the charge. For this, Longstreet has no defense.

Two factors temper any criticism of Longstreet. First, once he unleashed his two divisions on the afternoon of July 2, the troops fought as hard and as well as any seen in the war. Second, peering through the glasses of perfect hindsight, it is clear that Longstreet's objections to Lee's plans on July 2 and 3 were valid. Defensive forces had major advantages over attacking forces. But the student of the battle is left in a fog as to whether switching to defensive tactics at Gettysburg would have been successful for the Confederates. And there is no way of knowing whether a fourth Confederate division on July 3 would have made the difference in the outcome of Pickett's Charge.

Longstreet did no favors for himself after the war when he accepted a Federal position in New Orleans and endorsed Republican politics and policies. These only added to the attacks on his behavior at Gettysburg. His embracing Republican politics in 1867 did much to drive away his friends and business associates. In June 1867, the *New Orleans Times* published a letter from Longstreet that resulted in death threats against him and accusations of his being a traitor to the South. The final act that cemented Southern disdain for him was his acceptance in 1869 of the position of surveyor of customs for the port of New Orleans. The appointment came from a former nemesis of the Confederacy, President Ulysses S. Grant. Former Confederates never forgave Longstreet for this act.[23]

In the 1890s Longstreet turned to his memoirs. If the controversy swirling around him had cooled slightly, his writings refueled the fire. Longstreet criticized Lee in print, going so far as to call Lee's official report "disingenuous" when Lee discussed the third day at Gettysburg.[24] In his memoirs, Longstreet returned to the theme that the Union army could not be dislodged from its position and his proposed flanking movement should have been implemented.[25]

How close was the Confederacy to victory on the second and third days of the battle? Longstreet's actions and words combine in a fog so dense, while we desperately try to peer through it and discover an answer to the question of what happened at Gettysburg, in the end we are left with only opinion and conjecture.

16

Sickles

Hero or Goat?

THE WORD *COLORFUL* IS inadequate to describe the life and personality of Maj. Gen. Daniel E. Sickles, commander of the Union 3rd Corps. Sickles summed up his life best when he wrote, "I have said to you that I do not deem it a wise course, nor recommend it to any friend; but I have adopted it; it is mine, and I will follow it come what may."[1] Born in 1819, Sickles came to be associated with Tammany Hall politics by 1843. When he married at age thirty-two, his bride was only sixteen. With his law degree, he kept several positions prior to the Civil War, including state assembly-man, corporation counsel, secretary to the minister of Great Britain, militia officer, state senator, and congressman (Democrat). Living beyond his means and guilty of many personal indiscretions, he became a notorious public figure in 1859 when he gunned down Philip Barton Key, son of Francis Scott Key, in the neighborhood of the White House. Sickles had uncovered a love affair between Key and his wife, Teresa. At his murder trial, he claimed to have killed Key while in a fit of rage that caused him "temporary insanity," a first for the legal world. He was acquitted. If he had further ambitions for higher office, they ended when he publicly for-gave his wife—a taboo according to nineteenth-century American double standards. The Sickles returned to New York in relative obscurity, and he reopened his law practice.[2]

When the war broke out, Sickles led an effort to raise, not just a regi-ment, but an entire brigade. It became known as the Excelsior Brigade and

Daniel E. Sickles

consisted of the 70th, 71st, 72nd, 73rd, and 74th New York. Perhaps out of patriotism, perhaps out of a desire for high command, Sickles found motivation and was soon in command of the brigade. By November 1862, Sickles was a major general and a corps commander.[3] As he approached Gettysburg on July 1, the politician-general was at the head of thirteen thousand men—the 3rd Corps.

Sickles's corps was camped less than twenty miles from Gettysburg, between Taneytown and Emmitsburg, Maryland, on the morning of July 1. That day the general received a succession of conflicting orders. Army commander Maj. Gen. George Gordon Meade, per the Pipe Creek circular, directed him to guard the army's left flank in the Emmitsburg area.[4] (See chapter 8, "What Is the Pipe Creek Line?") At variance with those orders, Sickles received messages from 1st Corps commander John F. Reynolds to bring his corps forward. Reynolds's first communication was received prior to the Pipe Creek circular. After Reynolds's death, 11th Corps commander Oliver O. Howard contacted Sickles, urging him to advance toward Gettysburg. Shortly after 3:00 p.m., Sickles set his corps in motion, destination Gettysburg.[5] It was a good decision. Had the battle continued after the 3rd Corps arrived on July 1, the additional Union troops would have been of immeasurable support as well as a morale booster for the men of the 1st and 3rd Corps.[6] As night fell, the 3rd Corps scrambled to find a position on the southern end of Cemetery Ridge.

On the morning of July 2, Sickles was uneasy with the placement of his men in the Union line. Despite scattered skirmishing, no attacks had been made by either side. The inactivity allowed him to examine the ground occupied by his corps. The southern end of Cemetery Ridge dips lower than the surrounding area. To the west, he could see the higher ground of the Peach Orchard—a setting that reminded him of the scene of Chancellorsville, when Confederate artillery exploited the higher ground to shell his position. To seek permission to move his corps, Sickles journeyed to

Meade's headquarters. In response, Meade asked his chief of artillery, Henry J. Hunt, to look into the matter, particularly with regard to the placement of his artillery.[7] Hunt was the best artillerist in the Union army, and his opinion would be valuable.

While Hunt and Sickles rode to the intersection of the Emmitsburg Road and the Wheatfield Road, Sickles presented his idea of moving his corps forward to occupy the high ground to his front.[8] Hunt appreciated the merit of the higher ground, but he also saw problems with advancing the 3rd Corps to occupy it. Such a movement would break the line, disconnecting the 3rd Corps from the 2nd Corps on its right; the 3rd Corps alone did not have sufficient men to cover the bulge in the line that would result from the advance. Nevertheless, Sickles requested permission to move forward, but Hunt would not grant it. Instead, Hunt returned to Meade to discuss the position.[9]

Sickles remained unsatisfied, and another piece of the puzzle fell into place when he sent Maj. Henry E. Tremain to Meade's headquarters with three messages. First, his last two brigades had arrived. Second, Hiram Berdan's sharpshooters had returned from a reconnaissance after running into Confederate troops. Third, did the commanding general have orders for how the Emmitsburg Road should be used by the Union supply wagons?[10] When Tremain returned to Sickles, the 3rd Corps commander was not satisfied with Meade's replies. Sickles took matters into his own hands and, acting on his own initiative, he ordered his corps forward to the Peach Orchard.

While the corps was moving up, Sickles received three messages from Meade that called for a meeting of the corps commanders. Despite his desire to oversee placement of his men, he could not ignore the army commander's requests. Sickles left his troops for the meeting at Meade's headquarters. Meanwhile, Meade learned that all was not well with his left flank—the sector occupied by the 3rd Corps. He rode toward the 3rd Corps position to see for himself what was going on and encountered Sickles on the road. Grasping what was happening, Meade lost his temper but realized that he had to act to support Sickles; he told Sickles to stay put and he would send more men.[11]

Time, however, had run out for Sickles. The methodical, unending en echelon attack planned by the Confederates had reached the point of execution. The Confederate army attacked Sickles's advanced corps before Union reinforcements could arrive. First came two divisions of Longstreet's 1st Corps, then a division from A. P. Hill's 3rd Corps struck Sickles's line before the 3rd Corps could dig in to its new position. By the time it was over, Sickles's corps had been mauled and pushed back, disorganized, a remnant of the force that had marched to Gettysburg. Meade acted as quickly as he could, throwing the 5th Corps and parts of the 2nd, 6th, and 12th Corps into the killing ground that carried such simple names as the Peach Orchard, the Wheatfield, the Trostle farm, the Rose Woods, the Stony Hill, the Devil's Den, the Triangular Field, Little Round Top, and Bloody Run. Eleven Confederate brigades waged a deadly dance with twenty-two Union brigades. When it was over, three hours later, fifteen thousand casualties were strewn on the countryside.[12]

The mystery of Sickles's action does not lie in whether he had the authority or orders to move his corps. He didn't. Had Sickles almost lost the

Sickles returned to Congress after the war and was instrumental in the establishment of the Gettysburg National Military Park. He frequently revisited the battlefield and is pictured below in a wheelchair at the fiftieth anniversary of the battle.

battle of Gettysburg, only to be saved by reinforcements and the hard fighting of Union soldiers? Or had his corps acted as a breakwater, absorbing the blows of the Confederate army and blunting the enemy's attack? The Confederates almost prevailed. At one time, only the 1st Minnesota stood in the way of Cadmus M. Wilcox's Alabama brigade and Cemetery Ridge. Farther north, on the ridge, Ambrose Wright's Georgians made it to the crest, just south of the soon-to-be-famous Copse of Trees, only to be forced back. Did these units fail because too much energy and men had been expended trying to get there, or would they have not even come that close had Sickles maintained his original position on Cemetery Ridge?

As with most what-ifs of Gettysburg, there is no answer. The Confederate attack did not follow Lee's plan. It started to unravel as soon as it began. If Sickles had not moved his corps, there is every possibility that Lee's plan would have come undone on its own.

What we do know is that controversy blew up after the battle. Two sides aligned with two opposing views: Sickles saved the Union army on July 2 or Sickles's actions almost destroyed the army. Matters quickly came to a head in early 1864 during the hearings on Gettysburg before the Committee on the Conduct of the War, where Sickles worked to claim credit, at the expense of Meade, for the Union victory in Pennsylvania. There was no shortage of opinions, and the arguments endure to the present. The fog of the debate will exist until the last book about Gettysburg is written.

17

Mahone and Anderson

$\mathcal{T}$HE FRENCH PHRASE *en echelon* is parsed as "by rung" or "by step" or "by grade." The term is widely used in geology and the military. When applied to military tactics, en echelon is difficult to employ, because it requires co-ordination and communication. Such an attack requires the close attention and participation of the commanders as to when to launch the next "step." The purpose of the tactic is to force the enemy to strip his defenses from the center or opposite flank, thus weakening those areas. When an en echelon attack hits the weakened areas, a breakthrough results. At least, that is the theory.

On July 2, Lee decided to employ the tactic to destroy the Union army. Starting on the Confederate right flank, Lee planned to launch one brigade at a time, slowly moving the attack toward the center of the line—an en echelon attack.[1] Upon hearing the sound of battle coming from Long-street's corps, Richard S. Ewell would attack the Union right flank at Culp's and Cemetery hills.[2]

This attack did not begin until the late afternoon of July 2, but it pro-gressed nonetheless. As with most combat plans, the plan immediately started to come undone when the first Confederate brigades altered their courses to meet the threats coming from the Union positions—notably the advanced front presented by Daniel E. Sickles's 3rd Corps. When the lines of blue and gray met, new names entered the lexicon of the American Civil War: Little Round Top, the Wheatfield, the Rose farm, the Peach Orchard,

Bloody Run, and Devil's Den. The second action—or lack of action—to break down came on the Confederate left when Ewell did not move forward as instructed. Four long and bloody hours passed before the Confederate 2nd Corps moved forward to attack Culp's and Cemetery hills.

Still the en echelon attack was working, and Meade was forced to shift his troops to defend his left flank. The 5th Corps was sent to aid the heavily pressed 3rd Corps. From the center of the Union line, elements of the 2nd Corps headed south and into the burgeoning conflict. From the Union right flank, a division from the 12th Corps abandoned the Culp's Hill area to reinforce the left flank. Finally, units from the 6th Corps were reassigned to shore up the final positions from Cemetery Ridge to Little Round Top and beyond.

After James Longstreet's two divisions were fully engaged, the attack progressed with divisions from A. P. Hill's corps. Success seemed to be at hand when a brigade of Georgians under Brig. Gen. Ambrose Ransom "Rans" Wright advanced across the open fields to the crest of Cemetery Hill. But Wright had no support; units on his left and right had not advanced alongside him and thus could not reinforce the gain. Wright did not realize the attack had broken down, that the brigades to his left were not moving forward. This breakdown occurred in Richard Anderson's division, namely William Mahone's brigade. The reasons for this failure have been in a fog since the battle.

Anderson's star was on the rise. He was one of a select few to be considered for corps command. From the battles of the Peninsula campaign in 1862 to Chancellorsville two months before Gettysburg, he had shown the necessary qualities for a combat leader. Modest and unselfish, Anderson's affable personality allowed him to avoid conflict with those who had much larger egos.[3] Gettysburg, though, was not his finest hour. His division arrived late on July 1, but it was not ordered into combat immediately. On July 2, his division took up a position on Seminary Ridge. His right flank would connect with the left of Longstreet's corps. The division was to be deployed from right to left as follows: a brigade of Alabama regiments under Cadmus M. Wilcox, Perry's Florida Brigade under Col. David Lang (brigade commander Edward Aylesworth Perry was suffering with typhoid when the battle commenced), the Georgia Brigade of Ambrose R. Wright,

Carnot Posey's brigade of Mississippians, and finally, William Mahone's brigade.[4] The en echelon attack was to follow that order.

One by one, the brigades went forward across the fields to attack the Union line on the Emmitsburg Road. Heavy fighting marked the progress of all the brigades. Despite being pushed back, the Union line severely punished the approaching Confederates. After crossing the Emmitsburg Road, the attack slowed. William Barksdale's Mississippi Brigade had been on Wilcox's right. Barksdale's effort and success can only be described as magnificent. Battering and wrecking Union brigades, the Mississippians' clout seemed to power the Confederate attack forward. As the brigade approached the Plum Run depression, new resistance arose. Fatigue and combat losses finally caught up with the brigade, and the Mississippians came first to a standstill and then fell back.[5] Wilcox's Alabamians ran into their own problems when confronted with the unexpected charge of the 1st Minnesota. Similarly, Perry's Florida Brigade was having problems with the 19th Maine and 42nd New York. Help was needed to push the Federals back.[6]

Even with the brigades to his right stalled, Wright's Georgians pushed forward with sheer determination and fought their way to the top of Cemetery Ridge, the farthest advance of the day for the Confederate plan. Looking to his left, Wright saw Posey's Mississippians stalled at the Emmitsburg Road. With the Union resistance stiffening, requests for help were sent back by Posey, Wilcox, and Wright. Mahone's brigade was next in line, but Mahone never responded—his brigade never moved an inch. The en echelon attack fell apart. No more Confederate units advanced.

Why did Mahone not move forward? Mahone never explained.[7] His official report is brief and makes no mention of receiving any orders or requests to join the fight on July 2. Mahone admitted to being posted in support of William J. Pegram's batteries; his brigade only engaged in skirmishing with the enemy on July 2 and 3.[8] The net result was that Mahone's brigade had the lowest casualty rate of any Confederate infantry brigade at Gettysburg: 102 out of 1,542 men.[9] Many Confederates wondered why.

Anderson's report created a bigger mystery. He confirmed his brigades had gone into action "in the manner directed." After praising his men for their effort, Anderson acknowledged the units "were compelled to retire.

They fell back in the same succession in which they had advanced—
Wilcox's, Perry's, Wright's, and Posey's."[10] No mention is made of Mahone;
Anderson gives no indication of the role Mahone was to play in the attack.
His report indicated the brigades attacked en echelon, but he gave no rea-
son for the breakdown. If Mahone had been held in reserve, why would
Anderson not confirm this? Like Mahone, Anderson never addressed this
issue in his official report or after the war.

Also lacking in Anderson's report is any explanation of why he did
nothing to support Wright. Such support was critical, as Wright pointed
out to Porter Alexander the next afternoon, when he said, "The real difficulty is to stay there after you get there."[11]

The breakdown of the attack left two tragic consequences. First, Lee
wrote in his official report, "Wright gained the crest of the ridge itself, driving the enemy down the opposite side." Lee also admitted that Wright was
separated from any possible supporting regiments and "compelled to
retire."[12] Did this temporary breaching of the Union line inspire Lee to for-
mulate Pickett's Charge the next day? The army commander also wrote,
"The result of this day's operations induced the belief that, with proper concert of action, and with the increased support that the positions gained on
the right would enable the artillery to render the assaulting columns, we
should ultimately succeed, and it was accordingly determined to continue
the attack."[13] Perhaps Lee should have met with Wright after the fighting on
July 2.

The second unfortunate consequence was the mortal wounding of
Maj. Gen. Dorsey Pender. His division was to the left of Anderson's. When
the attack broke down, Dorsey rode toward Anderson's division to find out
why. As he headed south along the line, he was wounded in the leg by an
artillery shell; he later died on July 18.[14] His loss deprived the Confederacy
of a first-rate officer—a loss Lee could ill afford.

With the breakdown playing a major role in the fighting on July 2, the
failure of Mahone and Anderson attracts much interest. Regrettably, their si-
lence has left the breakdown of the July 2 attack in a fog that cannot be
cleared.

18

What's in a Name?

*W*HEN VISITING THE ANTIETAM battlefield, one is struck by the lack of geographical features other than the area of the Burnside Bridge. Very little effort is required to imagine the same scenery and landscape in middle America. The geography of Gettysburg, on the other hand, is as varied as the men who fought there. To the west the ridges traverse the landscape from north to south, like great waves of an ocean heading toward the town. Two of the ridges—Seminary and McPherson's—fuse northwest of the town at Oak Hill. This rise dominates the view to the south, east, and west. Since the time of the battle, the ridges have taken on legendary names: Seminary, the Ripple, McPherson's, Herr, Knoxlyn.

Lying north of the town is a great flat area known as the Gettysburg Plain. Dominated by Oak Hill to the west, it is a poor defensive position but ideal for maneuvering. The town lies on the southern edge of this plain but gradually rises in elevation as it becomes part of Cemetery Hill. To the east of Cemetery Hill stands the equally prominent tree-covered Culp's Hill. Running south, Cemetery Ridge slowly fades into lower ground as it approaches the two substantial prominences now known as the Little Round Top and Big Round Top.

These geographical features gave rise to names that live on in history and clearly identify areas of the battlefield. Some reflect—such as the Slaughter Pen or the Valley of Death—the fighting that occurred here. Oth-

The boulder-strewn slope of Little Round Top often has been confused with Stony Hill, a prominence one thousand yards west of Little Round Top.

ers describe physical features: the Peach Orchard, the Wheatfield, the Railroad Cut. Some sites have names with cloudy histories, such as Devil's Den.

While battlefield visitors can employ these now-familiar landmarks as well as signs and maps to identify places where they are, the soldiers who fought here had no such aids. Their after-action reports thus create their own fog. After the armies left the area, many of those who wrote about the battle did not return to Gettysburg until after the war. They used the landmarks they could remember to describe their actions and positions.

A prime example of this is Joseph B. Kershaw's report. He makes several references to a "rocky mountain, a "stony hill," a "stone wall," and a "stone house" in his report—which he submitted on October 1, 1863.[1] We now know that he was referring to Little Round Top, Stony Hill, and a stone wall and house on the John Rose farm. Later, in 1876, Kershaw referred to Stony Hill as a "rocky knoll," but by then he had learned that the stone house belonged to Rose.[2] In the years after the battle, Little Round Top came into prominence, but not Stony Hill. Without visiting the battlefield and knowing only of Little Round Top, the confusion of the two hills generates another fog of battle.

Little Round Top is a thousand yards east of Stony Hill. They are separated by Devil's Den–Houck's Ridge, the Wheatfield woods, and the Wheatfield. The Peach Orchard lies five hundred yards to the northwest. Both hills have woods, and both slopes are dotted with large stones and boulders. Adding to the confusion, from the Confederates' perspective, there were trees behind both hills. The major difference between the two is elevation. Stony Hill is more than a hundred feet lower than Little Round Top. Adding to the mistaken identity, in the years after the war, Stony Hill was overgrown with trees that obscured the sight of rocks and boulders from the south, as Kershaw would have remembered the landscape. In recent years, the National Park Service's program to restore wood lines to the historic timeframe of the battle has resulted in the removal of the nonhistoric trees on Stony Hill, allowing an unobstructed view of Kershaw's "stony hill."

With fourteen brigades of infantry from both armies fighting in and around the Wheatfield next to Stony Hill, students of the battles frequently have a difficult time deciphering movements per the firsthand accounts of the participants. The unintentional confusion of Little Round Top and Stony Hill often stymie everyone.

19

The Savior of Little Round Top

IN 1993 THE MOVIE *Gettysburg* was released. The Ted Turner production was based on Michael Shaara's Pulitzer Prize–winning *Killer Angels*. The plot, however, focuses on only two parts of the battle: Col. Joshua Lawrence Chamberlain's 20th Maine on July 2 at Little Round Top and Pickett's Charge on July 3. In the months after the release of the movie, a new mythology of Gettysburg began to emerge: Chamberlain and the men from Maine won the battle on the slopes of Little Round Top. Chamberlain's actions were indeed critical to the preservation of the Union position on Little Round Top and the left flank of the Army of the Potomac. But was the action "the" critical factor at Gettysburg?

Little Round Top is a rocky hill rising 150 feet above the valley to the west and 100 feet above the valley separating it from Big Round Top. At the time of the battle, the larger hill was covered with trees, but the western slope of Little Round Top was barren. Boulders dotted the western face, making the hill a strong defensive position.

Earlier on July 2, the hill was to be the left flank of Maj. Gen Daniel E. Sickles's 3rd Corps as it stretched south along Cemetery Ridge. But Sickles's unauthorized westward advance to the Peach Orchard salient left Little Round Top uncovered and Sickles embroiled in controversy. (See chapter 16, "Sickles: Hero or Goat?") On the Confederate side, Lee never deemed the hill as worthy of capture and focused instead on Cemetery

Strong Vincent

Hill. Envisioning an attack from the Emmitsburg Road, with the troops perpendicular to the road, Little Round Top only came into play when Longstreet's assault on the afternoon of July 2 veered to the east, placing the hill in harm's way.

Lee's plan of attack was based on intelligence from an early morning reconnaissance. But the Southern troops encountered a very different situation in the late afternoon. Rather than being empty, the Emmitsburg Road, the Peach Orchard, the Wheatfield, and Devil's Den were all in the possession of Sickles's 3rd Corps. As men from Evander M. Law's Alabama Brigade and Jerome B. Robertson's Texas Brigade stepped out to the attack, both brigades headed farther east then contemplated, toward Devil's Den and the Round Tops. Lee's plan was undone in the opening phase of the attack when his infantry had to made adjustments to meet the new position of the Union line. Law's and Robertson's brigades were under the command of an experienced and qualified combat leader, John Bell Hood. Any chance that the brigades might change course in the face of this new development on the battlefield was lost when Hood was wounded and taken from the field.

After Sickles's move to the salient, Little Round Top would have been barren except for the perceptive eyes and quick action of Maj. Gen. Gouverneur K. Warren, chief of engineers for the Army of the Potomac. While surveying the battlefield from the crest of Little Round Top, Warren spotted movement in the distance from the waiting Confederate assault columns. He and his staff immediately began to search for units to fortify the hill. Harvard-educated twenty-six-year-old Col. Strong Vincent was among the first to respond. Vincent rushed his 5th Corps brigade up the mountain and into a line of battle. Despite being in command of the brigade for only five weeks, he demonstrated the many traits of a successful field commander.[1] Disregarding earlier orders, Vincent's men barely arrived prior to the initial attacks on Little Round Top. Vincent placed Chamberlain's 20th Maine in position on the left flank—the very end of the Union line.[2]

Next to respond to Warren's call for troops was twenty-eight-year-old Brig. Gen. Stephen H. Weed, who commanded another 5th Corps brigade. Weed was a graduate of the West Point class of 1854.[3] When the right flank of Vincent's brigade began to falter under Confederate pressure, Weed's lead regiment—the 140th New York, commanded by Col. Patrick O'Rorke—crested the hill and crashed into the Confederates pushing hard on the right flank of the 16th Michigan. O'Rorke was killed in the action,

Stephen H. Weed

but his unit repulsed the Confederates and preserved Vincent's right flank.[4] The three trailing regiments of the brigade filled in the right side of the forming battle line. Little Round Top was quickly transformed into a Union bastion with eight regiments from two brigades fighting to hold the hill at all costs.[5]

Lt. Charles Hazlett's battery from the 5th Corps artillery brigade executed a miraculous climb up the steep eastern side, through trees and over rocks. Horses and gunners strained at every step to pull the guns to the crest of the hill. Men from the infantry (including Gouverneur Warren) pitched in to move the thirty-eight hundred pounds of gun and caisson to the top of the critical hill.[6] Once there, the deep-throated roar of these 10-pounder Parrotts added to a deadly rain of iron on any Confederates attempting to reinforce the advance on Little Round Top.

Hazlett's Battery D, 5th U.S. Artillery had a long and storied history back to the Revolutionary War that included the assault at Trenton.[7] But the unit paid a high price for this latest chapter in its history: the death of Hazlett.

The Confederates exerted maximum effort, but they could not dislodge the Federals from Little Round Top. Complicating matters further, the weather was very warm. Uphill fighting is arduous and difficult at best, thus fatigue became an issue for both sides. In addition, the terrain broke up the initial advance, so the Confederates were not fighting as unified brigades. The Texans intermixed with the Alabamians. The 4th and 5th

Joshua Lawrence Chamberlain

Texas found themselves alongside the Alabama Brigade without their proven commander; Jerome Robertson was with the 1st Texas and 3rd Arkansas and directing the fighting in Devil's Den. Command in the Alabama Brigade became disjointed when brigade commander Evander Law was compelled to assume command of the division after Hood was wounded.

The 15th and 47th Alabama facing Chamberlain's 20th Maine on the southeastern flank of Little Round Top had to go up and over Big Round Top. They were short of water and fighting off sharpshooters every inch of the way. Both Law's and Robertson's brigades assaulted the hill one way or another. The fight was far more than the struggle between the 15th and 47th Alabama and the 20th Maine. But this is not to diminish or trivialize Chamberlain's actions.

At the time of the battle, Chamberlain was thirty-four years old. A native of Maine, his family was no stranger to combat. His ancestors had fought in the Revolutionary War and the War of 1812. By vocation, Chamberlain was a professor of rhetoric and languages. He took advantage of a two-year sabbatical to enlist in the Union army. Bowdoin College leaders were greatly dismayed by this, but they failed to convince the governor to refuse Chamberlain's enlistment.[8] Although he had no military training, he was commissioned the lieutenant colonel of the 20th Maine in August 1862. Intelligent and resourceful, he quickly learned the art of war. Before the battle of Gettysburg, his wartime service gave no indication of the great things ahead. Held in reserve at Antietam in September 1862, later the 20th Maine suffered dearly during the many charges against the stone wall at Marye's Heights in Fredericksburg. Succeeding to regimental command just prior to the battle of Chancellorsville, there was little for Chamberlain to do when his unit was held in reserve because of illness.[9]

Chamberlain possessed the "right stuff," being able to act and react despite his own fears in battle. Despite the smoke of the battle that swirled around Little Round Top on the afternoon of July 2, Chamberlain responded and countered the moves made by the two Alabama regiments intent on sweeping his command from the field. With the battle coming to a climax, both sides exhausted and no decisive moment that either could claim, Chamberlain was confronted with dwindling numbers and very little remaining ammunition when he made the only aggressive choice he could. He had many reasons to pull back or await a final Confederate onslaught. Instead, he chose to attack, and his place in history was assured. He ordered his men to fix bayonets and to charge downhill and into the Confederate ranks.

The Alabama and Texas troops below were equally if not more exhausted than Chamberlain's men. The heat, dwindling numbers, and the cold steel of the Maine men's bayonets convinced many to withdraw and others to surrender their weapons. The right side of the Union line held, breaking the Confederate attack.

The cost of the repulse was high, with more than 980 killed and wounded on both sides. The grim reaper's list included Union commanders Vincent, Weed, O'Rorke, and Hazlett.[10] In the end, the stand of the Union army on Little Round Top cannot be credited to any one individual or unit. As is the case in most battles, a series of events and actions by many individuals evoked the final outcome of the conflict. Contrary to popular opinion, Chamberlain alone did not win the battle of Gettysburg or even the fight for Little Round Top. To elevate him to such a lofty height, belies the efforts and sufferings of so many others. Yet Chamberlain receives many laurels for this victory—because he was one of the few field officers to survive the fighting. It would be wise to appreciate his actions on the battlefield without placing him above all others. With that perspective, the fog of Gettysburg recedes a little so that we can see the others who sacrificed so much for their country, so we can appreciate their efforts and know their names.

20

The Broken 11th Corps

$\mathcal{F}$OR THE MEN OF the Union 11th Corps, hope filled their breast during the end of June 1863. As the corps moved toward Gettysburg, the soldiers realized this could be their last chance, a last opportunity for redemption, a last opportunity to savor the sweet taste of victory, and a last opportunity to clear their name. The 11th Corps had been formed in September 1862 and was assigned to the Army of the Potomac. Having missed the battle of Fredericksburg in December, the men were able to reap the misery of Ambrose E. Burnside's "Mud March."[1] Unknown to the soldiers, the worst was to come in the next two battles in which they would fight.

In May 1863, near the Wilderness church in northern Virginia, two miles west of the crossroads known as Chancellorsville, the 11th Corps was the unlucky recipient of Stonewall Jackson's devastating flank attack. Blame was quickly attached to the men of the corps when it should have gone to their commanders, including Maj. Gen. Oliver O. Howard, who had ignored the warning signs of the flank movement.[2]

The role of Howard and other commanders mattered little to the remainder of the Army of the Potomac, for the 11th Corps was comprised of foreign troops with foreign names. Brigade and regimental commanders included the names of Hans Boebel, Gotthilf Bourry, Wladimir Krzyzanowski, August Otto, Carl Schurz, Alexander Schimmelfennig, George von Amsberg, Delteo von Einsiedel, Leopold von Gilsa, Adolph von Hartung, and Adolph von Steinwehr. Ignored in the corps were the more "American" names such as Allen, Ames, Lockman, Osborn, Robinson, Smith, and Williams. Bigotry against immigrants, both soldiers and citizens, was as prevalent as summer rain. Maj. Gen. Francis C. Barlow, commander of the 1st Division in the 11th Corps, had a low opinion of his own men and drilled them repeatedly in the name of military discipline. As a result, the men had an equally low opinion of Barlow.[3] The 11th Corps' reputation had been made at Chancellorsville, and as with their individual nationalities, this reputation would hang on the men like a yoke for oxen.

Still, there were opportunities to redeem one's reputation. As the 11th Corps marched into Gettysburg, morale improved as they saw the approaching battle as one of those opportunities to prove their mettle. Now they were on their own turf: Pennsylvania—the Union. The Rebels had invaded, and it was time to avenge the sting and scorn of Chancellorsville.

The morning of July 1 began well enough for the men. They had camped at Emmitsburg, a scant seven miles from Gettysburg, in perfect position. In the early morning they began to move to Gettysburg via the Emmitsburg Road. Normal traffic jams of the nineteenth-century variety developed, but on the whole, the corps moved steadily northward after moving east and north on the Taneytown Road.[4] The closer the troops came to Gettysburg, a sense of urgency developed and the men increased their pace. The route, however, became more difficult, because of a morning rain that turned the roads to mud.[5]

Early in the afternoon the immigrant soldiers entered Gettysburg by the Taneytown Road and hurried through the heart of town toward the flat ground to the north, known as the Gettysburg Plain.[6] The atmosphere was different; the people who watched from the side of the road were Union people. Cheering the soldiers on, the citizens also handed out water to the parched men racing through town on the double quick.[7]

To their disgust, the first day at Gettysburg would prove to be neither a day of salvation nor redemption for the 11th Corps troops. Again the commanders failed to equal their Confederate counterparts, leaving the corps' right flank unprotected. A devastating attack was delivered by one of the Confederates' finest brigades: five Louisiana infantry regiments under Brig. Gen. Harry T. Hays. When the right flank of the 11th Corps began to collapse, the remaining brigades could not stand their ground. Simultaneously, the Union 1st Corps, to the west of Gettysburg, was worn down and could no longer hold its line. The great retreat through Gettysburg was on. The 1st Corps, however, would not bear the same stain of the retreat as the 11th Corps, because it had been fighting since the morning and had repeatedly repulsed the Confederates, giving as it good as it was taking. As the Union forces re-formed and assembled on Cemetery Hill, there was no dissection of what had gone wrong, only that the 11th Corps had broken again.

On July 2, the corps was kept on Cemetery Hill with Adelbert Ames's division at the base of East Cemetery Hill, the regiments lined up along the Brickyard Road. Desultory skirmishing and artillery fire made life dangerous as well as uncomfortable.[8] When Longstreet launched his attack on the Union left, the 11th Corps watched for any advance by Confederate infantry on its front. With darkness starting to cover the battlefield, the men spotted two Confederate brigades advancing to the attack. For the second time in two days the 11th Corps faced Hays's Louisiana Brigade, this time with Isaac E. Avery's North Carolina brigade on the Tigers' left flank.

The popular story tells of Confederates sweeping away the 11th Corps line at the base of East Cemetery Hill and advancing up the hill to the Union guns, where darkness, Federal reinforcements, and the lack of Confederate reinforcements forced the attackers back down the hill toward their starting point. This version of events includes yet another instance of the 11th Corps breaking in unison and allowing the Confederates to sweep up the hill in an unbroken line. This last part of the tale of the fighting is inaccurate. If the encroaching darkness hampered the Confederates, it also was of no help to the defenders of the hill. A sharp rise in the area fronting the 153rd Pennsylvania and 68th New York protected the approaching Confederate line. The distance is short, allowing the Union defenders one or perhaps two shots before the Confederates were on the men in blue. The Union men fought, but the Confederates had momentum. The impression of Union soldiers watching the gray line advance and running in panic is simply not true.

The Confederate uphill attack was in groups of men, not neatly organized lines of battle. The reason for this is simple: not all of the 11th Corps regiments broke. The 17th Connecticut, 41st New York, and 75th Ohio remained in the line in total or in parts. Continuing the fight, those

Confederates advancing had to go around these knots of resistance to move higher on the hill.[9]

One final fog engulfed the men of the 11th Corps after Gettysburg. A brigade of the 2nd Corps, the Gibraltar Brigade, was sent to help repel the attack. Eight months after the battle—and continuing for the next fifty years—a debate began as to whether the Rebels were repulsed by the 2nd Corps soldiers or the 11th Corps troops or a combination of the two.[10]

A July 2 story demonstrates the frustration of the 11th Corps soldiers. During the attack on Culp's Hill, four of the corps' regiments were sent to assist Brig. Gen. George S. Greene's defense. After the successful fight, an anonymous officer remarked to the 82nd Illinois commander, "If you had been here yesterday instead of that damned 11th Corps, we would not have been driven back." To which the commander replied, "You are a miserable hound, sir. I and my regiment belong to that same 11th Corps you are speaking of, and we did no worse fighting yesterday."[11]

The immigrant stigma was still evident in 1888 at the dedication of the monument to the 74th Pennsylvania. Capt. Paul Rohrbacker addressed the gathering: "As free men, not as hirelings, did they offer their life for the preservation of this land, and thus paid off a long-standing debt. Thus they paid old debts to the great patriots who sowed also for us the seed of freedom. Were these soldiers less patriotic because they spoke German and sang German songs? Were they as defenders of our glorious flag less valiant, were the blows dealt by them less vigorous because they were given by German arms? Let the deeds of the Seventy-fourth Pennsylvania, on the first day's fight at Gettysburg, answer these questions."[12]

The 11th Corps continued to defend its honor until the end of the war. Justified or not, the 11th Corps was cut loose from the Army of the Potomac. The 1st Division was sent to Charleston Harbor in August 1863. The remaining men were sent to the Army of the Cumberland in Tennessee in September. Since then the record and performance of the 11th Corps at Gettysburg has slowly emerged from the fog of accusations of cowardice and weakness. The corps is now judged by the decisions of its officers and not by the men's ability or desire to fight nor their ethnicity.

21

It Wasn't That Close

At times, the truth is difficult to accept, and the growth of conspiracy theories is a natural outgrowth of tragedy. The battle of Gettysburg was no different, not as a conspiracy, but in accepting the truth of the whys and explanations of the battle. After the war, when Southern veterans looked for reasons and scapegoats, the myth of the lost opportunity at Culp's Hill emerged.

For the men on the left flank of Lee's army on the evening of July 2, the fighting was confused. The smoke of nineteenth-century weapons obscured battlefields during daylight attacks. The Confederates at Culp's Hill encountered the powder smoke, the increasing darkness, the wooded ground of unfamiliar terrain, and a very determined lot of Union soldiers under Brig. Gen. George S. Greene on Culp's Hill. After the war, Confederates learned of the dispositions of Union troops when their commanders called a halt to the attack. A possibility of success soon turned into an assumption—followed by a certainty. The Confederates had halted short of a golden opportunity to take the Baltimore Road and fall upon the rear of the Union army.

In the years after the war, this belief became prevalent, especially as an element in the deflection of criticism from Lee for the loss at Gettysburg. The notion conjures an image of a brigade of Confederates moving splendidly through a field into the unsuspecting rear of the Union line, forcing a mass panic. The reality reveals a much different image: it wasn't that close. The results of the evening were created by several interrelated factors: the topography, the unknown, the darkness, George S. Greene, Richard S. Ewell, and James Longstreet.

The topography of Culp's Hill is not easily discerned on the modern battlefield of Gettysburg. The hill has two peaks, with the upper hill being sixty feet higher than the lower hill. A saddle of land bridges the two elevations. Numerous boulders covered the hill, providing both cover and an impediment to an attacking force. At the time of the battle, the trees were very few in number. Today, it requires a strong effort to hike through the trees and undergrowth at the height of the summer growing season. The modern woods on the battlefield create an almost impenetrable fog, blocking a clear view of the nature of the terrain. To understand the relation between the two elevations, despite today's forest, should help any student of the battle to comprehend what happened here in the evening of July 2.

An understanding of Lee's assault plan for July 2 also is an element of understanding how the evening played out. Longstreet's men were to be the principle attacking force. At the sound of his guns, Ewell was to make a demonstration and convert the effort into a full-blown attack should circumstance allow.[1] Longstreet's en echelon attack was to draw Union reserves from the center or right flank of the Union line. With the center or right weakened, Ewell's assault on either the center or the right flank would break the line. To that end, the attack was working. In addition to the brigades from the Union 2nd Corps sent to the Union left, elements of the 12th Corps were also ordered to the left flank. Twelfth Corps commander Henry W. Slocum left the right flank to Greene's brigade—five regiments totaling 1,350 men.[2] This decision would prove to be wise.

Greene was up to the task. When Ewell's attack finally came, Greene extended his line and sent for reinforcements. His brigade needed every man available since the attacking force consisted of Edward Johnson's full division. In response to Greene's request, help arrived in the form of regiments from the 1st, 2nd, and 11th Corps, adding 750 men to Greene's defenders.[3]

Perhaps the most valuable assets at Greene's disposal were the topography and the quickly erected breastworks. The north slope of Culp's Hill is steep and difficult to traverse. The grade of the hill relaxes as the mound curves to the east and then south. When on defense, holding the high ground is always beneficial, and on this day, the Union soldiers held the high ground, on which they had constructed breastworks for further protection.

On the opposite side, Johnson's Confederates faced an arduous route. After sloshing through Rock Creek, they were to climb the hill they faced, fighting all the way. Scattered trees and boulders hindered their forward movement, but at the same time, these natural objects provided cover for those who momentarily halted to fire on the defenders.

George S. Greene

Darkness conceals and hides. It proved to be a valuable ally to the Union defenders by masking the terrain, a terrain Confederate commanders had not scouted prior to the attack. Unable to take full advantage of the ground, and with Greene's defensive perimeter holding firm, the Confederates had to feel their way to the Union line in the deepening darkness. Lt. Col. Simeon T. Walton, commander of the 23rd Virginia, ordered his men to cease fire and sent a single volunteer forward to discern if the troops in front of them were friend of foe.[4] Such action begs the question, is this anyway to attack the enemy?

After the war, with the smoke cleared from the battlefield, veterans realized the Confederates who captured the lower height of Culp's Hill had come within six hundred yards of the Baltimore Pike (the inviting rear area of the Union army) and possible victory. The normal reaction is to bemoan missing such an apparent opportunity. But it wasn't that easy. To place yourself in the shoes of those Confederates on these lower heights, you would have been surrounded in darkness and facing the unknown, unsure of what was in front of you. Your regiment or brigade could have collided into a much larger Union force and faced catastrophe. Such unknowns are a liability difficult to overcome in battle.

Confederate veterans claim that if Ewell had sent his men forward earlier, there would have been sufficient daylight to sustain the attack. How much earlier? If Ewell were prompt in launching his offensive, would the Union forces on Culp's Hill have been diverted to the left to meet Longstreet's attack? It seems improbable. Without that shifting of troops, Johnson's division would have faced the entire Union 12th Corps.

Adding to the improbability of Confederate success, around 10 p.m., John W. Geary's 12th Corps division was returning from a sojourn to the left flank at the same time that the attack on Culp's Hill was winding down. A Confederate volunteer who had been sent forward to scout the scene had reported he had seen wagons on the Baltimore Pike, and Johnson decided the Union army was retreating. The brave volunteer had failed to see Geary's returning men, but they were there.[5] In addition to these troops, Thomas H. Neill's 6th Corps brigade and John C. Robinson's 1st Corps division were also available. Historian Edwin B. Coddington wrote, "The lost opportunity of the Confederates, which had been fleeting at best, to envelop the right of the Union army existed less in actuality than in the minds of broken-hearted veterans seeking the reason why. . . . If Johnson's men had seized the pike, it is questionable whether they could have held it."[6] The men in blue were simply too numerous to exploit the opportunity.

Writings and speeches after the war may have emphasized this so-called lost opportunity, but these words spun a fog of the reality of the fighting on the evening of July 2. This fog of the alleged lost opportunity should clear with a real grasp of the situation Edward Johnson's Confederates faced that dark night on a rocky hill.

22

The Essential Business Meeting

$\mathcal{T}$HE HOUR WAS VERY late on July 2 when George Gordon Meade called together his corps commanders. It seemed like a wise decision. The fighting of the last two days had been dreadful, with losses in men and material at substantial levels. Without doubt, the time was right to take stock of where the army stood and assess its capabilities for the following day. Author Noah Andre Trudeau called the meeting "an executive session."[1]

The summit was held at Meade's headquarters at Lydia Leister's farmhouse. By modern standards, the home was little more than a small cabin. The cramped, hot room to be used was dreadfully small, perhaps ten by ten or ten by twelve feet. Squeezing into the room were twelve men—Meade, chief of engineers Gouverneur K. Warren, chief of staff Daniel Butterfield, Henry W. Slocum, Winfield S. Hancock, John Gibbon, Alpheus S. Williams, David B. Birney (who had succeeded the wounded Sickles), George Sykes, O. O. Howard, John Sedgwick, and John Newton.[2] Chief of artillery Henry J. Hunt begged off to attend to his batteries.

The night's discussion began with an assessment of manpower followed by an appraisal of ammunition, food, and the other supplies necessary for battle. Then the commanders discussed the army's position at Gettysburg. Finally, in what seemed like a good idea at the time, Meade allowed chief of staff Butterfield to pose three questions to the group. (In retrospect, Meade probably regretted this act for the rest of his life.) First, should the army

Lydia Leister's home served as Meade's headquarters during the battle.

stay or retire to another position? Second, should the army attack? Third, how long should the army wait for the enemy to attack?

The consensus was to stay at Gettysburg, remain on the defensive, and wait one day for Lee to attack again.[3] Although the answers and teamwork between the commanders was a good sign, after the battle, the topic of the meeting became fodder for Meade's critics to assert that Meade did not want to fight but rather to retire to the Pipe Creek line. (See chapter 8.)

One of Meade's critics was Maj. Gen. David B. Birney, commander of the 3rd Corps' 1st Division. Birney had been a lawyer prior to the war, but after sensing the coming war in 1860, he began studying military tactics. After Sickles's wounding at the Trostle farm, Birney succeeded to command the 3rd Corps.[4] Birney's March 1864 testimony before the Committee on the Conduct of the War was decidedly anti-Meade (as well as anti–West Point and anti-Democrat). With the skill of an experienced attorney, Birney's carefully chosen words created an impression that the July 2 council was divided, with Meade not wanting to continue the fight. Both allegations were untrue.[5]

Why did Birney assail Meade? The history between the two men provides ample evidence of perceived slights by Meade against Birney. At the

December 1862 battle of Fredericksburg, Meade had accused Birney of failing to support him when he almost broke Stonewall Jackson's line. Two additional friction points emerged during the Gettysburg campaign. With the wounding of Sickles. Birney took over command of the 3rd Corps, but Meade appointed Hancock to command both the 2nd and 3rd Corps. Birney protested, but Meade confirmed the order. Birney perceived this demotion as a personal slight. A second affront followed when, six days after the battle, William H. French replaced Birney as corps commander.[6] Interestingly, shortly after his testimony before the committee (which failed to remove Meade from command), Birney approached Meade to mend fences.[7] Birney's death from typhoid fever in October 1864 precluded any postwar dialogue between the two men.[8]

Of course, the most colorful and controversial personality to assert the same allegations against Meade was former 3rd Corps commander Daniel E. Sickles. He was eager to take credit for the victory at Gettysburg (by breaking up Longstreet's attack on July 2), and so he indirectly informed the Committee on the Conduct of the War that Meade wanted to retreat from Gettysburg and re-form his line at Pipe Creek.[9] But Sickles was not at

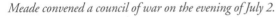

Meade convened a council of war on the evening of July 2.

the council of war; he had been removed from the battlefield when his right leg was severely injured. What Sickles knew of the meeting likely came from Daniel Butterfield.

The most damaging claims against Meade came from Butterfield, Meade's former chief of staff and also Joseph Hooker's chief of staff. Well connected politically and an able administrator, Butterfield rose quickly in rank during the war, but he was disliked by many and was derisively nick-named "Little Napoleon."[10] After Meade assumed command of the army, he had no time to name his own chief of staff prior to the breakout of fighting at Gettysburg.

By 1864, Butterfield believed that Meade had insulted him on two occasions. First, Meade had only eight days' seniority over Butterfield, and Meade had replaced Butterfield as 5th Corps commander in December 1862. Second, to ease his pain after the loss of the corps command, Hooker had appointed Butterfield as his chief of staff. Butterfield lost that position after suffering a slight wound on July 3, and Meade relieved him on July 5, much to the relief of many staff officers.[11] Finally, Butterfield was always loyal to Hooker and owed no allegiance to Meade.[12] It is little wonder that Butterfield struck back during his testimony before the Committee on the Conduct of the War.

Butterfield was determined to discredit Meade before the committee. Through lies and carefully editing, Butterfield recast the events of the battle. According to Butterfield, Meade advised him in the late morning of July 2 to be fully informed of the status and position of the army in the event of any contingency. Butterfield claimed this order indicated Meade was intent on retreating from Gettysburg.[13] Following this line of reasoning, Butterfield's testimony about the July 2 war council further demonstrated Meade's lack of desire to fight at Gettysburg.[14]

So it went for Meade, who was forced to spend time defending his reputation from allegations that he never wanted to fight at Gettysburg and thus the task fell to others to achieve victory. An old adage states, "Councils of war never fight." Yet an astute reading of the minutes of the July 2 war council does not reveal a timid Meade, but rather a general in search of opinions and answers. The fog of Meade's intention at the war council quickly dissipates in this light.

Part 4

July 3

Death Everywhere

23

Prelude to Pickett's Charge

$\mathcal{B}$EFORE DIVING DEEP INTO the fog of Pickett's Charge, an understanding of the troops involved in the charge will help light the path. Three basic elements should be kept in mind when reading of the attack.

First, the plan was Lee's. He assigned the task to Longstreet, although Longstreet's attitude was less than enthusiastic. The composition of the charge involved three divisions: one from Longstreet's corps and two from A. P. Hill's corps. You will find references to the charge as Lee's Charge, Longstreet's Charge, and Pickett's Charge. For simplicity's sake, I have used the traditional moniker of Pickett's Charge.

Second, the Confederates made the understanding easier when the units were named after their commanders (Birkett D. Fry's brigade, Henry Heth's division, A. P. Hill's corps). The problem was caused because the battle lasted more than one day and the unit's original commander was wounded and replaced. Hence, William D. Pender's division is called Isaac R. Trimble's division during the charge and Heth's division is referred to as J. Johnston Pettigrew's division. Books on Gettysburg will use one name or the other. If unfamiliar with the battle, one could look forever trying to find Trimble's division on the first two days of the battle and never find it.

Third, the numbers can be confusing. Early estimates ranged from 17,000 to 20,000.[1] Longstreet's memoirs set the number at 15,000.[2] As more historians delved into the numbers, the final assessments range from 10,500 to 13,000.[3] The major problem is the actual number of men in the two divisions from Hill's corps. Heavily battered in the fighting on July 1, these divisions did not make a formal accounting of their losses between July 1 and their involvement in the charge on July 3. As George E. Pickett had not been involved in combat on the first two days, the size of his division is easier to assess.

Pickett's division: Pickett's division (Longstreet's corps) contained three brigades, which were commanded by Richard B. Garnett, James L. Kemper, and Lewis A. Armistead. All of the troops were from Virginia.

Heth's division: Heth's division (A. P. Hill's corps) contained three brigades. The division's command structure had been juggled after the losses of July 1. The division had been the first to make contact with the Union army and had paid a high price in so doing. On July 3, the division was commanded by Brig. Gen. J. Johnston Pettigrew (Heth had been wounded on July 1). The division's brigades were a diverse group from five states. Col. Birkett D. Fry was commanding James J. Archer's brigade (Archer had been captured on July 1). Command of Pettigrew's brigade had been passed to Col. James K. Marshall after Pettigrew's promotion to divisional commander. Brig. Gen. Joseph R. Davis retained command of the Mississippi brigade. Likewise, Col. John M. Brockenbrough remained at the head of his troops throughout the battle. Elements of the division included two Alabama regiments, three Mississippi regiments, five North Carolina regiments, three Tennessee regiments, and four Virginia regiments.

Pender's division: William D. Pender had been mortally wounded on July 2. Maj. Gen. Isaac R. Trimble had been with the army but unassigned to any command. He was given Pender's division, but there was no time for Trimble to introduce himself to his troops prior to the afternoon charge on July 3. Only two of his four brigades were involved in the charge: Brig. Gen. James H. Lane's brigade and Brig. Gen. Alfred M. Scales's brigade, which was led by Col. William L. J. Lowrance (Scales had been wounded on July 1). The two brigades consisted of ten North Carolina regiments. Both brigades had been hammered severely on the first day of the battle and were far from top combat form.

Anderson's division: A fourth division from Hill's corps was used in a futile attempt to support the right wing of the charge. Richard H. Anderson's division sent two brigades forward, but they were too late and too little to help Pickett's division. It was a needless loss of life. Brig. Gen. Cadmus M. Wilcox led five Alabama regiments while Col. David Lang commanded Edward Aylesworth Perry's three-regiment Florida brigade (Perry was ill and out of action when the battle began). Both units had been involved in combat the previous day, with Wilcox's unit being the target of the near suicidal charge of the 1st Minnesota.

Artillery: Batteries from all three corps were used in the assault and were commanded by Col. E. Porter Alexander from Longstreet's corps.

24

The Absent
A. P. Hill

*T*HE SEARCH FOR A Confederate scapegoat for the loss at Gettysburg has ranged far and wide. First Corps commander James Longstreet has always been a lightning rod for the stinging criticism of veterans and historians. Second Corps commander Richard S. Ewell has never been able to escape Stonewall Jackson's ghost regarding his decision not to press the attack on the first day of the battle. Cavalry commander Jeb Stuart is also one of the controversial commanders at Gettysburg. In addition to these, the final member of Lee's principal Gettysburg lieutenants, Maj. Gen. A. P. Hill's name is no less embroiled in controversy than the others. Mystery and fog follow his legacy at the battle, and his critics ask, where was he?

Hill's contributions to the battle are difficult to enumerate or understand. His 3rd Corps was the first in combat on July 1 west of Gettysburg. On July 2 the corps occupied the center of the Confederate line, and one of his brigades almost found victory on Cemetery Ridge. On July 3 two of the three divisions in Pickett's Charge came from Hill's command. But the general's personal contributions on this battlefield are foggy.

The thirty-seven-year-old Virginian had served in the regular army since his graduation from West Point in 1847 until the split in the Union. His Confederate service, however, was not exactly smooth. Often argumentative with his superiors, Hill had been arrested twice and threatened with court-marital. Lee transferred him from Longstreet's corps to Stonewall Jackson's corps to avoid one of these unpleasant quarrels. Soon Hill came

Ambrose Powell Hill

into conflict with Jackson and was arrested over marching procedures. Only necessity saved him from being held out of command.[1] Hill's saving attribute was his ability, at times, to be one of the best divisional commanders in the Confederate army in battle. So good was he in those times that Lee had told Jefferson Davis that, next to Jackson and Longstreet, Hill was the best commander he had.[2] Moving fast and hitting hard, Hill's men won laurels at the Seven Days' battles, Cedar Mountain, and Chancellorsville. Hill and his light division achieved immortality for their actions in saving the right flank of Lee's army at Antietam in September 1862. Although he stumbled at Second Manassas and Fredericksburg, Hill was still held in high regard by both Confederate and Union commanders. After being wounded at Chancellorsville, he came to Gettysburg as a corps commander for the first time.[3] At Gettysburg, his performance would be less than sterling.

* * *

The mystery of A. P. Hill begins on June 30. After Lee's discovery that the Union army was farther north than anticipated, and with Stuart's cavalry out of touch, Lee ordered his army to concentrate in and around the Cashtown or Gettysburg area "as circumstances might require." The morning of June 30 found Hill's corps camped near Cashtown, waiting for the other two Confederate corps to arrive.[4] With time on their hands, division commander Harry Heth sent a brigade to Gettysburg to search for supplies. J. Johnston Pettigrew marched his 2,775-man North Carolina brigade to the Lutheran Seminary three-quarters of a mile west of Gettysburg. While surveying the town, the officers spotted the long line of John Buford's Union cavalry arriving from the south. Pursuant to his orders not to force a fight, Pettigrew withdrew to Cashtown and reported his finding to his superiors.[5]

For Pettigrew, his conversations with his superiors must have made him feel like a child whose parents would not believe he had seen a ghost. First

Heth and then Hill refused to believe he had seen regular Union cavalry at Gettysburg; both asserted that Pettigrew saw only a home guard or scattered vedettes (mounted pickets in front of a larger body of troops). Pettigrew drew one of his aides, Lt. Louis Young, into the conversation. Young, whom Hill knew from prior service, had clearly seen the strength of the Union force. Still Hill did not believe that Federal troops were anywhere near Gettysburg. With a blindness that defies understanding, Hill allowed Heth to proceed to Gettysburg the following day for supplies and the famous "shoes" (see chapter 7, "The Shoes, Always the Shoes").[6]

In 1877, Heth attempted to explain Hill's permission by explaining that Lee had advised Hill that the Union forces were still at Middleburg and had not struck their tents. But historian Harry Pfanz pointed out, "If [Lee] said [this], this made no sense."[7] Lee already knew that the Union army was on the move, and lacking Stuart's reconnaissance, each day's situation was fluid. Hill needed to rely on his subordinates for his own understanding of the situation, and to ignore what he was told cannot be justified.

Hill wrote very little about the conversation between Pettigrew, Heth, and himself in his official report other than to report that Heth suggested that Pettigrew did not know the size of the force in front of him (Pettigrew). Hill then added a very disturbing line in the official report: "A courier was then dispatched with this information to the general commanding, and with orders to start Anderson (another division) early; also to General Ewell, informing him, that I intended to advance the next morning and discover what was in my front."[8]

Was Hill looking for a fight? If so, it was against Lee's orders to avoid a general engagement until the entire army was rejoined. Heth's official report mentions only that he was ordered "to move at 5 a.m. in the direction of Gettysburg."[9] Was Hill simply blind to the reconnaissance of his own troops?[10] Either way, the mystery and fog regarding Hill's state of mind had begun.

* * *

For A. P. Hill, July 1 brought more questions. His headquarters were established at the Cashtown Inn on the evening of June 30. The next morning, Hill remained at Cashtown while Heth pushed his division to Gettysburg and became embroiled with Buford's Union cavalry and then the Union 1st Corps. The battle of Gettysburg had begun. Despite the sound of guns to the west, Hill made no effort personally to head toward the sound of the fighting to determine the situation. Lee arrived at Cashtown around noon. Amazingly, Hill could not tell his commander what was happening. He did offer that he was not feeling well and that Heth knew not to initiate a general engagement.[11]

Lee's presence did much to either inspire or embarrass Hill, or it at least improved his physical condition since he immediately mounted his horse and rode to the sound of the guns in the east, toward Gettysburg. Lee followed later, and by 3 p.m. he was at Knoxlyn Ridge, the site of the first shots of the battle between Heth's infantry and Union vedettes. He conferred with A. P. Hill and then Heth. At 3:30 Lee made the decision to continue the battle.[12] The remarkable absence in the after-action reports is the lack of any particular passage referring to Hill's actions prior to Lee's arrival. It appears he did little to alter the events of the afternoon of July 1, that is, until late in the afternoon. With Richard H. Anderson's division now arriving on the field, there was an opportunity for the Confederates to push the Union troops on both flanks. Two of Hill's three divisions under Heth and Pender were fought out for the day. With those divisions unavailable, Anderson would have to be the trump card. However, neither Lee nor Hill recorded any thoughts of possibly using Anderson to assist Richard S. Ewell's 2nd Corps in the Confederates' attempts to take the hills south of Gettysburg. In hindsight, historians can recognize an opportunity was being lost. Anderson's attack, in concert with Ewell's corps, would not be.[13]

One of the South's best generals, A. P. Hill was neither fast nor hard hitting on the first day of the battle. The combat had largely driven itself. Hill was never a major factor. On his first day of combat as a corps commander, Hill was a nonentity. No one has been able to explain his leisurely approach. Hill's official report reflects caution and a desire not to lose rather than a desire to win.[14]

*   *   *

Dawn on July 2 presented Hill a new opportunity to display those qualities that had won Lee's admiration. Instead, it would be another day of mental absence from the battle and subject Hill to the worst criticism of the battle. His inaction forced Lee's attack to break down. Hill never adequately explained his actions of this day, leaving historians in another fog.

Lee's plan for the day was to renew the offensive. His tactics for the attack would be risky, an en echelon attack.[15] Beginning with Longstreet's corps on his right, brigades would be sent in individually; along the Confederate line, units to the left waited their turn to advance. The idea was to allow the Union left to be enveloped by Longstreet's veteran corps. Or if Union reinforcements from the center of the line were sent to aid in the fight against Longstreet, Hill's brigades would penetrate the Union center. Finally, at the sound of Longstreet's guns, Ewell was to attack the Union right on Culp's Hill and East Cemetery Hill.[16] It was a risky tactic; failure by one brigade to advance could bring the whole attack to a halt. At the end of the day, the plan had indeed failed. Puzzled and perplexed, Lee needed look no further then his three corps commanders—Longstreet, Ewell, and Hill—for culpability. (Longstreet's is discussed in chapter 15, "Someone Blundered.")

Ewell's attack failed to materialize until dark, after Longstreet's corps was spent. However, for a short time, there was an opportunity in the center of the Union line. With Longstreet's men mauling the Union 3rd Corps, elements of the 2nd, 5th, and 12th Corps were being shifted on the battlefield to stop the Confederate tide. Even with Ewell's inaction, it would be up to Hill's corps to take advantage of the shifting Union troops.

The en echelon attack requires the division and corps leaders to be in contact with the brigade commanders directing the timing of the attack. Brigade commanders cannot be left to their own devices. Postwar criticism of Longstreet centers on his mood and activity prior to the launching of the attack; condemnation of Longstreet does not concentrate on the handling of his corps on July 2 during the attack. As his corps went into action, Longstreet was active, even holding back the eager William Barksdale and his Mississippi brigade until the right moment. Barksdale's brigade then unleashed one of the magnificent charges of the war and broke the Union salient at the Peach Orchard.

As the en echelon attack moved northward along the Confederate lines, Longstreet's corps became wholly engaged. The next division in line belonged to Richard H. Anderson in Hill's corps. The brigades from left to right were

Cadmus M. Wilcox's Alabamians, David Lang's Floridians, Ambrose R. Wright's Georgians, Carnot Posey's Mississippians, and finally William Mahone's Virginians, who were posted just behind Edward L. Thomas's brigade in William D. Pender's division. Wilcox's brigade set off around 6 p.m., followed by Lang and then Wright.[17] Shortly thereafter, the attack broke down. With Wright's fourteen hundred Georgians making progress, Posey sent his regiments forward, almost piecemeal. Mahone never ordered his fifteen hundred Virginians to move forward. All of this happened at a critical time for Wright: his men had reached the crest of Cemetery Ridge. Union reinforcements soon repulsed the Georgians because Confederate reinforcements did not follow immediately.[18] Why did Thomas and Mahone fail? Pender's division, to the left of Mahone, was ready to go, and when Pender set off to find out when to go, shrapnel from an artillery blast mortally wounded him. Without his leadership, the division did not move forward. Without support, Wright was forced to withdraw under increasing Union pressure.

Where was corps commander A. P. Hill or division commander Richard Anderson? Why weren't they following the attack to ensure the plan was executed? Neither Hill nor Anderson ever answered these questions. Their official reports do not comment on the action. No explanation was offered afterward.[19] The fog of this mystery comes from Hill's own report. Confirming that he was to cooperate with Longstreet in the attack, Hill offers high praise for the three brigades that made the charge. But the report simply stops after these commendations. No reason was given for any action after the beginning of the charge, no explanation was offered of where he was during the attack.[20] Perhaps Mahone was ordered not to attack, to stay in support. Such an idea does not fit with Mahone's position, since his brigade was deployed to continue the en echelon attack.[21] Mahone is also silent as to what occurred, and in the understatement of the battle, wrote, "The brigade took no special or active part in the actions of that battle beyond that which fell to the lot of its line of skirmishers."[22]

*   *   *

On the final day of the battle, A. P. Hill was again strangely quiet in the planning and execution of Pickett's Charge. Longstreet was given overall command of the attack, using his last fresh division (Pickett's) and two of Hill's divisions (Pender's [Trimble's] and Heth's [Pettigrew's]). In addition, Hill's third division (Anderson's) was to be "ready to take advantage of any success which might be gained by the assaulting column, or to support it, if necessary."[23]

There is no evidence that Hill, at any time, undertook an appraisal of the condition of his men after the battering the divisions took on July 1 and 2. That information might have affected Lee's attack plan for the third day. In hindsight, we recognize those two divisions may not have been the best troops to send forward, but Lee's field commanders failed to give him any opportunity to alter the plan.

During the advance, the two brigades on the left (John M. Brockenbrough's and Joseph Mayo's) came to a halt and then retreated. Joseph R. Davis's brigade made it to the Emmitsburg Road, but due to flanking fire, it too gave way. Given the instructions regarding Richard H. Anderson's division on the left flank, Hill had the opportunity to reinforce the left flank when it began to melt away in the early stages of the forward movement—but there is no evidence he made any effort to assist.[24] Longstreet eventually asked for his help, but it was too late.[25]

Criticism of Hill's actions on July 3 must recognize that the attack itself was not under Hill's control, but as a corps commander, he had opportunity to be of invaluable assistance. He was not. A Confederate artilleryman on the scene believed Hill appeared "dazed, if not confounded at the scene before him."[26]

Where was Hill? The question refers not to his physical presence but rather his mental involvement in the battle. It appears his mind was not "in the game." We don't know why this was and are left with an impenetrable fog of Gettysburg. Hill's lack of contribution to the battle cost Lee and the Confederacy, and cost them dearly.

25

Fog or Smoke?

$\mathcal{A}$T 1 P.M. ON July 3, preceding the gray advance known as Pickett's Charge, two signal guns initiated the largest cannonade of the Civil War. One hundred seventy-two heavy guns bellowed flying iron and white smoke. Union gunners responded from 166 artillery pieces. As the cannonade continued and the Confederate assault began, Union artillery chief Henry J. Hunt brought another 54 guns to bear on this sector of the battlefield.[1] Today, we look at two fogs that swirl around this cannonade. Did the Confederates overshoot because the powder smoke obscured their view of the Union line—or was their aim that bad? How damaged were the two opposing lines after the barrage?

The cannonade prior to the attack literally created the largest fog of the battle. Smokeless gunpowder came years later. With cannon firing and the subsequent explosions, it is a wonder that anyone could see anything. Almost as famous as Pickett's name is in the charge is the Confederate artillery's inaccuracy. Far too many shells passed over the Union line and fell to the rear. A maelstrom of fire and metal encircled Union commander George G. Meade's headquarters at the Leister house on the Taneytown Road. Union Pvt. N. Eldred described the hellish scene erupting around him: "It seemed to me that the heavens were on fire."[2]

Meade, however, remained calm during the cannonade, despite the destruction of his headquarters. The porch steps and columns were blown away. Shells ripped through the house while Lt. Washington A. Roebling and Gen. Seth Williams studied a map.[3] Sixteen horses tied to a picket fence were killed during the barrage.[4] As noted earlier, it was during this time that chief of staff Daniel Butterfield was wounded by a shell fragment.

Meanwhile, Meade regaled his staff with an anecdote of the 1846 battle of Palo Alto during the Mexican War. Gen. Zachary Taylor found a teamster hiding behind an overturned ammo cart during a cannonade. Told that no spot was safer than another, the teamster replied, "It kind o' feels so." The staff, however, found little humor in the story.[5] Eventually, the intense fire forced Meade to move a half mile farther east to Power's Hill.[6]

Although the eastern slope of Cemetery Ridge was to the rear of the main Union line, artillery chief Hunt saw that most of the Confederate shells fell in this area.[7] The popular explanation centers on the Confederacy's poorly trained artillery crews failing to aim their guns accurately. But this fog is more myth than fact. Was the literal fog of powder smoke from the muzzles of the Confederate guns the cause of their overshooting their intended targets? The acrid smoke of the guns burned the eyes of the gunners and blocked their vision. Add the return fire of the Union guns and exploding caissons behind the lines, and one can begin to envision the field engulfed in flame and smoke.

There are other factors to consider. In 1863, artillery shells were an inexact science that involved fuses exploding at inopportune times. Edwin B. Coddington suggested that both sides had a tendency to overshoot their targets.[8] At Gettysburg it is easy to forget the overshoots of the Union artillery as they benefited the Union when they landed among the prostrate Confederate infantry. Waiting to advance, these foot soldiers were helpless to defend themselves from the iron rain and exploding shells.

Correcting the gunners' aim was difficult because this was based on experience and sightlines. Fairfax Downey emphasized this point when he wrote that the shells landing beyond Cemetery Ridge were "lost" to the Confederate gunners as they did not see them land and were unable to adjust their aim.[9]

Overlooked and rarely discussed are the thoughts of the man who was given the task of aligning the Confederate guns. Longstreet's chief of artillery, Col. E. Porter Alexander, was a respected leader, but he found himself having to place eighty of his eighty-four guns in a parallel line with the Union forces.

Unable to enfilade the Federal positions, only a perfect shot could harm the Union guns and infantry. After the war, Porter raised this argument: the parallel line was ineffective.[10] His point was clearly demonstrated when Pickett's troops advanced and the Union guns on the southern end of the line were able to enfilade and damage the advancing infantrymen.[11]

The second part of the cannonade myth would have one believe that very little (if any) damage was suffered by the Union line from the Confederate guns. Five Union batteries had been placed near the Copse of Trees—from north to south they were George A. Woodruff's, William A. Arnold's, Alonzo H. Cushing's, T. Frederick Brown's, and James M. Rorty's. With two batteries on either side of the trees, Cushing's battery was the target of the spear point of the coming attack. Confederate fire was heavy, and Woodruff was forced to ask for help from a New York regiment to help man the guns after many of his men were injured or killed.[12] Rorty lost half of his guns and sixty-two of sixty-five men. Infantry volunteers from the 13th Vermont and 19th Massachusetts helped to carry on the fight. A Confederate shell hit a nearby limber, and the resulting explosion killed Rorty.[13]

What is not mysterious or engulfed in a fog was the punishment suffered by Cushing's battery. As the Confederate infantry advanced, Cushing had only two remaining working guns. He was mortally wounded but would not leave the battery. Fifty men from the 71st Pennsylvania were needed to help man the guns. Lt. Frank Haskell of John Gibbon's staff described the onslaught: "Our artillerymen upon the crest budged not an inch, nor intermitted, but, though caisson and limber were smashed, and the guns dismantled, and men and horses killed, there amidst smoke and sweat, they gave back, without grudge, or loss of time in the sending, in kind whatever the enemy sent, globe, and cone, and bolt, hollow or solid, an iron greeting to the rebellion, the compliments of the wrathful Republic."[14]

But the Union possessed what the Confederacy lacked—reinforcements. While the Southern gunners could only attempt to harass the Union line in fear of hitting their own men, the Union line received fresh batteries and ammunition to punish the approaching butternut infantry, thanks to its ever-present commander, Henry J. Hunt.[15]

The final analysis shows a myriad of reasons as to why the Confederate gunners missed their targets with a majority of their shots. Placing all blame on poor aim creates a fog that should not be. On the receiving end of the Confederate barrage, the image of Union soldiers standing in the front lines, watching the shells pass overhead, was never the true representation of those two hours on the afternoon of July 3.

26

Pickett and Who?

$\mathcal{O}$F THE NAMES ASSOCIATED with Gettysburg, the two most prominent are Abraham Lincoln and Confederate Maj. Gen. George E. Pickett. Described as swashbuckling, dapper, and dashing, Pickett's division of 5,473 men spearheaded the grand assault of July 3. The mere mention of Pickett's Charge conjures visions of a one-mile-wide gray wave marching steadily into a cataclysmic storm of Union fire, men dying for old Virginia and for the Confederacy. The moment was immortalized generations later by William Faulkner, one of America's masters of prose, in his 1948 novel *Intruder in the Dust*:

> For every Southern boy fourteen years old, not once but whenever he wants it, there is the instant when it's still not yet two o'clock on that July afternoon in 1863, the brigades are in position behind the rail fence, the guns are laid and ready in the woods and the furled flags are already loosened to break out and Pickett himself with his long oiled ringlets and his hat in one hand probably and his sword in the other looking up the hill waiting for Longstreet to give the word and it's all in the balance. . . . This time. Maybe this time with all this much to lose and all this much to gain: Pennsylvania, Maryland, the world, the golden dome of Washington itself to crown with desperate and unbelievable victory the desperate gamble, the cast made two years ago.

The vivid passage stirs emotions in all students of the charge, and it prompts many to wish they were there at that climactic moment. But, alas, even Faulkner contributes to the misconceptions surrounding the assault.

The term *Pickett's Charge* is a misnomer. In reality, his was just one of three divisions that emerged from the tree line of Seminary Ridge. Soldiers from five states constituted the charge. Finally, the attack was far more complex than a simple forward motion of infantry.

The offensive belonged to Lee, not Pickett nor Longstreet. Lee changed his plans for a pincer move on the morning of July 3 when the Union army took the initiative and launched a dawn attack on Lee's left flank, forcing his left wing away from Culp's Hill. With his left now unavailable, the concept emerged for a targeted charge on the center of the Union line. This Plan B was to exploit a massive artillery bombardment that would soften the supposedly weak center of Meade's line on Cemetery Ridge. Next, Longstreet's 1st Corps would act as a spear and pierce the line.

As soon as he heard Lee's plan, Longstreet protested. Two of his divisions, Lafayette McLaws's and John Bell Hood's, had been badly used up in the previous day's fighting. Only Pickett's division was at full strength, having arrived on the battlefield too late on July 2 to participate in the fighting. Lee accepted Longstreet's assessment and chose to replace McLaws's and Hood's men with one and a half divisions from A. P. Hill's 3rd Corps. J. Johnston Pettigrew led the full division, and Isaac R. Trimble's men would make up the balance, with two of his four brigades. Thus the assault involved soldiers from Alabama, Mississippi, North Carolina, Tennessee, and Virginia.

Unfortunately for the Confederate effort, Hill and his staff would fail Lee badly. The six brigades from Hill's corps selected for the attack also had been badly used up during the first day's fighting at McPherson's farm and at the Lutheran Seminary. As damaged as McLaws's and Hood's divisions were after July 2, the units selected from Hill's corps were in no better shape. Nevertheless, the plan moved forward.

As it evolved on the ground between Seminary Ridge and Cemetery Ridge, the attack initially contained not one spearhead but two, separated some distance by the trees on Seminary Ridge. Trimble's and Pettigrew's divisions constituted the northern flank of the attack, with Pickett's division covering the south. Trimble's and Pettigrew's troops were to move straight toward the Union line while Pickett's brigades would have to execute a series of left-flank marches, slowly merging with the right side of Trimble and Pettigrew's line to present a united front prior to the moment of contact with the enemy. That was how it was planned: one attack carried out by two halves, which were to join near an angle in the Union line on Cemetery Ridge.

Despite the complexity of the operation, Lee decided to add another division, or at least part of it, to the assault. Richard H. Anderson's division of Hill's 3rd Corps was to act as a shield for Pickett's vulnerable right side. Two of Anderson's brigades were detailed for this work: Cadmus M. Wilcox's and David Lang's. This protective detail soon melted away when the charge began, partly due to a lack of centralized leadership: Anderson's troops were not under Pickett's command—the very division they were assigned to assist.

Altogether, eleven brigades from four divisions from two corps were involved in the attack, and yet the assault has been immortalized as Pickett's Charge. How did this happen?

Newspapers laid the foundation of the misnaming of the attack, principally Southern dailies. In his report of the day's events, *New York Tribune* correspondent Whitelaw Reid incorrectly placed Pickett's division in the vanguard of the assault, with Hill's men in support. Evidence suggests that this was based on mistaken information rather than designed to be an intentional slight. At the same time, Richmond's five major newspapers catered to local interests and heralded Pickett's division as the main element of the day's action. In turn, many other papers across the South forwarded the information to their readers as fact, and the legend was born.[1]

In the 1870s, as Gettysburg gradually became a tourist destination, the heretofore barely mentioned Copse of Trees began to emerge as the symbolic High Water Mark of the Confederacy. The division that fought around and in front of the trees was Pickett's. If this point on the battlefield was to be the High Water Mark, then the Confederacy would be well served by emphasizing the desperate and heroic effort exerted here by Pickett's men. The Northern public gracefully slipped into the same thoughts. After all, if the Richmond papers acclaimed Pickett's troops as the cream of

Southern soldiery, then the Army of the Potomac had vanquished the best the South had to offer. The result was the denigration of the other brigades to a sublevel below Pickett's Virginians.

To this muddling of the facts should be added the pervasive desire to simplify complex issues and events, especially legendary historical events. Few have explained it better than historian Carol Reardon: "From the time the battle smoke cleared, Pickett's Charge took on this kind of chameleon like aspect and, through a variety of carefully constructed nuances, adjusted superbly to satisfy the changing needs of Northerners, Southerners, and finally the entire nation. In the immediate postwar years, the gallantry and sacrifice of the Confederate infantry on July 3 gave Southerners some much needed heroes to help ease the pangs of defeat and, in some ways, to validate and represent all that was right about the Lost Cause."[2]

The fog that ignores five of the states to the benefit of one state should be lifted forever.

27

North Carolina vs.
Virginia

$\mathcal{C}$APT. W. R. BOND was a staff officer from North Carolina in the Army of Northern Virginia at Gettysburg. In 1888, he published a booklet entitled *Picket or Pettigrew?* in which he described himself as a "Sometime Officer Brigade Staff Army of Northern Virginia."[1] Bond's pamphlet was written in response to a twenty-five-year debate over which state's troops advanced farther during the July 3 charge: Virginians or North Carolinians. The debate included an argument over who suffered and/or sacrificed more men. Bond added his opinion to the many who sought to establish who had been the bravest participants in the noblest charge of the Civil War. The argument, however, spews only fog and masks the true lesson of the charge.

Union troops defended a low stone wall at the apex of the charge. The wall ran north and south in front of the Copse of Trees. North of the trees, the wall made a ninety-degree turn to the east and then another ninety-degree turn to the north. This angle sparked part of the controversy. Today, three markers at the angle afford some insight into the debate. The marker honoring Lewis A. Armistead is inside the angle. He was Pickett's only brigade commander to advance beyond the wall. The monument marks where Armistead was mortally wounded after leading his Virginians into the angle. Erected in 1988, the marker has the simple inscription "Brigadier General Lewis A. Armistead C.S.A. fell here July 3, 1863."[2]

To the north, approaching the east-west segment of the stone wall, approximately twenty yards from the Union line, is another monument.

This one is dedicated to the 26th North Carolina and its actions during the charge on July 3. The first day of fighting at Gettysburg had been a ghastly day for the 26th North Carolina; it collided with the renowned Iron Brigade and suffered dearly in the ensuing fighting. Despite its losses that day, the Tar Heel unit was ordered to participate in the great charge. The marker's inscription pays tribute to those men of the 26th North Carolina who advanced within "ten paces" of the Union line before being forced back. The Tar Heels claimed they had planted their flag on the stone wall before succumbing to enemy fire.[3] This monument was erected in 1986. It is farther east of the Armistead marker, implying a farther advance by North Carolinians than Virginians.

Farther north, near the Brian barn, another Confederate marker was placed just a few feet from the wall to commemorate the efforts of the 11th Mississippi, part of Joseph R. Davis's brigade in Pettigrew's division. The remnants of the unit advanced within twenty-five feet of the Union defenders. Here a group of Mississippians faced the choice of surrender or "become the flying targets of a thousand muskets." These men choose surrender and were helped over the wall by Union troops.[4] The Mississippi marker (erected in 2000) is farther east of both the 26th North Carolina marker (erected in 1986) and the Armistead marker (erected in 1888). Hard to overlook is the fact that the monuments were placed farther east as time passed. The placement of the markers reflects the debate over which state's troops advanced farther during the charge.

A second part of this debate focuses on allegations that other units broke and doomed the charge to failure. On July 23, 1863, recriminations of who had faltered in the charge began with an article by *Richmond Enquirer* correspondent Jonathan Albertson. He described Pickett's men as heroic and brave. In contrast, the men of Pettigrew's division "wanted of firmness of nerve and steadiness of tread which so characterized Pickett's men." Albertson also described the soldiers to Pickett's left as "raw troops." After placing Pickett's division in the glory of combat, he described Pettigrew's division as being in "utmost confusion" and "flying, apparently panic stricken, to the rear."[5]

The intended impression was that cowardly North Carolinians had abandoned Pickett's Virginians to their own fate. What Albertson failed to mention was that one of the first units to break on the far left was John M. Brockenbrough's brigade of Virginians. But Brockenbrough's men did not withdraw because of cowardice. The unit was demoralized after having a succession of commanders, after being handled badly in the past, and after a horrible mauling during the first day's fighting. Given this recent experience, the brigade should never have been placed on the flank of the attack.[6]

The debate as to who performed the most valiantly at Gettysburg was not restricted to veterans of the battle. In 1877, the *Raleigh Observer* sent questionnaires to veterans seeking information as to whose troops had faltered and doomed the charge to failure.[7] The die had been cast, and opinions proliferated in speeches, papers, and letters well into the twentieth century.[8] More is the pity, for the debate creates a fog around the pertinent and essential point. Whether the most valiant Southern soldiers on the battlefield were from Alabama or Florida or Mississippi or North Carolina or Tennessee or Virginia, what was asked of these men was so monumental that we are left with the difficult task of comprehending why they went forward. After scanning the Union line from Seminary Ridge and comparing that view to the one from the fence on the Emmitsburg Road, the magnitude of the charge overwhelms the senses. Lee had not given his army a demanding task, the mission his soldiers undertook was an impossible task. Students of the battle cannot fret over or debate which state's troops advanced the farthest; rather, they should wonder how any of the Confederates made it as far as they did.

Pickett's Charge demonstrates how far men will go when fighting for their ideal of how they should be governed. It is a lesson that still applies today to the world's trouble spots.

28

Where Is Pickett?
Where Is Pickett's Report?

IN 1825, JOHN QUINCY ADAMS, a son of the second president of the United States, secured his place in history when he became the country's sixth president. That same year, on January 25, George Edward Pickett was born in Richmond, Virginia, not knowing that destiny had reserved his place in history. After a fateful day in July 1863, his name and actions on the fields south of Gettysburg would be engulfed in the fog of controversy.

Pickett's path to this prominent position in the history of the Civil War was not marked by spectacular achievements as a child or as a young soldier. His family was not wealthy, despite having a home in Richmond and a plantation at Turkey Island. His father did, however, have connections. In 1842, the young man obtained an appointment to West Point. Abraham Lincoln did not nominate him for this appointment, as purported by a seemingly never-ending myth. In reality, a friend of Pickett's uncle obtained the nomination from Illinois congressman John T. Stuart.[1]

Pickett ranked last in his class when he was graduated from West Point in 1846. After serving in the Mexican War, his unit was transferred to Texas. In 1855 he was transferred to Washington Territory in the Pacific Northwest. While serving with Gen. William Harney, hostilities were narrowly avoided between the United States and Britain over the occupation of San Juan Island between the Washington Territory and Vancouver Island. Cooler heads prevailed, and Harney lost his command.[2] When the

Civil War broke out in 1861, Pickett resigned his commission and joined the Confederate army.[3]

At Gettysburg, Pickett's division was not at full strength. Two of his five brigades were elsewhere: Micah Jenkins's brigade was in North Carolina and Montgomery D. Corse's brigade was at Hanover Junction.[4] Nevertheless Pickett was eager for action. His division had not fought as a whole unit since 1862 and had missed the great victory at Chancellorsville.[5] As the last division in the long line of the Army of Northern Virginia, Pickett's Virginians had not arrived in time for the fighting on July 1 or July 2. Pickett's appointment with destiny would come the following day.

The story of Pickett's Charge has been told and retold countless times. No matter how many times it is repeated, it always ends the same: the three divisions in the charge are repulsed, blame is passed around, but the men are honored as heroes even if there is a dispute over who advanced the farthest (see chapter 27, "North Carolina vs. Virginia"). Not only was Pickett's division devastated, so was Pickett himself.[6]

In the years after the war, the charge took on a universal quality not found in other great times of combat in the war. Rather than get caught up in the commanders and state pride, one must recognize that the valor displayed on the field of Gettysburg came from within the men whose feet trod this ground under fire. Despite the debate over who broke first, glory and honor were accorded those who participated in one of the South's "finest hours."

Still, Pickett himself became the center of attention in Virginia. Yet in 1894 one of Pickett's men made a shocking accusation. Maj. Kirkwood Otey of the 11th Virginia posed the question of where Pickett was during the charge, arguing that Pickett was not with his division during the charge. Otey claimed that, after having his wounds bandaged, he saw Pickett at the "whiskey wagon."[7] He enlarged his criticism by pointing out that neither Pickett nor any member of his staff had been injured during the attack.[8]

The response was immediate and included full denials of any drunkenness or cowardice by those who knew or had been with Pickett. Pickett died in 1875, and it was left to his chief supporters, his wife, and members of his division to defend him. Unfortunately, for several years, rumors and

innuendoes would not go away.[9] The attack
on Pickett always seemed to include an attack on not only his place during the battle
but also his fondness for alcohol.[10]

To clear the fog of Pickett's performance,
historians point out that Pickett was where he
should have been and that he acted as a commander should have acted during an operation such as the frontal assault his men were
making. The idea of a commander on horse-
back, pointing his sword toward the enemy is
romantic fantasy and finds no basis in the re-

George E. Pickett

ality of the battlefield—unless the commander wished to be the first to die.
During the Civil War, division commanders needed to be behind their men.
The distance allowed them to see their entire command, to respond to
changing conditions, and to send for reinforcements when appropriate.
During the charge, Pickett saw a threat to his right flank. Kemper's brigade
was on the right and was being struck hard by a flanking attack of George J.
Stannard's Vermont brigade. Pickett also witnessed the slow disintegration
of the brigade on the left flank in Pettigrew's division.[11] As a result, he sent
four of his staff to the rear with messages.

One wonders where Pickett's place would be in Confederate lore if he
had been wounded or killed in the attack. Luck has more to do with becoming a casualty then any other factor in combat. No matter how much
training one has or how good a soldier one is, luck may be the sole determination if one is a casualty. Thus was the case with Pickett and his staff; despite the flying lead, the group's luck held and none were injured.

Pickett did not explain where he was during the charge in his official
report because there is no report. Lacking such firsthand testimony, students of the battle find themselves in one of the most frustrating fogs of the
battle. It was not that Pickett failed to write a report; he did. Lee, however,
rejected it.[12] Lee wrote that Pickett and his men "have crowned yourselves
with glory."[13] Nevertheless, the army commander advised Pickett to "guard
against dissensions which the reflections in your report would create." Pickett was ordered to destroy the original and all copies of his report. An aide

to Pickett witnessed the general's anger when he received the order to destroy his report.[14]

One of those who saw the report was Pickett's immediate superior,
James Longstreet. He later wrote that Pickett's report was not the problem as
much as the report "was made in writing and of official record." Pickett's account, apparently, was not self-laudatory but contained accusations against
other commanders. Pickett's brother claimed that not all copies of the report
were destroyed, one was sent to an uncle in Richmond. When Union troops
occupied the Confederate capital in April 1865, the uncle burned the
report.[15]

Was Pickett critical of Lee? It seems unlikely, if we believe Longstreet's
account of the report. If Pickett was critical of the commanding general,
would this account for Lee's criticism of Pickett after the loss at the battle of
Five Forks when Lee, referring to Pickett, asked, "I thought that man was
no longer with the army?"[16] Considering Lee's demeanor, such criticism was
as strong as he would allow. Did the destroyed report account for the icy
rapport between the two men after the war? In 1870 Pickett encountered
John S. Mosby just after Mosby had visited with Lee. Mosby convinced
Pickett to meet with Lee, and the two men went to Lee's home. Afterward,
Mosby described the meeting as "embarrassing" and reported that when
the two had left the general's home, Pickett said to Mosby, "That old man
. . . had my division massacred at Gettysburg."[17] Was the report the problem or did Pickett continue to resent his division's fate at Gettysburg? All of
these questions could be answered if the report still existed. But in the end,
we will never know.

29

The Ignored and Neglected Child

THE PARCEL OF LAND sits east of Gettysburg between Hanover and York roads. A mobile-home park sits on the southern end. The remaining area is farmland. A single National Park Service road cuts through its midst. If this particular part of the battlefield, known as East Cavalry Battlefield, were a child, it could sue its parents for nonsupport. Visitors to this ground find themselves alone. Rarely can more than two cars be seen parked along the road. The battlefield is on the National Park Service map, but it fails to garner any interest from visitors as an important part of the battle. That's a shame, for the fight on this rolling land of crops and pastures carries its own mystique and share of colorful characters.

Why does the East Cavalry Battlefield lay concealed in a fog of anonymity? Further still, why are all the other cavalry battle sites at Gettysburg shrouded in obscurity? Controversy can be found at the cavalry fields. Add to the mix a cast of attention-grabbing characters, and the cavalry fighting is ripe for unending discussion. Cavalry was involved in the fighting in five different areas: the fight in the fields west and north of Gettysburg preceding the arrival of the Union infantry, the East Cavalry Field, the field on the Slyder farm, Brinkerhoff's Ridge, and Fairfield.

On the morning of July 1, the actions of Buford's cavalry division were textbook examples of a delaying action. The story of his men are well documented and mentioned in general histories of the battle as well as histories of the first day at Gettysburg. His troopers bought the time needed for the

Union 1st Corps to arrive. Any attempt to relate the story of the fighting on July 1 without incorporating the cavalry feats would make the day's events incomprehensible. Heavily traveled park roads routinely take visitors to the areas where Buford's troopers made multiple stands. Unfortunately, many visitors leave the battlefield with the impression that there was little cavalry action after July 1 until July 3, when Union and Confederate cavalry clashed east of Gettysburg.

Faring not so well are the other areas of cavalry combat. One locale, Brinkerhoff's Ridge, is seemingly lost in a fog, imperceptible to many visitors. Situated on Hanover Road, south and west of the larger East Cavalry Field, fighting occurred here late on July 2. Part of the reason for this cloak of invisibility is that the property is privately owned. The land is not part of the national park nor is it marked with monuments. Traffic also is a problem, and there are precious few places to pull over and explore the area. Nonetheless, the combat here had a bearing on the actions of the armies on both July 2 and July 3.

At Brinkerhoff's Ridge two veteran infantry brigades guarded the left flank of the Southern army. On July 2, Brig. Gen. Albert G. Jenkins was to move his cavalry brigade to the flank to relieve the infantry, but the horsemen never made it. Jenkins was wounded north of Gettysburg, and his successor never led the brigade to its assigned position.[1] Shortly, the Confederate foot soldiers found themselves in a serious skirmish with Union cavalry under Brig. Gen. David M. Gregg, a very quiet, unassuming thirty-year-old whose cousin was the governor of Pennsylvania.[2]

At first glance, this fighting seemed inconsequential to the overall events of Gettysburg, but further examination shows otherwise.

One of the two Confederate units at Brinkerhoff's Ridge was the famed Stonewall Brigade. Skirmishing with Gregg's troopers on July 2 deprived the Confederate attack on Culp's Hill of a veteran brigade. Whether the fourteen hundred men of the Stonewall Brigade would have made a difference at Culp's Hill is arguable.[3] Of equal importance is that Gregg, the Union cavalry commander, recognized the importance of the ground east of the ridge.[4] One other person recognized this as well. Jeb Stuart arrived on the scene late in the fighting and saw the same thing that Gregg saw.[5] The table was set for the next day's actions.

The final day of the battle witnessed three different and unrelated cavalry actions. The most visible of these occurred to the east of Gettysburg, near Brinkerhoff's Ridge. Centered on the Rummel farm, the battle featured dismounted cavalry and charges. This confrontation featured two of the nineteenth century's most high-profile celebrities: Stuart and Union Brig. Gen. George A. Custer. Sadly, a modern fog has developed with the notion that the fight on East Cavalry Field was between Stuart and Custer. The titles of two recent books go so far as to use the phrase "Custer vs. Stuart."[6] Reality shows the fight was between Stuart and Gregg, commander of the 2nd Division of Union cavalry. Custer's brigade of Michigan cavalry was in the fight, but so were two other Union cavalry brigades.

The plan for the Confederate cavalry was simple: loop around the Union right flank and see what harm they could do. Stuart's four brigades of cavalry and battery of horse artillery approached the area of fighting the previous day. A fog of wonder surrounds one of the participating brigades: for some inexplicable reason, Albert Jenkins's horsemen each carried only ten rounds of rifle ammunition.

As the Confederates drew near, Gregg approached Custer, who was attached to H. Judson Kilpatrick's division. Although ordered to return to the Union left flank, Custer had no objection to Gregg's request to stay and face the approaching Southern troopers.[7] During the fight, Custer provided one of the most memorable Gettysburg moments as he was leading the 5th Michigan in a charge against Wade Hampton's cavalry with his famous cry, "Come on, you Wolverines!"[8] Skirmishing, charging, countercharging, the three-hour fight was pure cavalry, and in the end it was Stuart who withdrew his forces to the north of Gettysburg.[9] The two armies lost more than four hundred men on the field.[10] Gregg had won. For Stuart, it was an ignominious end to a dreadful campaign.

The fourth area of cavalry combat is on the southern part of the main battlefield, just north and northwest of Big Round Top. There is much sadness on this part of the field for it is hard to justify the action here. If Gregg's tangle with Stuart preserved the Union right flank from further harm, the Union cavalry charge on the Confederate right flank gained nothing, not time, not territory. The Union commander, Brig. Gen. H. Judson Kilpatrick, received command of the 3rd Cavalry Division on June 28, three days before the battle. Aggressive to a fault, Kilpatrick determined his troopers needed to charge the Confederate infantry in and around the Slyder farm after Pickett's Charge. The terrain was rugged and rocky.[11] Despite protests from brigade commander Elon Farnsworth, the charge was carried out. The only result was a good many empty Union saddles—including Farnsworth's.[12] After the battle a controversy arose as to whether Farnsworth killed himself rather than surrender.[13] Perhaps the senseless nature of the charge and its lack of meaning to the battle are why the action on Slyder's farm fails to garner much interest among park visitors. This oversight is a pity. The farm is in pristine condition.

The final locale of cavalry combat is the key as to why it too is overlooked by the vast majority of visitors. The site is away from the battlefield, north of Fairfield on a road known as the Fairfield-Ortanna Road. On a nearby ridge, elements of the 6th U.S. Cavalry clashed with the 6th, 7th, and 11th Virginia Cavalry. A Confederate battery also added its weight to the fight. Four hundred Union troopers were following orders to block Confederate reinforcements or wreak havoc in the Confederate rear area. What the Union horsemen found were sixteen hundred well-seasoned Confederate troopers, and they were in no mood to be pushed around. At the end of the fight, the Union force had lost 60 percent of its men, including two hundred captured.[14] The Confederates reported losses of fifty-eight men. As with Brinkerhoff's Ridge, the land is privately owned and not conducive to large groups of visitors.

Knowing about these five sites in and around the battlefield should satisfy any visitors curious about cavalry action at Gettysburg. In recent years more books on the cavalry at Gettysburg have been published, and slowly the fog encircling these areas is thinning. With the exception of the Kilpatrick fiasco, all of them played significant roles in the battle.

30

One More Needless Death

The smoke and the shot, thick as molasses
Down the Baltimore Pike and the passes.
Capt'n said a young girl was dead.
Shot in the kitchen, baking bread.
— "The Ballad of Jennie Wade" by Bob Welch[1]

AFTER TWO DAYS OF brutal combat, the morning of July 3 promised only more heat and death. Sitting in the middle of the maelstrom was the home of John and Georgia McClellan. Inside the small house were six very frightened people—Georgia; her newborn son, Louis Kenneth McClellan; her mother, Mary Wade; her younger brother, Harry Wade: her sister, Jennie Wade; and a six-year-old boarder under the care of the Wades, Isaac Brinkerhoff. The house was a modest brick building divided into two homes on the northern slope of Cemetery Hill. A Union skirmish line now engulfed the home. Confederates were perilously close, just a few hundred feet to the north, in buildings on the southern edge of town. It was a dangerous place for a soldier, let alone any civilian. Early that morning, a single shot from a Confederate rifle passed through two doors and struck twenty-year-old Jennie Wade in the back, killing her instantly.[2] No one doubts had the Confederate soldier realized what sorrow his bullet would cause, he would have never squeezed the trigger. Jennie Wade's death was one part of a trilogy of tragedy involving her, a Union soldier, and a Confederate soldier—a tragedy and a mystery that appears to be more Hollywood script than a heartbreaking story from the battle.

This tragedy begins prior to the war with Mary Virginia "Jennie" Wade, Johnston "Jack" Skelly, and Wesley Culp. All were native to the Gettysburg area and knew each other. A nineteenth-century town of twenty-five hundred allows for familiarity among the residents. Culp's uncle owned a hill to the southeast aptly named Culp's Hill. At the base of the hill was Spangler's Spring, a popular picnic area for the townspeople. It is easy to envision these three individuals playing as children near the spring or perhaps playing games in the streets and fields around Gettysburg.[3] As time passed the three matured, and the relationship between Jack and Jennie became close.[4] Legend holds that their friendship began to look like a future marriage.[5]

Strengthening the ties of small-town life, Jack's brother worked for a carriage maker alongside Wesley Culp. Just before the war, the carriage maker moved to Shepherdstown, Virginia, and Wesley and Jack's brother moved with the business to start a new life. As the dark clouds of war formed, the two young men realized a decision would have to be made soon. When war did break out, the Gettysburg natives chose to return to their hometown, but Wesley decided to stay in Shepherdstown. His decision was never understood by his family and resented by the townspeople of Gettysburg.

As a member of the local Hamtramck Guards, Wesley enlisted as a private in Company B of the 2nd Virginia (soon to be part of the famous Stonewall Brigade). He never shared with anyone his reasons for choosing this course.[6] Did he ponder the possibility of fighting against friends from his hometown? On the other side of the Mason-Dixon Line, Jack Skelly enlisted in the Union army. By June 1863, he was a member of the 87th Pennsylvania Infantry.[7] Did he imagine the prospect of being in combat against Wesley Culp?

At this point, the story follows its strange path toward tragedy. As Lee's invasion wound its way northward in June 1863, Winchester, Virginia, was again occupied by Confederate troops after a brief battle. Among the Union soldiers taken prisoner lay Jack Skelly with an arm wound. Confederate Wesley Culp encountered some prisoners from his hometown of Gettysburg and learns of Skelly's wounding. He visited him in the Taylor House Hospital, and a deep fog descends on the story: Jack allegedly gave Wesley a message should he return to Gettysburg. Neither Jack nor Wesley left a written record of the message's content; we are left to wonder whether it was a word of encouragement to home or perhaps to someone in particular, someone dear to his heart.[8] Legend declares the message to be a marriage proposal to Jennie Wade.

The story comes to an inevitable climax when Lee's army clashes with Meade's at the hometown of the three characters of this tragedy—Gettysburg. Jack Skelly lies seriously wounded near Winchester; Wesley Culp approaches Gettysburg with the Confederate army; and Jennie Wade goes about her daily routine despite the threat of war fast approaching.

As the first day of battle began north and west of town, Jennie and her mother decided that the family should move from their home on Breckenridge Street farther south to stay with Georgia and her newborn. Jennie's sister, Georgia, had given birth to her son just days before, on June 26.[9] Since her husband was in the Union army, it only made sense to consolidate the family for safety and help.

Flush with victory on the first day, Confederates took control of the town. Union forces were in full retreat, running through town but rallying on Cemetery Hill, on which stood the McClellan home. No longer a place of refuge, the home was now the center of fierce skirmishing. As the McClellan home was on the hill's northern slope, it was in the direct line of fire from the Confederates.

Although evening fell, deadly shots continued hitting the house into the night and throughout the next day. At one point, a Confederate artillery shell pierced the north side of the roof and lodged itself in the south wall, failing to explode. Meanwhile, Jennie and her mother kept busy, baking bread and trying to help the wounded soldiers around the house without endangering themselves. July 2 would be another long night for the anxious family.

Wesley Culp's regiment arrived in Gettysburg on July 2, and Culp was allowed to visit his two sisters in town. For his sisters, Wesley recounted his conversation with wounded Jack Skelly and reported that he had a message for Jack's mother. When pressed for the contents of the message, he only replied that they could receive the news from Mrs. Skelly. With the refusal to expand on the message, the evening came to a close as Wesley walked out of the house and out of their lives forever.[10]

The morning of July 3 held no promise of a better day than the previous two. After breakfast, Jennie Wade read from the biblical book of Psalms: "Though War should rise against me." The words were ominous and prophetic. At approximately 8:30 a.m., the fatal bullet struck Jennie Wade in the back as she was kneading dough for bread. The bullet passed through her body and lodged in her corset.[11] She fell dead—the only civilian killed during the battle. Found in the pocket of her apron was a photograph of Jack Skelly.

At an unknown time that morning, approximately a mile southeast of the McClellan home and just past Culp's Hill and Spangler's Spring, the 2nd Virginia engaged in skirmishing with Union forces. After the battle, the 333-man regiment counted its casualties. Compared to the slaughter elsewhere on the battlefield, the number of men lost was light: only three dead. One of them was Wesley Culp.[12]

On July 12, just nine days after the deaths of Jennie Wade and Wesley Culp, Jack Skelly died of his wounds at the Taylor House Hospital in Winchester, Virginia.

> She was carried to the cellar I have heard.
> One more needless death in Gettysburg.
> —"The Ballad of Jennie Wade" by Bob Welch[13]

Mysteries still surround this story line. Unlike a Hollywood script, this is a true story, but fog clings to the ending. Neither Jennie Wade, Jack Skelly, nor Wesley Culp left a written record of these events. The gist of Skelly's message to his mother through Culp has never been revealed. He did not share it with anyone else, and if he did, the message was never relayed to her. Jack was equally reticent. Fellow soldiers claimed not to know of the message.[14]

Only through second-hand sources has the story been pieced together. Two books revealed the story as we know it: *Jennie Wade: The True Story of Jennie Wade, A Gettysburg Maid*, by John White Johnston (1917) and *The Jennie Wade Story*, by Cindy Small (1991). Relying on secondary sources, mainly newspapers from Gettysburg to Pittsburgh, and private papers, the story has been carefully researched. Complicating their efforts, the sources are not from the time of the battle, but rather date from 1873 and later. Although the story is simple, both Johnston and Small scrutinized the record to determine their veracity.

Indirect sources confirm the story but without specifics. The history of the 87th Pennsylvania mentions the story twice and describes Jack Skelly as "a good fellow and a brave soldier who fell mortally wounded."[15] Skelly's photograph is prominently displayed in the book, seemingly lending credence to the story.[16] The regimental history was published in 1901, sixteen years before Johnston's work on Jennie Wade. The author of the regimental history may have simply retold the story without confirming the facts. Since then, the story has been repeated countless times in other works and publications.

The Wade family did not have a good reputation in Gettysburg at the time of the battle. Cindy Small weighs the family's status as a reason for possible doubts about the truthfulness of the story. Jennie's father, James, had been committed to the Adams County Almshouse in 1852 after a series of run-ins with the law and other unknown activities. With the father in the almshouse, young Harry was born in 1855, leaving many people wondering who the father might be.

After the battle, seventy-year-old John Burns, the only civilian to participate in the battle, demonstrated a negative attitude toward Jennie. He accused her of many things and dismissed the story of her making bread for Union soldiers at the time of her death as something from the imagination of a newspaper correspondent. No reason can be found to explain Burns's attitude,[17] but because he

Jennie Wade, the only civilian killed during the battle, was buried in Evergreen Cemetery.

was a hero of the battle, people paid attention to his opinions—or perhaps his rantings.

The questions about the story cast sufficient doubt on the truthfulness of the story of Skelly's message to his mother. However, neither these questions nor the delay in the telling of the story is sufficient to dismiss it as untrue. We want to believe the story because it is a good story. But the lingering question remains, was there a message? Piecing the story together 50 or 130 years after the event can only confirm that we will never know the true story with absolute certainty.

*   *   *

After her death, Jennie Wade's body was carried to the cellar where she lay until the battle was over. She was then buried behind the McClellan house. Six months later her body was moved to the German Reformed Church. Her final resting place is in Evergreen Cemetery, taken there in November 1865.

The site of Wesley Culp's death is not known. One account claims he climbed onto a rock for a better view and was shot in the forehead. A Confederate soldier supposedly told the Culp family where he was buried, but the family maintained they never recovered his body. The only evidence anyone ever found on the field was a part of Culp's rifle with his name carved into the stock.[18] Some have wondered if Culp's body was buried in secret so as to prevent its desecration by angry townspeople. With the atmosphere of confusion after the battle and thousands of dead in the field, many believe he was secretly interred in Evergreen Cemetery. The cemetery has no record of any such burial.[19]

Johnston "Jack" Skelly was buried at Winchester. In the fall of 1864 his body was moved to Gettysburg and interred in Evergreen Cemetery. When Jennie's body was moved to the Evergreen Cemetery, the two found their final rest only seventy-seven yards apart.[20]

Georgia McClellan and her family moved to Iowa after the battle. There she spent the remainder of her life and was the driving force behind the placement of a monument to Jennie at her gravesite. The Iowa Women's Relief Corps erected the monument in the cemetery in 1901. Today, one of two twenty-four-hour-a-day American flags marks Jennie's final resting place. The other flag flies over the grave of John Burns.[21] In 1922, a metal marker was placed in front of Jennie's birthplace at 242–246 Baltimore Street.

> The sun rose over Gettysburg today.
> Dried the blood in the wheat field where I lay.
> Shone on cannons, firing one by one.
> And on the grave of a girl not twenty-one.
> —"The Ballad of Jennie Wade" by Bob Welch[22]

Part 5

The Battle Over

31

The Attack of July 4

$\mathcal{A}$s THE SUN ROSE on the morning of July 4, the sight and stench of the battlefield overwhelmed any unlucky civilian who ventured out to survey the landscape. More than a few soldiers felt the same. Three days of combat had left more than fifty thousand casualties, the carcasses of thousands of horses, discarded military equipment, and smoke from a thousand fires. Added to this assault on the senses were the vivid memories of the fighting alongside friends and compatriots who were now horribly wounded or dead.[1] What thoughts, emotions, and ideas did the soldiers entertain as they contemplated what this day might bring? How many were feeling the effects of combat fatigue? How many even cared? Were their senses numb to the thought of a fourth day of deadly struggle?

With the dawning of the sun the two commanding generals had quite different matters on their hands. On Seminary Ridge, Lee had already started to implement his next move: an orderly withdrawal to the mountains to the west and a return to the safety of Virginia. Of foremost importance to him was transporting the wounded back. Lee also straightened his lines on Seminary Ridge, abandoning the town and Culp's Hill and the Wheatfield.

George Gordon Meade used the day to evaluate the condition of his army, celebrate Independence Day, and maintain a watchful eye on the enemy. Not until the evening did he decide his next step. After meeting with his corps commanders, Meade directed the 6th Corps to "find out the position and movements of the enemy." Their advance was to begin at 4:30 on July 5.[2]

This day of combat "inactivity" laid the groundwork for second-guessers as to whether Meade could or should have struck Lee on July 4. Critics point to two aspects of the status of the Confederate army on July 4. First, Lee had no more reserves. Second, the Confederate army had suffered badly and it was far from home.

Likewise, if Meade were to assume the offensive at Gettysburg, he had several factors to consider. First, information from his corps commanders was anything but positive for seizing the initiative on July 4. Five of the army's six corps had been heavily engaged at Gettysburg. Casualties were high. Only the fourteen-thousand-man 6th Corps was up to strength, having suffered less than 2 percent casualties. Four of the corps had sustained heavy losses, from the 50 percent casualty rate of the 1st Corps to 20 percent of the 5th Corps. The 12th Corps had lost 11 percent, but it was the smallest of all the corps and was firmly entrenched on Culp's Hill.[3] Second, only two of the Union corps commanders favored taking the offensive, a clear sign the commanders knew what the fighting had been like, realized the advantage of their current position on the ridge, and acknowledged the condition of their men.[4] Third, reports indicated Confederate wagon trains were in motion.[5] Meade knew this meant Lee was either re-

Meade's army pursues Lee after Gettysburg.

treating or attempting to outflank the Union army. Fourth, while the 6th Corps had suffered the least, its units were scattered across the entire Union line. How long would it take to pull the regiments, brigades, and divisions together? What chance was there of maintaining an element of surprise for the pending Union assault? What other forces could support the 6th Corps in this attack? Could the 6th Corps deal a deathblow to Lee's army? Fifth, reports from the 5th Corps indicated that Lee still held a strong position on Seminary Ridge with his flanks refused, bent back to guard the flanks.[6] Obviously the Confederate army had sustained major losses, but were Lee's men now like a wounded tiger, more dangerous then ever? Finally, why would Union troops fare any better than the Confederates had on July 2 and 3, crossing the same open ground? Battle-hardened Southerners had failed to dislodge Meade's army from Cemetery Ridge, and they no doubt welcomed an opportunity to turn the tables on a Union advance.

In the afternoon, natural events asserted their authority, overruling additional assaults by either blue or gray. A thunderstorm followed by heavy rain dowsed the countryside, preventing further bloodshed and cleansing the fields of the raw devastation wreaked here over the past three days.

Unfortunately for Meade, he handed his critics an argument after the battle. A message of thanks to his troops was a proper protocol for the commanding general's headquarters, but Meade summarized the battle as "greater efforts to drive from our soil every vestige of the presence of the invader." When Abraham Lincoln read it, he said, "Drive the invaders from our soil. My God is that all?"[7] The president understood that the destruction of Lee's army was the major steppingstone to victory; at the same time, Lincoln did not have all the information Meade had on July 4. Nevertheless, a foundation for second-guessing Meade's performance at Gettysburg was laid. Could the Army of Northern Virginia have been destroyed at Gettysburg? It is a fog that can never be cleared.

The allegation that Meade should have destroyed Lee on July 4 was the least of Meade's problems after the battle and after the war. For ten days after the battle, Meade followed Lee's movements back to Virginia, searching for an opportunity to engage Lee in battle. After the Confederate army crossed the Potomac at Falling Waters, no further opportunity was at hand.

Distress over Lee's escape was felt no higher than in the White House. In a July 21 letter to Gen. Oliver O. Howard, Lincoln wrote, "I was deeply mortified by the escape of Lee across the Potomac, because the substantial destruction of his army would have ended the war."[8] Failure to demolish the Army of Northern Virginia led to accusations that Meade ignored the Union's best opportunity to end the war in July 1863. This debate was not confined to letters, newspapers, or periodicals. The Committee on the Conduct of the War, which was controlled by Radical Republicans with a deep suspicion of Democrats and West Pointers, took up the issue.[9]

Meade and his lieutenants had earned the victory at Gettysburg, but there was a problem. In Union military circles there were more than enough egos who wanted their share of the credit. An easy step toward helping one's self-image and self-promotion was to denigrate the roles played by others in the victory. Not all soldiers in the two armies were looking out only for themselves, but enough saw the victory as an opportunity to cause problems for others. None was better at the game than the original 3rd Corps commander at Gettysburg, Daniel E. Sickles.

Wounded on the second day of the battle, Sickles was a major thorn in Meade's side in front of the Committee on the Conduct of the War. Sickles asserted that his forward movement on July 2, while being against Meade's orders, provoked combat at a time when Meade was hesitant to move. By initiating the contact, Sickles claimed that he alone was responsible for the victory at Gettysburg.[10] To bolster his assertion, Sickles's testimony outlandishly ignored the fighting on the first day. "We in the army do not regard the operations of the two corps under General Reynolds as properly the battle of Gettysburg," he said. "We regard the operations of Thursday and Friday, when the whole army was concentrated as the battle of Gettysburg."[11]

In this accusatory atmosphere it was no surprise that the committee also labored over Meade's failure to destroy Lee after Gettysburg. The Confederates had escaped, and someone had to bear the blame for the lost opportunity. Meade was the obvious target. To be sure, many had hoped in the days after Gettysburg, with Lee's army wounded and retreating, a prospect to end the war was presented to the Union commanders.

Yet in the days immediately after the battle of Gettysburg, Meade focused on knowing where Lee was marching his army. He pushed John Sedgwick's 6th Corps forward, not to engage the enemy, but to obtain information on Lee's movements. Meanwhile, Lee hoped that Meade would attack with the Confederate army's back to the South Mountains and the two passes available.[12] The thought of Lee's wanting to be attacked would cause any opposing commander to hesitate and deliberate such action.

As both armies worked their way toward Williamsport and Falling Waters, their cavalries continued a deadly game of skirmishing, always looking to exploit an opening. Could Meade have moved more rapidly and brought Lee to bay? There is no answer to this question that would satisfy students of the battle. As with Richard S. Ewell's failure to attack on the first day of Gettysburg, so Meade's actions after the battle leave all wondering if he could have found the place and time to attack Lee and further damage or destroy the Confederate army.

By July 12, the Confederates were building pontoon bridges and guarding the approaches to the Potomac River at Falling Waters and Williamsport.[13] While Lee waited, he strengthened his already formidable defenses with the Union army only two miles away. In a council of war on the same day, Meade met with the corps commanders who had studied these defenses. Despite Meade's own desire for a frontal assault, his generals voted seven to two against the action, factoring in the Confederates' entrenchments and the ground the Union troops would have to cover.[14] Right or wrong, the decision not to attack was made on July 13. That evening,

This rear-guard action near Falling Waters in Maryland was the concluding action of the Gettysburg campaign.

Meade ordered four divisions forward the next day to unmask Lee's defenses, but it was too late. The Army of Northern Virginia had escaped.[15]

Whether or not the Union army could have destroyed Lee on July 14, even with Lee's back to the river, remains a foggy question. Criticism followed Meade for the rest of the war and after it over his decision not to attack Lee on either July 4 or July 13.

32

In Harm's Way

$\mathcal{O}$VERLOOKED IN MANY ACCOUNTS of the battle, the civilians of Gettysburg were in harm's way before, during, and after the battle. Occupied by Confederates on the first day of the battle, the town itself remained in Rebel hands until July 4. For the residents, their ordeal did not end after the armies marched away. Regrettably, most visitors to the battlefield today do not have sufficient time to digest the many remarkable details of the battle, including the numerous stories of the townspeople. To many, the story of the only civilian killed, Jenny Wade, dominates the chronicle of the ordeal suffered by civilians during and after the battle (see chapter 30, "One More Needless Death"). But there is so much more, for the stories of the civilians vary from humor to tragedy, including a kidnapping that is seldom discussed in the histories of the battle.

More than eight hundred families in Adams County suffered losses, personal and material, because of the battle.[1] Their troubles began in late June, when Jubal Early's division arrived and rummaged for supplies. Shortly after their departure, John Buford's cavalry arrived and established vedettes to monitor the approach of the main body of Lee's army. After the fighting of July 1, many Union soldiers sought refuge from victorious Confederates in the homes of the citizens. Those citizens who accommodated these requests did so at great risk when Confederates began searching the town for Union stragglers. Corpses of soldiers and horses littered the streets. Add the July heat, and the odor of death permeated the town.

Farms were stripped of food, animals, and fencing.[2] The loss of food was critical for the farmers and townspeople, who could face shortages for the rest of the year. This included the loss of gardens found at every home in town. All foodstuffs disappeared as the soldiers consumed everything they found. Clothing also suffered the same fate.[3] After the battle, claims were submitted for twenty-five hundred animals either dead or missing.[4] Typical was the claim of the John Forney farm northwest of Gettysburg on the Mummasburg Road. The farm lost almost four thousand fence rails, sixty-two acres of lost crops, household property, and damage to the home as a result of its being used as a hospital.[5]

Individual personalities shone through the smoke of battle. Catherine "Katie" Guinn lived on a farm on the Taneytown Road. No longer in existence, the farm was just south of the national cemetery. Since it was very close to the battle line of the Union 2nd Corps, less than 150 yards, her home was used as a hospital and aid station. Katie, though, was a match for all the battle had to offer. Allegedly any Union soldier lacking a clear reason to be around her home was physically confronted and "beat up." One can only imagine the pounding an unlucky soldier suffered when he was found in her cellar and left dirt on her clean laundry.[6]

Proximity to windows placed every civilian in danger. At the Henry Jacobs home on West Middle Street, father and son ventured outside on July 2 to sit on the cellar door and listen to the cannonade. When whizzing bullets came too close, the two adventurers quickly returned to the cellar—a common refuge for all the townspeople. Shortly thereafter, a soldier in George Doles's Georgia brigade occupied the seat recently vacated by the Jacobses. From inside the cellar, the family heard the soldier groan, fall over, and slide off the cellar door. Despite the summer heat, few civilians ventured outside of their cellars.[7] Still, bullets wounded at least four civilians.[8]

Those homes along the paths followed by wounded soldiers toward their lines were soon occupied, creating further problems and tribulations for the homeowners. John and Martha Scott's store and home on Chambersburg Street was no exception. Wounded Union soldiers from the first day's fighting came to the home looking for aid. Confederate soldiers shortly followed and took a number of the Federals as prisoners. In the confusion, Martha hid a Union officer's sword.[9]

Artist Alfred Waud sketched this sharpshooting scene in the town.

Martha's sister Mary lived with the Jacobses, and she went to the Christ Lutheran Church on Chambersburg Street to assist with the wounded. After hours of caring for torn bodies and the dying, an artillery shell struck the church. Fearful of further shellings and overcome by the sights, smells, and sounds of human carnage in the makeshift hospital, she returned home.[10] On July 2, when she was unable to get help for a Union soldier, Mary sought out a local doctor to conduct an amputation in the house. Unwelcome guests arrived to the door, and five Confederate surgeons demanded that Martha cook for them.[11]

Yet more dangers stalked the civilians, such as captivity. While Confederate soldiers were looking for Union soldiers in hiding, fifteen-year-old Albertus McCreary made the mistake of wearing a Union kepi outside his home. As soon as they spotted McCreary's military headgear, two soldiers took him prisoner. Only the protestations of the father and the neighbors convinced the soldier in charge that the teenager may be foolish but he was not a soldier.[12]

The fate of several Gettysburg-area men has long been buried in the past and rarely mentioned. Taken prisoner, they were marched to Virginia and then to various prisons in the South. By 1865 all of the men returned—except for William Harper, who died at the prison at Salisbury, North Carolina. Harper was from Greenmount, Pennsylvania, and the Confederates also seized his son, Alexander. The group of civilian prisoners included the postmaster of Fairfield, Pennsylvania.[13]

In the months that followed the battle, soldiers with serious wounds continued to die in the hospitals erected around the town. Civilians also continued to die. With forty-five thousand to sixty thousand shells brought to the battle by the two armies, danger lay everywhere after the armies departed. Of course, it was not long before the locals engaged in relic hunting. In late July, a father and son were killed near Greenwood, Pennsylvania, while trying to open an artillery shell. A second son was seriously wounded. A young boy was killed in August, and in September a seventeen-year-old boy was killed in Maryland, both while dabbling with artillery shells. So it went, civilians dying who otherwise would have lived had the battle not occurred.[14]

33

Who Lived?
Who Died?

*F*IFTY-ONE THOUSAND IS A hard number to fathom, but fifty-one thousand men were either dead, wounded, or missing after the smoke cleared from Gettysburg. Yet the number is often recited without appreciating the scale of the casualties inflicted here. The names and the faces of those who sacrificed their lives and bodies are lost in the enormity of the sterile number. But from the time of the battle to the present, the actual number of men killed, wounded, and missing has been in a fog.

Poor communications, misidentifications, faulty record keeping, and false information led to many misunderstandings and wrong assumptions about battlefield casualties. Immediately after the battle, numerous reports included two Confederate corps commanders—James Longstreet and A. P. Hill—among the lists of the wounded, captured, or killed.[1] It would take time for those false bits of information to be sorted from the truth. For high-ranking officers such as Longstreet and Hill, newspapers were quicker in clarifying the facts for family and friends. For the families of common soldiers awaiting news of their loved ones, news was exceptionally slow in coming. The terrible news may come from a list of casualties printed in the newspaper or posted by the telegraph office or railroad station or via letter from an officer or a soldier, advising the family of the death or wounding of their loved one.

For the battle of Gettysburg, the *Official Reports* list the casualties for the Union as 2,834 killed, 13,713 wounded, and 6,428 missing, a total of

23,190.[2] Confederate losses are tallied at 2,592 killed, 12,709 wounded, and 5,150 missing.[3] This is the best calculation the compilers of the *Official Records* could make. The Confederate numbers are known to be inaccurate because several of the units that were heavily involved in the fighting did not report any missing soldiers. Additionally, the *Official Records* acknowledges that there are discrepancies in the numbers its sources provide. After the battle, the Union adjutant general records showed 12,227 Confederates (including wounded and unwounded) as being captured, compared to the *OR* number of 5,150.[4]

A prime example of the differing accounts on casualties for losses is Brig. Gen. James H. Lane's North Carolina brigade. The *OR* numbers report 41 dead and 348 wounded with no missing, a total of 389 casualties.[5] Lane's report in the *OR* records his total losses as 660.[6] Other units never reported their casualties, such as Joseph D. Moore's and John W. Lewis's batteries in Henry Heth's division.[7] A Herculean effort would be required to rectify the two numbers.

A second example of the difficulties in sorting out the numbers can be found in the only Florida brigade at Gettysburg. Col. David Lang led the brigade through the fighting on July 2 and July 3. Examination of John Busey and David Martin's *Regimental Strengths and Losses at Gettysburg* records that the unit lost 455 men of 742 engaged, leaving 287 men available for duty.[8] In a letter to his cousin on July 9, Lang stated, "Of the whole number (700) which I carried in I now have 220 for duty."[9] The numbers are close (287 v. 220), but they do not match. How does one rectify the difference?

This confusing fog has many sources. Although the Union army performed a complete muster roll on June 30, none was taken on July 4. Subsequent movements by the army after the battle meant that updated musters were not always completed.[10] Stragglers could never be accurately assessed. Union soldiers listed as killed in the *OR* were only those who were killed on the battlefield or died soon afterward.[11] Adversely, the Confederate numbers included soldiers who had died by the end of 1863.[12] Were all wounded men counted, including the walking wounded? How many of the missing were dead and their bodies never found? We have more questions then answers.

The extent of the casualties sustained by the two armies remained in a fog until the late twentieth century when historians scrutinized the battle records. Although the fog did not lift, it is less thick. In the years after the war, three sources were used to compile casualty numbers. *The War of the Rebellion: A Compilation of the Official Records of the Union and Confederate Armies* was published by the War Department over a twenty-one-year period from 1880 to 1901. The other two sources are William F. Fox's *Regimental Losses in the American Civil War, 1861–1865* (1889) and Thomas L. Livermore's *Numbers and Losses in the Civil War in America, 1861–65* (1901). Fox and Livermore were veterans of the war.

In the 1980s historians undertook a monumental effort to update the numbers. Works such as Robert Frick and Chris Ferguson's *The Gettysburg Death Roster: The Confederate Dead at Gettysburg* (1981) and John Busey and David Martin's *Regimental Strengths and Losses at Gettysburg* (1982) shed new light on the casualty numbers. Both of these works are in their fourth editions. Additional work includes Kathleen R. Georg and John W. Busey's *Nothing But Glory: Pickett's Division at Gettysburg* (1987), John W. Busey's *These Honored Dead: The Union Casualties at Gettysburg* (1988), and William Howard's *The Gettysburg Death Roster: The Union Dead at Gettysburg* (1991).

The latest research reveals a larger casualty list than previously known, particularly with regard to Confederates, whose casualties appear to number more than 23,000 with 4,649 dead.[13] Historians Busey, Ferguson, Frick, Georg, Howard, and Martin acknowledge that they have not found definitive numbers and their Confederate numbers are still understated, particularly for the dead, because there is a dearth of Confederate records.[14] Union numbers, however, remain fairly constant, around 23,000.[15] The latest works, however, catalog the Union dead at more than 5,000.[16]

With ongoing efforts to reexamine the numbers, a fair statement placing the total number of fatalities at Gettysburg in excess of 10,000 would be in line. The revised numbers come from greater scrutiny of the totals of wounded and missing. The overall number of casualties has not risen, but the battle has become deadlier, much more so than we realized. The fog is thinner, but it persists.

34

The Photographs Lie

AN OLD ADAGE ASSERTS, "Photographs never lie and photographs never forget." For better or for worse, the rapid technological advancements of the twenty-first century have shredded that allegedly wise saying. The ability to alter and revise photographs is within reach of anyone with a computer and certain graphics programs. At the time of the Civil War, photography was in its infancy. Today, we are the beneficiaries of the work of individuals who dedicated themselves to preserve primitive Civil War photography. These photography historians are unwrapping many of the mysteries surrounding the photographs of the conflict.

Although limited in number, the photographs and captions were taken at face value for more than a century. In 1975, a book appeared that blew away long-held assumptions and accepted facts. William Frassanito's *Gettysburg: A Journey in Time* opened many eyes and challenged everyone to look deeper into the photographs. His book followed a simple premise and exposed a number of lies associated with photography at Gettysburg.[1] Frassanito found the positions of the camera of the original photographs of Gettysburg and captured modern images to demonstrate how the scene had or had not changed. What followed was the realization that the earlier photographers had mislabeled their photographs, particularly photographs of the dead.

A prime example is the photograph on page 186. After the battle, various photographs were assumed to be Union corpses in the Wheatfield or the first day's field of battle near the McPherson farm. Frassanito found the rocks in the background and made a positive identification of the bodies as Confederates on the Rose farm.[2] As a result, the National Park Service removed the nonhistoric trees at the site so the increasing number of visitors who visited the area with Frassanito's book in hand would have a better understanding of the area. The book is an absolute must-have for any student of the battle.

How did the photographs come to be so badly mislabeled? To begin to answer this question, one must embrace the reality of 1863. If we were to project modern media methods on a major historical event like the battle of Gettysburg, we can imagine a horde of cameras and satellite uplinks descending on the crossroads like locusts on a field of grain. Video cameras would be everywhere. Journalists and their camera operators would be embedded with the regiments going into action. In fact, though, the only newsmen traveling with the armies during the Civil War were correspondents and artists with pencil and paper. These people attempted to tell the stories and record the scenes of the war for the masses. Although news traveled quickly over telegraph wires, the artists' renderings of the battle scenes

This image of dead Confederate soldiers on the Rose farm, who fell in action on July 2, has often been mislabeled as Union casualties of July 1 near McPherson's farm.

had to be transported physically to newspaper offices for publication. These did not appear in print until days or weeks after the battle.

Civil War photographers were not part of any news organizations, nor did news organizations supply the wagons of photographic equipment necessary to document the battlefield. These early photographers were entrepreneurs whose business was to sell their images to the public. These photographers blazed a new trail in the communications field: photojournalism. Traveling closely behind the armies, the photographers wasted no time in recording the scenes of a battlefield—after the fighting was over. Pioneer photographer Alexander Gardner (formerly of Mathew Brady's studio) and his assistant arrived on the battlefield in the late afternoon of July 5. The main body of their work was conducted the next day and included photographs of the dead at Gettysburg.[3] Mathew Brady and his assistants arrived in the area on July 15 and began photographing scenes of the battle. These photographers were followed by many more. The Tyson Brothers, Isaac and Charles, opened a studio in Gettysburg and sold views of the battlefield. Their assistants and later owners of the shop continued to photograph the area. Others, including Samuel Weaver, Peter Weaver, Hanson Weaver, Frederick Gutekunst, and Samuel Corlies, also preserved nineteenth-century views of this hallowed ground.[4]

During the 1960s, video of the Vietnam War brought the conflict into American living rooms via nightly newscasts. A hundred years earlier, private photographers' studios in New York and Washington brought the war into American parlors during the Civil War. A colorful, creative title for a photograph here and there might bring a faster sale. After all, sales were needed to continue the work they had begun. Who could correct such misinformation? The soldiers moved on with the armies and had seen the reality of the dead. Local citizens were not frequent visitors to the larger cities. Even if they had, they would not have necessarily spotted the misinformation. After all, during battles, civilians mostly sought refuge in their basements or fled the area for safety. Most likely, the locals were not in a position to know the content of the photographs.

While today we are vexed with the misidentified photographs, we are ever grateful to the wartime photographers for their work in documenting the war.

35

Ectoplasm or Imagination?

AFTER THE COLD WHITE winter weather of southern Pennsylvania, early each year the unmistakable signs of warm weather returning can be found around Gettysburg: increasing numbers of birds, grass greening, trees leafing, flowers blooming, growing numbers of vehicles and visitors to the national park, and offers of evening ghost tours. The tour guides for these ventures, outfitted in period garb and carrying a candle lantern, escort groups while relating ghostly stories and echoes of the battle. On the city square, along Baltimore Street or Steinwehr Avenue, visitors can join a ghost tour to hear the stories peculiar to the north side and the south side of town.

Ghost stories have long been a part of the Gettysburg history, but in recent years they have reached a crescendo of offerings. This expansion of the tours should surprise no one, considering the number of television shows on the alleged hauntings of various parts of America. Many people are fascinated with ghost stories, and Gettysburg offers a unique setting for spectral activity. In 1991, the first of a steadily increasing stream of books on the ghosts of Gettysburg was published.[1]

From the Cashtown Inn to the Evergreen Cemetery gatehouse, mysterious footsteps and moving furniture are common signs of the alleged ghostly energy of the battle. Buildings and farms used as hospitals are prime sites for ghostly appearances. On the fields where the fighting occurred, chills, cold winds on warm summer days, or momentary visions of soldiers are frequently reported. On a dark night on the field of Pickett's Charge, two explorers experienced a sudden drop in temperature from 33 degrees to 3 degrees?[2] Some intrepid souls have dabbled in spirit photography, hoping to reveal "ectoplasm" on the battlefield.[3]

Gettysburg or any battlefield is fertile ground for ethereal stories. A sadness can be felt on these fields where men suffered and died. Most left behind unfulfilled dreams and ambitions. Sweethearts, wives, and family were left without a final farewell or closure of family matters. Emotion was in no short supply when shot and shell shattered this air.

During my many trips to Gettysburg, I have been asked if I have encountered any ghosts. My first experience came in the early 1980s, when I heard the story of the Triangular Field south of Devil's Den. Supposedly, if you attempted to photograph this field, your camera would mysteriously malfunction. Having never believed in ghosts, I was nonetheless pondering the story as I headed to the field one day. My camera performed flawlessly in the Triangular Field on that day and every other trip I have made to the field. While stomping around the battlefield, I have never encountered any apparitions or wisps of ghostly spirit.

The most interesting story of a ghost on the field came during a conversation with a National Park Service ranger. During a discussion on the mortal wounding of Confederate Brig. Gen. William Barksdale on July 2, the ranger related that annually on the evening of July 2 at midnight, near the George Weikert farm, one could hear Barksdale's dog calling for his lost master. It was a sad and forlorn sound, neither barking nor howling, but clearly a sign of distress. But, he added, it helps to consume two or three beers before listening for the dog. Humor aside, encounters with vaporous forms is a personal matter that science struggles with proving.

The fog of ghosts at Gettysburg remains an unanswered question. Thousands of books, articles, letters, and pamphlets were written on the battle by historians and veterans. Examination of the articles, diaries, and journals of the men who fought here reveals little in offering proof of ghosts before, during, or after the battle.

Today, apparitions and spirits are not universally accepted. The lack of agreement leaves us with a problem. Do we believe the stories? Should visitors go on ghost tours? Perhaps visitors should remember that the collection of ghost stories of Gettysburg has no bearing on the events or outcome of the battle. In the study of history, phantoms are an afterthought, an addendum. The spectral tales and stories do not add to our understanding of the events at Gettysburg, but they are nonetheless entertaining and fascinating.

36

Under the Spreading Chestnut Tree

$\mathcal{U}$NDER THE SPREADING CHESTNUT tree, the village smithy stands," Henry Wadsworth Longfellow wrote in 1839. But under the trees of Gettysburg, a battlefield stands. The dense foliage provided cover for Civil War armies, masking their movements and intentions from opposing forces. The trees and dense undergrowth of modern Gettysburg hide only the ground they cover, forcing visitors to visualize some of the undulations of the land and the depth of the woods.

The terrain at Gettysburg is as varied as the people who have tread its fields, ridges, rocky outcroppings, and hills. To the northwest, Oak Hill dominates the flat area called the Gettysburg Plain. To the south and west, a series of ridges resemble ocean waves. Known as Knoxlyn Ridge, Herr Ridge, Seminary Ridge, and Cemetery Ridge, all played a part in the battle. South and southeast of Gettysburg, several hills rise and tower over the surrounding ground. Culp's Hill, Cemetery Hill, Powers Hill, Little Round Top, and Big Round Top fall within the boundaries of the battlefield park. The jumbled boulders of Devil's Den are remnants of a geological age whose name many have long forgotten. The soldiers may have thought of the masses of granite as protection or a hindrance, but today, children of all ages are enticed to climb around the natural playground. After surveying their immediate conquest, they look for more challenges.

In the twenty-first century, the trees and the growth of the town create the densest fog in visually understanding the battlefield of Gettysburg. The town is caught between the proverbial rock and a hard place, wanting to expand but not at the cost of destroying the fields that bring visitors and commerce. The National Park Service also has a similar predicament. The mission of the park is to restore as much of the battlefield as possible so that visitors can see an unspoiled landscape. But within the town's precincts, that much of the battlefield can never be recovered.

The trees are another matter. Critical to life in 1863, orchards were used for food and income. Wooded lots provided fuel for cooking and warmth in winter. In the decades after the battle, the small orchards declined in importance to everyday life. Farming practices and industrialization changed lives and the needs for orchards and wooded lots. Some orchards were abandoned while others were expanded. Following the law of nature, trees in the wooded lots multiplied without the intervention of livestock and/or man. As the connection between wood to fuel and cooking became more tenuous, the wooded areas expanded beyond the Civil War boundaries.

In 1999, the National Park Service implemented a plan to restore the wooded lots to their original dimensions.[1] Orchards and woods would be recreated or reduced to reflect conditions as they existed in July 1863. In an age of increasing recognition of the benefit of trees, the effort to recreate the battlefield caused and still causes outcry among various individuals and groups over the loss of tracts of trees. The protests miss an important point. Visitors and historians come to Gettysburg to see the battlefield as it was in 1863; they do not come to see the trees. A local historian succinctly stated, "This hallowed ground is called the Gettysburg National Military Park, not the Gettysburg National Forest."

In nineteenth-century America, trees were life-providing materials for farmers and townspeople. All assets were to be used, and livestock were permitted to graze under the canopy of leaves, reducing the undergrowth. Not so today. Touring the battlefield, visitors are often confounded by the burgeoning undergrowth, adding to the fog of Gettysburg. The jumble of growth makes it difficult, if not impossible, to envision the fighting, the movements of troops, and sightlines of the soldiers. This is particularly true of the woods near the McPherson farm, Culp's Hill, and the Round Tops.

The woods near the McPherson farm are called both the Herbst

Wartime artist Edwin Forbes painted this scene of the July 2 assault on Culp's Hill. He shows the woods on the hill as being much thinner than they are today.

Woods and the McPherson Woods. Herbst Woods is the correct moniker, as the Herbst family owned the lot. John Slentz's family occupied the McPherson farm while Edward McPherson was serving as assistant deputy to the newly founded Internal Revenue Service in Washington. McPherson's family never occupied the farm.[2] The woods sit south of the farm and were the scene of ferocious combat between the Union Iron Brigade and J. Johnston Pettigrew's brigade on July 1. On the western edge of the woods, Maj. Gen. John F. Reynolds was killed. The heavy growth makes it difficult to understand how Reynolds died. Looking into the woods, visualizing the combat is left to the imagination. In 1863, the woods were thinner and the undergrowth was nonexistent, providing only minor impediments to the soldiers. What can be done about the undergrowth and trees? The answer is simple: money. Whether this fog can be cleared depends on how much time and money can be spent in keeping the undergrowth at bay.

Similarly, the trees and undergrowth on Culp's Hill obscure the terrain and sightlines of the soldiers as much or more than they do in the Herbst Woods. A print of an Edwin Forbes's drawing after the battle (above) clearly demonstrates the openness of Culp's Hill at the time of the battle. Historians are anxious to have the same unobstructed views today, but for the present they content themselves with visiting the area in the off-season, when the leaves are gone and the undergrowth is subdued. Otherwise, an emerald fog blocks the critical views.

Still offering a view that allows appreciation of the fighting here is the western face of Little Round Top, which appears much as it did in 1863. The reverse slope, however, is covered with heavy growth and obscures the terrain traversed by Union regiments and batteries to reinforce the hill on the critical afternoon of July 2. Present-day visitors cannot easily imagine the sweating, straining, and slipping that occurred here while heavy cannon were hauled to the summit. A hillside road adds to the fog, giving the impression of an easy time in approaching the crest, but no road existed in 1863. For many years, the view of the base of Big Round Top from Little Round Top was clouded by the trees, covering the approach of the Confederate attack on July 2. In 2007, the process of moving the tree line began and now offers an unobstructed view of the area, including a toilet facility that had remained hidden for decades under the green umbrella of trees (see photograph below).

With each passing year and the slow return to the original woodlot lines, the protective coat opens to reveal the battlefield. Unobstructed views of the battlefield are all visitors and students of the battle have wanted. That green fog is beginning to clear.

The base of Big Round Top was cleared of trees in 2007. The triangle of land between the roads on the left now resembles its appearance in 1863, except for the rest facility that was previously hidden by trees.

37

Was the War Fought West of Gettysburg?

$\mathcal{T}$HE NATIONAL PARK AT Gettysburg has it all. A leisurely drive past solemn monuments on tree-lined roads while viewing the diverse landscape is a pleasant excursion. Human-interest stories attract a wide audience. But a reading of the events of the battle generates more questions most battlefield guides can answer in a day. What-if questions are endless and engrossing. On the battlefield, quiet contemplation of the bloody events leads to a deep appreciation and respect for the men who fought here those three days in July. Away from the battlefield, the museums, shops, lodgings, and restaurants provide diversions. Regrettably, immersion in the Gettysburg experience can lead to a mistaken view of the war. Gettysburg may seem to have been the pivotal battle that determined the outcome of the Civil War, but such a vision is mistaken.

Living in the Midwest has meant long and time-consuming road trips to follow my passion. But living in the Midwest has also given me a different perspective of the role Gettysburg played in the Civil War. The war was not won or lost here. A historical construction of the Civil War resembles a brick wall, built piece by piece over four years by millions of men and women, involving countless decisions and the vicissitudes of war.

Finding a historian who believes the war was won in the West is not difficult.[1] Such beliefs are based on considering the whole war, not just individual battles. The script for Ken Burns's *The Civil War* has an appropriate comment covering the totality of the Civil War:

The Civil War was fought in 10,000 places, from Valverde, New Mexico, and Tullahoma, Tennessee, to St. Albans, Vermont, and Fernandina on the Florida coast. . . . American homes became headquarters. American churches and schoolhouses sheltered the dying, and huge foraging armies swept across American farms, burned American towns. Americans slaughtered one another wholesale, right here in America in their own cornfields and peach orchards, along familiar roads and by waters with old American names.

In two days at Shiloh, on the banks of the Tennessee River, more American men fell than in all previous American wars combined. At Cold Harbor, some 7,000 Americans fell in twenty minutes. Men who had never strayed twenty miles from their own front doors now found themselves soldiers in great armies fighting epic battles hundreds of miles from home.[2]

When engulfed by the experience of Gettysburg, the possibility of losing sight of the other four years of the war should be avoided. A glance through a day-by-day almanac of the war serves as a reminder that the entire nation was involved politically, militarily, socially, and financially. A great many factors determined the outcome of the war.

Turning a thousand miles to the west, the victory at Vicksburg on July 4 had great implications for the war. The Union now controlled the Mississippi River, cutting off Arkansas, Louisiana, and Texas from the rest of the Confederacy and depriving Southern armies of men and material from those states. In addition, an entire army had been captured. If Lee's image had been tarnished at Gettysburg, Ulysses S. Grant's star was on the rise. In the North, jubilation doubled over news of the twin victories.[3] In the South, spirits tumbled into "despondency."[4]

How did Gettysburg gain a higher position in public recognition than Vicksburg? Several factors played a role. First, as Lee's army moved north in the campaign, the emotions of those in Washington went from calm to nervous to panic. Upon Lee's retreat, a huge weight had been lifted from the city.[5] The relief would cause many to look at Gettysburg as the saving battle of the war. Second, the war in the east and Gettysburg were in close proximity to the major newspapers.[6] It would be easier to obtain information from southeast Pennsylvania than from a river city in Mississippi. Third, Gettysburg was the largest battle fought on Northern

At Vicksburg, on July 4, 1863, the day after the fighting had concluded at Gettysburg, Confederate Gen. John C. Pemberton surrendered the Mississippi River stronghold to Union Gen. Ulysses S. Grant. This capitulation concluded forty-four days of siege, gave the North complete control of the central waterway, and effectively severed the Confederacy east and west.

soil, and after Lee's army left, visitors could tour the battlefield—not so with Vicksburg.

Not all leaders or citizens viewed Gettysburg as the greatest victory of the war in the days after the battle. One of these was Abraham Lincoln. Although the president was not at Gettysburg, he knew the key to victory was the destruction of Lee's army. Lincoln did not keep these thoughts to himself but verbalized them to several people:

> Our army held the war in the hollow of their hand, and they would not close it. We had gone through all the labor of tilling and planting an enormous crop, and when it was ripe we did not harvest it.—to John Hay, one of the president's secretaries[7]

> "Drive the invaders from our soil" My god! Is that all?—Lincoln's exclamation after reading Meade's message to the army after the battle[8]

I was deeply mortified by the escape of General Lee's troops across the Potomac, because the substantial destruction of his army would have ended the war.—letter to Oliver O. Howard, July 21, 1863[9]

The last quote is especially significant as it demonstrates Lincoln's understanding of the war. It was not until Lee surrendered that the celebration of the war's end could begin. After Lee's surrender at Appomattox Court House in April 1865, the Confederacy still had armies in North Carolina and Texas. But even the most fervent Southerners realized Lee's surrender was the conclusion of their fight for independence.

The twin defeats of early July 1863 were depressing for the Confederacy, but Jefferson Davis still believed the war could be won.[10] The road would be more difficult, but all was not lost. The Confederate victory at Chickamauga in September 1863 gave support to the Confederate president's beliefs.[11] But the summertime losses had far-reaching effects. Henry Hotze, a Confederate agent in London, wrote of difficulties in securing loans: "When the last lingering doubts about the events on the Mississippi were removed, and no hope remained of Lee again turning upon the enemy, the loan, despite the utmost exertions of its friends, fell with accelerating velocity." The Confederate losses at Gettysburg, Vicksburg, and Port Hudson combined to destroy the last of the Confederate credit in Europe.[12]

By the fall of 1863, the North's jubilant summer had been muted by the realization that the war could still be lost. The Union defeat at Chickamauga reminded all that the Confederacy was still a dangerous foe and far from beaten and demoralized. Much more blood would be shed.

After the Union victory at Gettysburg, two years of brutal combat in the eastern theater remained. New names would be entered in the military history book: Mine Run, Cold Harbor, Spotsylvania, the Wilderness, the Crater, Petersburg, Five Forks, and on and on. Still, it would be unfair to categorize Gettysburg as just another battle in the East. On those three days in July 1863, the Union army found itself and came to believe in itself and its ability to defeat Robert E. Lee. The battle could have been a victory for either the North or the South. Ramifications of a Confederate victory are purely conjectural. Unless the Army of the Potomac had vaporized after a loss at Gettysburg, it would have still been between Lee and Washington.

Perhaps the real meaning of Gettysburg can never be stated in one sentence. Perhaps the best tribute Gettysburg can bestow on its visitors is a desire to seek more information about the entire war. The awareness of the sacrifice paid by others in other states would lead all of us to a better understanding of the war.

Appendixes

Numbers and Units

The Fog of Order

*B*OTH ARMIES WERE AMERICAN. The soldiers spoke the same language. Soldiers had friends or relatives among the enemy. West Point had graduated a number of the officers in the two armies. Even the armies were organized similarly by corps, divisions, brigades, regiments, battalions, companies, troops, batteries, platoons, and messes.[1] Likewise the chain of command went from general to lieutenant general, major general, brigadier general, colonel, lieutenant colonel, major, captain, lieutenant, sergeant, corporal, and private.

Adding an interesting dimension to rank are brevet ranks. This followed a pattern in the French army by which officers were promoted unofficially on merit. Such promotions were temporary but could be made permanent if the proper paperwork was submitted through official channels. In the prewar army, brevets bestowed rank and all that came with it— except an increase in pay.

Despite the organizational similarities between the Union and Confederate armies, a fog in comparison develops over names and numbers. The Union army was methodical and numbered its units: 3rd Corps, 2nd Division, 3rd Brigade, 5th New Jersey. But for the new student, the numbers mean little if anything. In the Confederate army, units were named after their commanders. Although the three corps of the Army of Northern Virginia were numbered 1st, 2nd, and 3rd, the corps are generally referred to as Longstreet's, Ewell's, and Hill's. To add a little confusion to the Confederate army, some brigades were named for commanders who were not on duty during the battle of Gettysburg. Florida had one brigade at Gettysburg, and it's referred to as Perry's or Lang's brigade. Brig. Gen. Edward Aylesworth Perry was the brigade's commander, but he was ill, recovering from typhoid, in July 1863, and command of the brigade fell to Col. David Lang.[2] If one is unaware of this, it appears there are two Florida brigades at Gettysburg. Likewise, the Louisiana brigade lost its commander, Francis Nicholls, at Chancellorsville; Col. Jesse Williams commanded the brigade at Gettysburg. Thus the literature may refer to this brigade as Nicholls's or Williams's brigade.

Further complicating matters, the armies were not static. In the Army of the Potomac, units were transferred during reorganizations or commanders were taken ill, transferred, promoted, demoted, wounded, or killed. To know the organization of the Army of the Potomac at the battle of Antietam in September 1862 is not to know the same army at Gettysburg. Lee's army was no different. For example, Longstreet's corps was transferred to the Army of Tennessee in time for the battle of Chickamauga in September 1863.

Finally, the number of men in the two armies will never be known. Attendance was not taken as the regiments arrived at Gettysburg. The armies that fought here were not concise, finite units of men. Companies, regiments, and brigades were assigned to guard supply routes, lines of communications, or the rear of the army. Hard marching found soldiers dropping out of line from exhaustion, illness, heat stroke, or fear. Often missed in the details of the famous charge of July 2 by the 1st Minnesota is the fact that only seven of the regiment's ten companies were engaged here. The three other companies—C, F, and L—had been reassigned to other areas on the battlefield.[3] Company F would rejoin the regiment in time to repulse Pickett's Charge on July 3.[4] Thus the full strength of the 1st Minnesota cannot be assumed when examining actions attributed to the regiment at any given time.

The order of battle below can give one the wrong impression. For example, the 2nd Vermont Brigade was not involved in all the actions in which the Union 1st Corps was engaged. George J. Stannard's 2nd Vermont was assigned to the 1st Corps a week before the battle, on June 23,

1863, but the brigade was not part of the first day's fighting at Gettysburg. The 1st Corps was devastated in these early actions, but the Vermont Brigade was unscathed. In fact, the Vermonters' claim to glory came on July 3, when they ravaged the right flank of Pickett's division and then turned 180 degrees to repulse the late attack of two other Confederate brigades.[5]

While the Union army was larger in total manpower, the makeup of individual units within Confederate corps and divisions was larger than their Union counterparts. The average strengths of infantry regiments were close: 334 men per Confederate regiment vs. 298 per Union regiment.[6] But many false assumptions that opposing corps and divisions were numerically equal will lead to equally as many false expectations about outcomes on the battlefield.

The following orders of battle are lengthy but more complete than those found in most books on the battle of Gettysburg. More information tends to lessen the fog, thus offering a better understanding of the battle. The numbers of soldiers engaged and their losses come from the fourth edition of John Busey and David Martin's *Regimental Strengths and Losses at Gettysburg*. The information on batteries comes from the same book and Gregory Coco's *A Concise Guide to the Artillery at Gettysburg*. I have also endeavored to provide more information on changes in leadership from the regimental level and higher; too often, no reason is offered as to why the change occurred.

The following abbreviations are used: a = arrested, aw = accidental wound, c = captured; i = illness, k = killed; m = missing, mw = mortally wounded; nr = no return on casualty figures; p = promoted during battle; r = returned to previous command during battle; w = wounded.

The Union Order of Battle

Army of the Potomac
Maj. Gen. George C. Meade, commanding
xxx [full compliment] / x% [percent of casualties]

Army Headquarters

Maj. Gen. Daniel Butterfield, chief of staff (w)
Brig. Gen. Gouverneur K. Warren, chief of engineers (w)
Brig. Gen. Henry J. Hunt, chief of artillery
Brig. Gen. Marsena R. Patrick, provost marshal general
Brig. Gen. Seth Williams, assistant adjutant general
Brig. Gen. Rufus Ingalls, chief quartermaster
Dr. Jonathan Letterman, medical director
Capt. Lemuel B. Norton, chief signal officer
Lt. John R. Edie, acting chief ordnance officer
Command of the Provost Marshal General
5th Pennsylvania Cavalry
6th Pennsylvania Cavalry, Cos. E and I
Regular Cavalry (detachments from 1st, 2nd, 5th, and 6th Regiments)

1st Corps

12,220 / 50%
Maj. Gen. John F. Reynolds (k)
Maj. Gen. Abner Doubleday (r)
Maj. Gen. John Newton

1st Division: Brig. Gen. James S. Wadsworth
  1st Brigade: Brig. Gen. Solomon Meredith (w)
        Col. William W. Robinson
    19th Indiana: 308 / 68%: Col. Samuel Williams
    24th Michigan: 496 / 73%: Col. Henry Morrow (w)
        Capt. Albert Edwards
    2nd Wisconsin: 302 / 77%: Col. Lucius Fairchild (k)
        Lt. Col. George Stevens (k)
        Maj. John Mansfield (w)
        Capt. George H. Otis
    6th Wisconsin: 344 / 49%: Lt. Col. Rufus Dawes
    7th Wisconsin: 364 / 49%: Col. William W. Robinson (p)
        Maj. Mark Finnicum
  2nd Brigade: Brig. Gen. Lysander Cutler
    7th Indiana: 434 / 2%: Col. Ira Grover
    76th New York: 375 / 62%: Maj. Andrew J. Grover (k)
        Capt. John Cook
    84th New York (14th Militia): 318 / 68%: Col. Edward B. Fowler
    95th New York: 241 / 48%: Col. George H. Biddle (w)
        Maj. Edward Pye
    147th New York: 380 / 78%: Lt. Col. Francis C. Miller (w)
        Maj. George Harney
    56th Pennsylvania (9 Cos.): 252 / 52%: Col. J. William Hoffman

2nd Division: Brig. Gen. John C. Robinson
  1st Brigade: Brig. Gen. Gabriel Paul (w)
        Col. Samuel H. Leonard (w)
        Col. Adrian Root (w/c)
        Col. Richard Coulter (w)
        Col. Peter Lyle (r)
        Col. Richard Coulter
    16th Maine: 298 / 78%: Col. Charles Tilden (w)
        Maj. Archibald D. Leavitt
    13th Massachusetts: 284 / 65%: Col. Samuel H. Leonard (p,w)
    94th New York: 411 / 60%: Col. Adrian r. Root (w,c)
        Maj. Samuel A. Moffett
    104th New York: 286 / 68%: Col. Gilbert G. Prey
    107th Pennsylvania: 255 / 65%: Lt. Col. James MacThompson (w)

Maj. Alfred J. Sellers

2nd Brigade: Brig. Gen. Henry Baxter

12th Massachusetts: 261 / 46%: Col. James L. Bates (w)
Lt. Col. David Allen Jr.

83rd New York: 199 / 41%: Lt. Col. Joseph A. Mensch

97th New York: 236 / 53%: Col. Charles Wheelock (c)
Maj. Charles Northrup

11th Pennsylvania: 270 / 49%: Col. Richard Coulter (p,w)
Capt. Benjamin F. Haines (w)
Capt. John B. Overmyer

88th Pennsylvania: 273 / 40%: Maj. Benezet F. Foust (w)
Capt. Henry Whiteside

90th New York: 208 / 40%: Col. Peter Lyle (p,r)
Capt. Emanuel D. Roth

3rd Division: Brig. Gen. Abner Doubleday (p)
Brig. Gen. Thomas A. Rowley (a)
Maj. Gen. Abner Doubleday

1st Brigade: Col. Chapman Biddle (w)
Brig. Gen. Thomas Rowley (a)

143rd Pennsylvania: 465 / 54%: Col. Theodore B. Gates

142nd Pennsylvania: 336 / 63%: Col. Robert P. Cummins (k)
Lt. Col. A. B. McCalmont

151st Pennsylvania: 467 / 72%: Lt. Col. George F. McFarland (w)
Capt. Walter F. Owens
Col. Harrison Allen

2nd Brigade: Col. Roy Stone (w)
Col. Langhorne Wister (w)
Col. Edmund L. Dana

80th New York (20th Militia): 287 / 59%: Col. Edmund Dana (p)
Lt. Col. John D. Musser

121st Pennsylvania: 263 / 68%: Maj. Alexander Biddle

149th Pennsylvania: 450 / 75%: Lt. Col. Walton Dwight (w)
Capt. James Glenn

150th Pennsylvania: 400 / 66%: Col. Langhorne Wister (p,w)
Lt. Col. H. S. Huidekper (w)
Capt. Cornelius C. Widdis

3rd Brigade: Brig. Gen. George J. Stannard (w)

Col. Francis V. Randall
13th Vermont: 636 / 19%: Col. Francis Randall (p)
Maj. Joseph J. Boynton
Lt. Col. William D. Munson
14th Vermont: 747 / 17%: Col. William T. Nichols
16th Vermont: 661 / 18%: Col. Wheelock G. Beasey
Artillery Brigade: Col. Charles S. Wainwright
2nd Maine Light, Battery B (6 3-inch rifles): 117 / 15%: Capt. James A. Hall
5th Maine Light, Battery E (6 Napoleons): 119 / 19%: Capt. Greenleaf T.
Stevens (w)
Lt. Edward N. Whittier
1st New York Light, Battery L & E (6 3-inch rifles): 124 / 14%: Capt. Gilbert
H. Reynolds (w)
Lt. George Breck
1st Pennsylvania Light Battery B (4 3-inch rifles): 114 / 11%: Capt. James H.
Cooper
4th U.S., Battery B (6 Napoleons): 23 / 29%: Lt. James Stewart (w)

2nd Corps

11,226 / 39%
Maj. Gen. Winfield S. Hancock (p)
Brig. Gen. John Gibbon (r)
Maj. Gen. Winfield S. Hancock (w)

1st Division: Brig. Gen. John C. Caldwell
1st Brigade: Col. Edward E. Cross (k)
Col. H. Boyd McKeen
5th New Hampshire: 179 / 45%: Lt. Col. Charles E. Haggard
61st New York: 104 / 60%: Lt. Col. K. Oscar Broady
81st New York: 175 / 35%: Col. H. Boyd McKeen (p)
Lt. Col. Amos Stroh
148th New York: 392 / 32%: Lt. Col. Robert McFarlane
2nd Brigade: Col. Patrick Kelly
28th Massachusetts: 224 / 45%: Col. Richard Burnes
63rd New York (2 Cos.): 75 / 31%: Lt. Col. Richard C. Bently (w)
Capt. Thomas Touhy
69th New York (2 Cos.): 75 / 33%: Capt. Richard Moroney (w)
Lt. James J. Smith

88th New York (2 Cos.): 90 / 31%: Capt. Denis F. Burke

116th Pennsylvania (4 Cos.): 66 / 33%: Maj. St. Clair A. Mulholland

3rd Brigade: Brig. Gen. Samuel K. Zook (mw)

      Lt. Col. John Fraser

52nd New York: 134 / 28%: Lt. Col. Charles G. Freudenberg (w)

      Capt. William Scherrer

57th New York: 175 / 19%: Lt. Col. Alford B. Chapman

66th New York: 147 / 30%: Col. Orlando H. Morris (w):

      Lt. Col. John S. Hammond (w)

      Maj. Peter Nelson

140th Pennsylvania: 515 / 47%: Col. Richard P. Roberts (k)

      Lt. Col. John Fraser (p)

4th Brigade: Col. John Brooke

27th Connecticut (2 Cos.): 75 / 49%: Lt. Col. Henry C. Merwin (k)

      Maj. James H. Coburn

2nd Delaware: 234 / 36%: Col. William P. Bailey

      Capt. Charles H. Christman

64th New York: 204 / 48%: Col. Daniel Bingham (w)

      Maj. Leman W. Bradley

53rd Pennsylvania: 135 / 59%: Lt. Col. Richard McMichael

145th Pennsylvania (7 Cos.): 202/ 45%: Col. Hiram L. Brown (w)

      Capt. John W. Reynolds (w)

      Capt. Moses W. Oliver

2nd Division: Brig. Gen. John Gibbon (p)

      Brig. Gen. William Harrow

      Brig. Gen. John Gibbon

1st Brigade: Brig. Gen. William Harrow (p)

      Col. Francis E. Heath

19th Maine: 439 / 46%: Col. Francis Heath (p)

      Lt. Col. Henry Cunningham

15th Massachusetts: 239 / 62%: Col. George H. Ward (w)

      Col. DeWitt C. Baxter (w)

1st Minnesota (2nd Co. Minnesota Sharpshooters): 330 / 68%: Col. William Colvill Jr. (w)

      Capt. Nathan S. Messick (k)

      Capt. Henry C. Coates

82nd New York (2nd Militia): 355 / 54%: Lt. Col. James Huston (k)

Capt. John Darrow

2nd Brigade: Brig. Gen. Alexander S. Webb

69th Pennsylvania: 284 / 48%: Col. Dennis O'Kane (mw)

Capt. William Davis

71st Pennsylvania: 261 / 38%: Col. Richard Penn Smith

72nd Pennsylvania: 380 / 51%: Col. Dewitt C. Baxter (w)

Lt. Col. Theodore Hesser

106th Pennsylvania: 280 / 23%: Lt. Col. William L. Curry

3rd Brigade: Col. Norman J. Hall

19th Massachusetts: 163 / 47%: Col. Arthur Devereaux

20th Massachusetts: 243 / 52%: Col. Paul J. Revere (mw)

Lt. Col. George N. Macy (w)

Capt. Henry L. Abbott

7th Michigan: 165 / 39%: Lt. Col. Amos E. Steel (k)

Maj. Sylvanus W. Curtis

42nd New York: 197 / 38%: Col. James Mallon

59th New York (4 Cos.): 152 / 22%: Lt. Col. Max A. Thoman (k)

Capt. William McFadden

Unattached

Massachusetts Sharpshooters, Co. C: 42 / 19%: Capt. William Plumer

Lt. Emerson L. Bicknell

3rd Division: Brig. Gen. Alexander Hays

1st Brigade: Col. Samuel S. Carroll

14th Indiana: 191 / 16%: Col. John Coons

4th Ohio: 299 / 10%: Lt. Col. Leonard W. Carpenter

8th Ohio: 209 / 49%: Lt. Col. Franklin Sawyer

7th West Virginia: 234 / 20%: Lt. Col. Jonathan H. Lockwood

2nd Brigade: Col. Thomas A. Smyth (w)

Lt. Col. Francis E. Pierce

14th Connecticut: 172 / 38%: Maj. Theodore G. Ellis

1st Delaware: 251 / 31%: Lt. Col. Edward Harris (a)

Capt. Thomas B. Hizar (w)

Lt. William Smith (k)

Lt. John D. Dent

12th New Jersey: 444 / 26%: Maj. John T. Hill

108th New York: 200 / 51%: Lt. Col. Francis Pierce

10th New York Battalion: (detached): Maj. George F. Hopper

3rd Brigade: Col. George L. Willard (k)

 Col. Eliakim Sherill (mw)

 Lt. Col. James M. Bull

 39th New York (4 Cos.): 269 / 35%: Maj. Hugo Hildenbrandt (w)

 111th New York: 390 / 64%: Col. Clinton McDougall (w)

  Lt. Col. Isaac M. Lusk (w)

  Capt. Aaron B. Seeley

 125th New York: 392 / 35%: Lt. Col. Levin Crandell

 126th New York: 455 / 51%: Lt. Col. Eliakim Sherrill (p,mw)

  Lt. Col. James M. Bull (p)

Artillery Brigade: Capt. John G. Hazard

 1st New York Light, Battery B (4 10-lb Parrotts): 117 / 22%: Capt. Lames M. Rorty (mw)

  Lt. Albert S. Sheldon (w)

  Lt. Robert E. Rogers

 1st Rhode Island Light, Battery A (6 3-inch rifles): 117/ 27%: Capt. William A. Arnold

 1st Rhode Island Light, Battery B (6 Napoleons): 129 / 22%: Lt. T. Frederick Brown (w)

 1st U.S., Battery I (6 Napoleons): 112 / 22%: Lt. George A. Woodruff (mw)

  Lt. Tully McCrea

 4th U.S., Battery A (6 3-inch rifles): 126 / 30%: Lt. Alonzo Cushing (k)

  Sgt. Frederick Fuger

3rd Corps

10,674 / 39.5%

Maj. Gen. Daniel E. Sickles (w)

Maj. Gen. David B. Birney (r)

Maj. Gen. William H. French

1st Division: Maj. Gen. David B. Birney (p)

 Brig. Gen. J. H. Hobart Ward

 Maj. Gen. B. Birney (r)

1st Brigade: Brig. Gen. Charles K. Graham (w/c)

 Col. Andrew H. Tippin

 57th Pennsylvania (8 Cos.): 207 / 56%: Col. Peter Sides (w)

  Capt. Alanson H. Nelson

 63rd Pennsylvania: 246 / 14%: Maj. John A. Danks

68th Pennsylvania: 320 / 48%: Col. Andrew H. Tippin (p)
　　Capt. Milton S. Davis
105th Pennsylvania: 274 / 48%: Col. Calvin A. Craig
114th Pennsylvania: 259 / 60%: Col. Frederick F. Cavada (c)
　　Capt. Edward R. Bowen
141st Pennsylvania: 209 / 71%: Col. Henry J. Madill
2nd Brigade: Brig. Gen. J. H. Hobart Ward (p)
　　Col. Hiram Berdan
20th Indiana: 401 / 39%: Col. John C. Wheeler (k)
　　Lt. Col. William C. L. Taylor (w)
3rd Maine: 210 / 58%: Col. Moses B. Lakeman
4th Maine: 287 / 50%: Col. Elijah Walker (w)
　　Capt. Edward Libby
86th New York: 287 / 23%: Lt. Col. Benjamin L. Higgins (w)
124th New York: 238 / 38%: Col. Van Horne Ellis (k)
　　Lt. Col. Francis L. Cummins (w)
99th Pennsylvania: 277 / 40%: Maj. John W. Moore
1st U.S. Sharpshooters: 313 / 16%: Col. Hiram Berdan (p)
　　Lt. Col. Casper Trepp
2nd U.S. Sharpshooters (8 Cos.): 169 / 25%: Maj. Homer R. Stoughton
3rd Brigade: Col. P. Regis de Trobriand
17th Maine: 350 / 38%: Lt. Col. Charles Merrill
3rd Michigan: 238 / 19%: Col. Bryon R. Pierce (w)
　　Lt. Col. Edward S. Pierce
5th Michigan: 216 / 50%: Lt. Col. John Pulford (w)
40th New York: 431 / 35%: Col. Thomas W. Egan
110th Pennsylvania (6 Cos.): 152 / 35%: Lt. Col. David M. Jones (w)
　　Maj. Isaac Rogers

2nd Division: Brig. Gen. Andrew A. Humphreys
1st Brigade: Brig. Gen. Joseph B. Carr
1st Massachusetts: 321 / 37%: Lt. Col. Clark Baldwin
11th Massachusetts: 286 / 45%: Lt. Col. Porter Tripp
16th Massachusetts: 245 / 33%: Lt. Col. Waldo Merriam (w)
　　Capt. Matthew Donovan
12th New Hampshire: 224 / 41%: Capt. John F. Langley
11th New Jersey: 275 / 56%: Col. Robert McAlister (w)
　　Capt. Luther Martin (w)

        Lt. John Schoonover (w)

        Lt. Samuel T. Sleeper

  26th Pennsylvania: 365 / 58%: Maj. Robert L. Bodine

2nd Brigade: Col. William Brewster

  70th New York: 288 / 41%: Col. J. Egbert Farnum

  71st New York: 243 / 37%: Col. Henry1. Potter

  72nd New York: 305 / 37%: Col. John S. Austin (w)

        Lt. Col. John Leonard

  73rd New York: 349 / 46%: Maj. Michael W. Burns

  74th New York: 266 / 34%: Lt. Col. Thomas Holt

  120th New York: 383 / 53%: Lt. Col. Cornelius D. Westbrook (w)

        Maj. John R. Tappen

3rd Brigade: Col. George Burling

  2nd New Hampshire: 354 / 55%: Col. Edward L. Bailey (w)

  5th New Jersey: 206 / 46%: Col. William J. Sewell (w)

        Capt. Virgil Healey (w

        Capt. Henry H. Woolsey (w)

        Capt. Thomas C. Godfrey

  6th New Jersey: 207 / 20%: Lt. Col. Stephen R. Gilkyson

  7th New Jersey: 275 / 42%: Col. Louis R. Francine (mw)

        Maj. Fred Cooper

  8th New Jersey: 170 / 28%: Col. John Ramsey (w)

        Capt. John G. Langston

  115th Pennsylvania: 151 / 16%: Maj. John P. Dunne

Artillery Brigade: Capt. George E. Randolph (w)

        Capt. A. Judson Clark

  1st New Jersey Light, Battery B (6 10-lb Parrotts): 131 / 15%: Capt. A. Judson Clark

  1st New York Light, Battery D (6 Napoleons): 116 / 16%: Capt. George B. Winslow

  4th New York Independent Battery (6 10-lb Parrotts): 126 / 10%: Capt. James E. Smith

  1st Rhode Island Light, Battery E (6 Napoleons): 108 / 28%: Lt. John K. Buckly (w)

        Lt. Benjamin Freeborn

  4th U.S., Battery K (6 Napoleons): 113 / 22%: Lt. Francis W. Seeley (w)

        Lt. Robert James

5th Corps

10946 / 20%
Maj. Gen. George Sykes

1st Division: Brig. Gen. James Barnes
 1st Brigade: Col. William S. Tilton
   18th Massachusetts: 139 / 19%: Col. Joseph Hayes
   22nd Massachusetts: 137 / 23%: Lt. Col. Thomas Sherwin Jr.
   1st Michigan: 145 / 29%: Col. Ira C. Abbot (w)
        Lt. Col. William A. Throop
   118th Pennsylvania: 233 / 11%: Lt. Col. James Gwyn
 2nd Brigade: Col. Jacob B. Switzer
   9th Massachusetts: 412 / 2%: Col. Patrick R. Guiney
   32nd Massachusetts: 242 / 33%: Col. George Prescott
   4th Michigan: 342 / 48%: Col. Harrison H. Jeffords (k)
        Lt. Col. George W. Lumbard
   62nd Pennsylvania: 426 / 41%: Lt. Col. James C. Hall
 3rd Brigade: Col. Strong Vincent (mw)
        Col. James C. Rice
   20th Maine: 386 / 32%: Col. Joshua Chamberlain
   16th Michigan: 263 / 23%: Lt. Col. Norval E. Welch
   44th New York: 391 / 28%: Col. James E. Rice (p)
        Lt. Col. Freeman Conner
   83rd Pennsylvania: 295 / 19%: Capt. Orpeus S. Woodward

2nd Division: Brig. Gen. Romeyn Ayres
 1st Brigade: Col. Hannibal Day
   3rd U.S. (6 Cos.): 300 / 24%: Capt. Henry W. Freedley (w)
        Capt. Richard G. Lay
   4th U.S. (4 Cos.): 173 / 23%: Capt. Julius W. Adams Jr.
   6th U.S. (5 Cos.): 150 / 29%: Capt. Levi C. Bootes
   12th U.S. (8 Cos.): 419 / 22%: Capt. Thomas s. Dunn
   14th U.S. (8 Cos.): 513 / 26%: Maj. Gortius R. Giddings
 2nd Brigade: Col. Sidney Burbank
   2nd U.S. (6 Cos.): 197 / 34%: Maj. Arthur T. Lee (w)
        Capt. Samuel A. McKee
   7th U.S. (4 Cos.): 116 / 51%: Capt. David P. Hancock
   10th U.S. (3 Cos.): 93 / 55%: Capt. William Clinton

11th U.S. (6 Cos.): 286 / 42%: Maj. Delancey Floyd-Jones
17th U.S. (7 Cos.): 260 / 58%: Lt. Col. J. Durrell Greene
3rd Brigade: Brig. Gen. Stephen Weed (k)
 Col. Kenner Garrard
140th New York: 453 / 29%: Col. Patrick O'Rorke (k)
 Lt. Col. Louis Ermst
146th New York: 460 / 6%: Col. Kenner Garrard (p)
 Lt. Col. David T. Jenkins
91st Pennsylvania: 222 / 9%: Lt. Col. Joseph H. Sinex
155th Pennsylvania: 365 / 5%: Lt. Col. John H. Cain

3rd Division: Brig. Gen. Samuel W. Crawford
 1st Brigade: Col. William McCandless
 1st Pennsylvania Reserves (9 Cos.): 382 / 12%: Col. William Talley
 2nd Pennsylvania Reserves: 235 / 16%: Lt. Col. George A Woodward
 6th Pennsylvania Reserves: 327 / 7%: Lt. Col. Wellington H. Ent
 13th Pennsylvania Reserves: 301 / 16%: Col. Charles F. Taylor (k)
  Maj. William R. Hartshorne
 3rd Brigade: Col. Joseph Fisher
 5th Pennsylvania Reserves: 288 / 2%: Lt. Col. George Dare
 9th Pennsylvania Reserves: 325 / 1%: Lt. James M. Snodgrass
 10th Pennsylvania Reserves: 401 / 1%: Col. Adoniram J. Warner
 11th Pennsylvania Reserves: 327 / 13%: Col. Samuel D. Jackson
 12th Pennsylvania Reserves: 276 / 1%: Col. Martin d. Hardin
 Artillery Brigade: Capt. Augustus Martin
 3rd Mass. Light, Battery C (6 Napoleons): 115 / 5%: Lt. Aaron F. Walcott
 1st New York Light, Battery C (4 3-inch rifles): 62 / 0%: Capt. Almont Barnes
 1st Ohio Light, Battery L (6 Napoleons): 113 / 2%: Capt. Frank C. Gibbs
 5th U.S., Battery D (6 10-lb Parrotts): 68 / 19%: Lt. Charles E. Hazlett (k)
  Lt. Benjamin F. Rittenhouse
 5th U.S., Battery I (4 3-inch rifles): 71 / 31%: Lt. Malbone F. Watson (w)
  Lt. Charles C. MacConnell

6th Corps

14,074 / 1.7%
Maj. Gen. John Sedgwick

General Headquarters
   1st New Jersey Cavalry, Co. L
   1st Pennsylvania Cavalry, Co. H

1st Division: Brig. Gen. Horatio G. Wright
  Provost Guard: 4th New Jersey (3 Cos.)
  1st Brigade: Brig. Gen. A. T. A. Torbert
    1st New Jersey: 265 / 0%: Lt. Col. William Henry Jr.
    2nd New Jersey: 357 / 2%: Lt. Col. Charles Wiebecke
    3rd New Jersey: 295 / 1%: Lt. Col. Edward L. Campbell
    15th New Jersey: 413 / 1%: Col. William H. Penrose
  2nd Brigade: Brig. Gen. Joseph J. Bartlett
    5th Maine: 307 / 0%: Col. Clark S. Edwards
    121st New York: 429 / 1%: Col. Emory Upton
    95th Pennsylvania: 323 / 1%: Lt. Col. Edward Carroll
    96th Pennsylvania: 323 / 1%: Maj. William H. Lessig
  3rd Brigade: Brig. Gen. David A. Russell
    6th Maine: 395 / 0%: Col. Hiram Burnham
    49th New York: 289 / 0%: Lt. Col. Thomas M. Hulings
    119th Pennsylvania: 423 / 1%: Col. Peter C. Ellmaker
    5th Wisconsin: 423 / 0%: Col. Thomas S. Allen

2nd Division: Brig. Gen. Albion P. Howe
  2nd Brigade: Col. Lewis A. Grant
    2nd Vermont: 465 / 0%: Col. James H. Walbridge
    3rd Vermont: 381 / 0%: Col. Thomas O. Seaver
    4th Vermont: 399 / 1%: Col. Charles B. Stoughton
    5th Vermont: 309 / 0%: Lt. Col. John R. Lewis
    6th Vermont: 346 / 0%: Col. Elisha L. Barney
  3rd Brigade: Brig. Gen. Thomas H. Neill
    7th Maine (6 Cos.): 216 / 3%: Lt. Col. Selden Connor
    33rd New York (detachment): 63 / 0%: Capt. Henry J. Gifford
    43rd New York: 370 / 1%: Lt. Col. John Wilson
    49th New York: 376 / 1%: Col. Daniel D. Bidwell
    77th New York: 385 / 0%: Lt. Col. Winsor B. French
    61st Pennsylvania: 386 / 1%: Lt. Col. George F. smith

3rd Division: Maj. Gen. John Newton (p)
        Brig. Gen. Frank Wheaton

1st Brigade: Brig. Gen. Alexander Shaler
   65th New York: 290 / 3%: Col. Joseph E. Hamblin
   67th New York: 349 / 1%: Col. Nelson Cross
   122nd New York: 414 / 11%: Col. Silas Titus
   23rd Pennsylvania: 489 / 3%: Lt. Col. John F. Glenn
   82d Pennsylvania: 291 / 2%: Col. Isaac Bassett
2nd Brigade: Col. Henry L. Eustis
   7th Massachusetts: 335 / 2%: Lt. Col. Franklin P. Harrow
   10th Massachusetts: 378 / 2%: Lt. Col. Joseph B. Parsons
   37th Massachusetts: 591 / 8%: Col. Oliver Edwards
   2nd Rhode Island: 364 / 2%: Col. Horatio Rogers Jr.
3rd Brigade: Brig. Gen. Frank Wheaton (p)
         Col. David J. Nevin
   62nd New York: 237 / 5%: Col. David Nevin (p)
         Lt. Col. Theodore B. Hamilton
   93rd Pennsylvania: 245 / 4%: Maj. John L. Nevin
   98th Pennsylvania: 368 / 3%: Maj. John B. Kohler
   102nd Pennsylvania: 103 / 0%: Col. John W. Patterson
   139th Pennsylvania: 464 / 5%: Col. Frederick H. Collier (aw)
         Lt. Col. William H. Moody
Artillery Brigade: Col. Charles H. Tompkins
   1st Mass. Light, Battery A (6 Napoleons): 135 / 0%: Capt. William H.
      McCartney
   1st New York Independent, 1st Battery (6 3-inch rifles): 103 / 12%: Capt.
      Andrew Cowan
   3rd New York Independent Battery (6 10-lb Parrotts): 111 / 0%: Capt.
      William A. Harn
   1st Rhode Island Light, Battery C (6 3-inch rifles): 116 / 0%: Capt. Richard
      Waterman
   1st Rhode Island Light, Battery G (6 10-lb Parrotts): 126 / 0%: Capt. George
      W. Adams
   2nd U.S., Battery D (6 Napoleons): 126 / 0%: Lt. Edward B. Williston
   2nd U.S., Battery G (6 Napoleons): 101 / 0%: Lt. John H. Butler
   5th U.S., Battery F (6 10-lb Parrotts): 116 / 0%: Lt. Leonard Martin

11th Corps

9,242 / 41.2%
Maj. Gen. Oliver O. Howard (p)
Maj. Gen. Carl Schurz
Maj. Gen. Oliver O. Howard (r)

1st Division: Brig. Gen. Francis C. Barlow (w)
    Brig. Gen. Adelbert Ames
  1st Brigade: Col. Leopold von Gilsa
   41st New York (9 Cos.): 218 / 34%: Lt. Col. Detto Von Einsiedal
   54th New York: 189 / 54%: Maj. Stephen Kovacs (c)
       Lt. Ernst Both
   68th New York: 232 / 60%: Col. Gotthilf Borry
   153rd Pennsylvania: 499 / 42%: Maj. John F. Frueauff
  2nd Brigade: Brig. Gen. Adelbert Ames (p)
       Col. Andrew Harris
   17th Connecticut: 386 / 51%: Lt. Col. Douglas Fowler (k)
       Maj. Allen G. Brady
   25th Ohio: 220 / 84%: Lt. Co. Jeremiah Williams (c)
       Capt. Nathaniel J. Manning (w)
       Lt. William Malone (w)
       Lt. Israel White
   75th Ohio: 269 / 69%: Col. Andrew L. Harris (p)
       Capt. George B. Fox
   107th Ohio: 458 / 46%: Col. Seraphim Meyer (a)
       Capt. John M. Lutz

2nd Division: Brig. Gen. Adolph von Steinwehr
  1st Brigade: Col. Charles R. Coster
   134th New York: 400 / 63%: Lt. Col. Allan H. Jackson
   154th New York: 240 / 83%: Lt. Col. D. B. Allen
   27th Pennsylvania: 284 / 39%: Lt. Col. Lorenz Cantador
   73rd Pennsylvania: 291 / 11%: Capt. D. F. Kelly
  2nd Brigade: Col. Orlando Smith
   33rd Massachusetts: 493 / 9%: Col. Adin B. Underwood
   136th New York: 484 / 23%: Col. James Wood Jr.
   55th Ohio: 329 / 15%: Col. Charles B. Gambee
   73rd Ohio: 338 / 43%: Lt. Col. Richard Long

3rd Division: Maj. Gen. Carl Schurz (p)
        Brig. Gen. Alex. Schimmelfennig (m)
        Maj. Gen. Carl Shurz
    1st Brigade: Brig. Gen. Alex. Schimmelfennig (p)
        Col. George von Amsberg
        82nd Illinois: 318 / 35%: Col. Edward Salomon
        45th New York: 375 / 60%: Col. George von Amsberg (p)
            Lt. Col. Adolphus Dobke
        157th New York: 409 / 75%: Col. Philip P. Brown Jr.
        61st Ohio: 247 / 22%: Col. Stephen J. McGroarty
        74th Pennsylvania: 334 / 33%: Col. Adolph Von Hartung (w)
            Lt. Col. Alexander von Mitzel (c)
            Capt. Gustav Schleiter
            Capt. Henry Krauseneck
    2nd Brigade: Col. W. Krzyzanowski
        58th New York: 195 / 10%: Lt. Col. August Otto
            Capt. Emil Koenig
        119th New York: 263 / 53%: Col. John T. Lockman (w)
            Lt. Col. Edward F. Lloyd
        82nd Ohio: 312 / 58%: Col. James S. Robinson (w)
            Lt. Col. David Thomason
        75th Pennsylvania: 208 / 53%: Col. Francis Mahler (w)
            Maj. August Ledig
        2nd Wisconsin: 446 / 49%: Lt. Col. Hans Boebel (w)
            Capt. John W. Fuchs
    Artillery Brigade: Maj. Thomas W. Osborne
        1st New York Light, Battery I (6 3-inch rifles): 110 / 10%: Capt. Michael
            Weidrich
        13th New York Independent Battery (4 3-inch rifles): 141 / 9%: Lt. William
            Wheeler
        1st Ohio Light, Battery I (6 Napoleons): 127 / 10%: Capt. Hubert Dilger
        1st Ohio Light, Battery K (4 Napoleons): 110 / 14%: Capt. Lewis Heckman
        4th U.S., Battery G (6 Napoleons): 115 / 15%: Lt. Bayard Wilkeson (mw)
            Lt. Eugene Bancroft

12th Corps

9,788 / 11%
Maj. Gen. Henry W. Slocum
Brig. Gen. Alpheus S. Williams

1st Division: Brig. Gen. Alpheus S. Williams (p)
          Brig. Gen. Thomas H. Ruger
 1st Brigade: Col. Archibald L. McDougall
  5th Connecticut: 221 / 3%: Col. Warren W. Packer
  20th Connecticut: 321 / 9%: Lt. Col. William B. Wooster
  3rd Maryland: 290 / 3%: Col. Joseph M. Sudburg
  123rd New York: 495 / 3%: Lt. Col. James C. Rogers
          Capt. Adolphus H. Tanner
  145th New York: 245 / 4%: Col. E. L. Price
  46th Pennsylvania: 262 / 5%: Col. James Selfridge
 2nd Brigade: Brig. Gen. Henry H. Lockwood
  1st Maryland Potomac Home Brigade: 674 / 15%: Col. William P. Maulsby
  1st Maryland Eastern Shore Infantry: 532 / 5%: Col. James Wallace
  150th New York: 609 / 7%: Col. John H. Ketcham
 3rd Brigade: Brig. Gen. Thomas H. Ruger (p)
          Col. Silas Colgrove
  27th Indiana: 339 / 32%: Col. Silas Colgrove (p)
          Lt. Col. John R. Fesler
  2nd Massachusetts: 316 / 43%: Lt. Col. Charles R. Mudge (k)
          Maj. Charles F. Moore
  13th New Jersey: 347 / 6%: Col. Ezra A. Carman
  107th New York: 319 / 1%: Col. Nirom M. Crane
  3rd Wisconsin: 260 / 4%: Col. William Hawley

2nd Division: Brig. Gen. John W. Geary
 1st Brigade: Col. Charles Candy
  5th Ohio: 299 / 6%: Col. John H. Patrick
  7th Ohio: 282 / 6%: Col. William R. Creighton
  29th Ohio: 315 / 12%: Capt. Wilbur F. Stevens (w)
          Capt. Edward Hayes
  66th Ohio: 399 / 6%: Lt. Eugene Powell
  28th Pennsylvania: 303 / 9%: Capt. John Flynn
  147th Pennsylvania (8 Cos.): 298 / 7%: Lt. Col. Ario Pardee Jr.

2nd Brigade: Col. George A. Cobham Jr. (r)

    Brig. Gen. Thomas L. Kane (i)

    Col. George A. Cobham Jr.

  29th Pennsylvania: 357 / 18%: Col. William Rickards Jr.

  109th Pennsylvania: 179 / 7%: Capt. Frederick L. Gimber

  111th Pennsylvania: 191 / 12%: Col. George A. Cobham Jr. (p)

    Lt. Col. Thomas M. Walker

3rd Brigade: Brig. Gen. George S. Greene

  60th New York: 273 / 19%: Col. Abel Godard

  78th New York: 198 / 15%: Lt. Col. Herbert von Hammerstein

  102nd New York: 230 / 13%: Col. James C. Lane (w)

    Capt. Lewis R. Stegman

  137th New York: 423 / 32%: Capt. David Ireland

  149th New York: 297 / 19%: Col. Henry A. Barnum—shared command with Lt. Col. Charles B. Randall (w)

Artillery Brigade: Lt. Edward D. Muhlenberg

  1st New York Light, Battery M (4 10-lb Parrotts): 90 / 0%: Lt. Charles Winegar

  Pennsylvania Independent Battery E (6 10-lb Parrotts): 139 / 2%: Lt. Charles A. Atwell

  4th U.S., Battery F (6 Napoleons): 89 / 1%: Lt. Sylvanus T. Rugg

  5th U.S., Battery K (4 Napoleons): 72 / 7%: Lt. David H Kinzie

Cavalry Corps

11,846 / 7%

Maj. Gen. Alfred Pleasonton

1st Division: Brig. Gen. John Buford

 1st Brigade: Col. William Gamble

  8th Illinois: 470 / 2%: Maj. John L. Beveridge

  12th Illinois (4 Cos.): 233 / 9%: Col. George H. Chapman (commanded 2 units)

  3rd Indiana (6 Cos.): 313 / 10%: Col. George H. Chapman (commanded 2 units)

  8th New York: 580 / 7%: Lt. Col. William L. Markell

 2nd Brigade: Col. Thomas C. Devin

  6th New York: 218 / 4%: Maj. William E. Beardsley

  9th New York: 367 / 3%: Col. William Sackett

17th Pennsylvania: 464 / 1%: Col. Josiah H. Kellogg

3rd West Virginia (2 Cos.): 59 / 7%: Capt. Seymour B. Conger

Reserve Brigade: Brig. Gen. Wesley Merritt

6th Pennsylvania: 242 / 5%: Maj. James H. Haseltine

1st U.S.: 362 / 4%: Capt. Richard S. C. Lord

2nd U.S.: 407 / 4%: Capt. T. F. Rodenbough

5th U.S.: 306 / 2%: Capt. Julius W. Mason

6th U.S. (detached to HQ)

2nd Division: Brig. Gen. David McM. Gregg

1st Brigade: Col. John B. McIntosh

1st Maryland (11 Cos.): 285 / 1%: Lt. Col. James M. Deems

Purnell (MD) Legion, Co. A: 66 / 0%: Capt. Robert E. Duvall

1st Massachusetts: (detached with HQ): Lt. Col. Greely S. Curtis

1st New Jersey: 199 / 5%: Maj. M. H. Beaumont

1st Pennsylvania: 355 / 1%: Col. John P. Taylor

3rd Pennsylvania: 335 / 6%: Lt. Col. E. S. Jones

3rd Pennsylvania Artillery, Battery H: 52 / 0%: Capt. W. D. Rusk

3rd Brigade: Col. J. Irvin Gregg

1st Maine (10 Cos.): 315 / 2%: Lt. Col. Charles H. Smith

10th New York: 333 / 3%: Maj. M. Henry Avery

4th Pennsylvania: 258 / 1%: Lt. Col. William E. Doster

16th Pennsylvania: 349 / 2%: Lt. Col. John K. Robison

3rd Division: Brig. Gen. H. Judson Kilpatrick

1st Brigade: Brig. Gen. Elon J. Farnsworth (k)

Col. Nathan P. Richmond

5th New York: 420 / 1%: Maj. John Hammond

18th Pennsylvania: 509 / 3%: Lt. Col. William Brinton

1st Vermont: 600 / 11%: Lt. Col. Addison W. Preston

1st West Virginia: 395 / 3%: Col. Nathan Richmond (p)

Maj. Charles E. Capehart

2nd Brigade: Brig. Gen. George A. Custer

1st Michigan: 427 / 17%: Col. Charles H. Town

5th Michigan: 645 / 9%: Col. Russell A. Alger

6th Michigan: 469 / 6%: Col. George Gray

7th Michigan (10 Cos.): 383 / 26%: Col. William D. Mann

Horse Artillery

  1st Brigade: Capt. James M. Robertson
    9th Michigan Battery (6 3-inch rifles): 111 / 5%: Capt. Jabez J. Daniels
    6th New York Independent Battery (6 3-inch rifles): 103 / 1%: Capt. Joseph
      W. Martin
    2nd U.S., Batteries B & L (6 3-inch rifles): 99 / 0%: Lt. Edward Heaton
    2nd U.S., Battery M (6 3-inch rifles): 117 / 1%: Lt. A. C. M. Pennington Jr.
    4th U.S., Battery E (4 3-inch rifles): 61 / 2%: Lt. Samuel S. Elder
    3rd Pennsylvania Heavy Artillery, Battery H (2 3-inch rifles): 52 / 1%: Capt.
      William D. Rank (detached)
  2nd Brigade: Capt. John C. Tidball
    1st U.S., Batteries E & G (4 3-inch rifles): 85 / 0%: Capt. Alanson M. Randall
    1st U.S., Battery K (6 3-inch rifles): 114 / 3%: Capt. William M. Graham
    2nd U.S., Battery A (6 3-inch rifles): 74 / 16%: Lt. John H. Calef
    3rd U.S., Battery C (detached)

Artillery Reserve

2,376 / 242
Brig. Gen. Robert O. Tyler (i)
Capt. James M. Robertson

1st Regular Brigade: Capt. Dunbar R. Ransom (w)
    1st U.S. Battery H (6 Napoleons): 129 / 8%: Lt. Chandler Eakin
        Lt. Philip D. Mason
    3rd U.S. Batteries F & K (6 Napoleons): 115 / 20%: Lt. John G. Turnbull
    4th U.S. Battery C (6 Napoleons): 95 / 19%: Lt. Evan Thomas
    5th U.S. Battery C (6 Napoleons): 104 / 15%: Lt. Gulian V. Weir
1st Volunteer Brigade: Lt. Col. Freeman McGilvery
    5th Massachusetts Light, Battery F (6 3-inch rifles): 104 / 20%: Capt. Charles
      Phillips
    9th Massachusetts Light Artillery (6 Napoleons): 104 / 27%: Capt. John
      Bigelow (w)
        Lt. Richard S. Milton
    15th New York Independent Battery (4 Napoleons): 70 / 23%: Capt. Patrick
      Hart (w)
    Pennsylvania Independent, Batteries F & G (6 3-inch rifles): 105 / 27%: Capt.
      James Thompson (w)

2nd Volunteer Brigade: Capt. Elijah D. Taft
  2nd Connecticut Light, Independent Battery (4 James rifles, 2 12-lb howitzers): 93 / 5%: Capt. Albert F. Brocker
  5th New York Independent Battery (6 20-lb Parrotts): 146 / 2%: Capt. Franklin A. Pratt
  1st Connecticut Heavy, Battery B (detached): Capt. John W. Sterling
  1st Connecticut Heavy, Battery M (detached): Capt. Elijah Taft
3rd Volunteer Brigade: Capt. James F. Huntington
  1st New Hampshire Light, Batteries F & G (4 3-inch rifles): 86 / 4%: Capt. Frederick M. Edgell
  1st Ohio Light, Battery H (6 3-inch rifles): 99 / 7%: Lt. George W. Norton
  1st Pennsylvania Light, Batteries F & G (6 3-inch rifles): 144 / 16%: Capt. R. Bruce Ricketts
  West Virginia Light, Battery C (4 10-lb Parrotts): 100 / 4%: Capt. Wallace Hill
4th Volunteer Brigade: Capt. Robert H. Fitzhugh
  6th Maine Light Artillery Battery F (4 Napoleons): 87 / 15%: Lt. Edwin R. Dow
  1st Maryland Light, Battery A (6 3-inch rifles): 106 / 0%: Capt. James H. Rigby
  1st New Jersey Light Battery A (6 10-lb Parrotts): 98 / 9%: Lt. Augustin N. Parson
  1st New York Light, Battery G (6 Napoleons): 84 / 8%: Capt. Nelson Ames
  1st New York Light, Battery K, and 11th New York Battery (6 3-inch rifles): 122 / 6%: Capt. Robert H. Fitzhugh
Train Guard
  4th New Jersey Infantry (7 Cos.)

The Confederate Order of Battle

Army of Northern Virginia
Gen. Robert E. Lee, commanding
xxx [full compliment] / x% [percent of casualties]

Army Headquarters

Col. R. H. Chilton, chief of staff and inspector general
Brig. Gen. W. N. Pendleton, chief of artillery
Dr. Lafayette Guild, medical director
Lt. Col. Briscoe G. Baldwin, chief of ordinance
Lt. Col. Robert G. Cole, chief of commissary
Lt. Col. James L. Corley, chief quartermaster
Maj. H. E. Young, judge advocate general
Col. A. L. Long, military secretary and acting assistant adjutant general
Lt. Col. Walter Taylor, aide de camp and assistant adjutant general
Maj. Charles Marshall, aide de camp and assistant military secretary
Maj. Charles S. Venable, aide de camp and assistant inspector general
Capt. S. R. Johnson, engineer

1st Corps

20,941 / 37%
Lt. Gen. James Longstreet

McLaws's Division: Maj. Gen. Lafayette McLaws
   Kershaw's Brigade: Brig. Gen. J. B. Kershaw
      2nd South Carolina: 412 / 41%: Col. John D. Kennedy (w)
         Lt. Co. F. Gaillard

3rd South Carolina: 407 / 21%: Maj. Robert C. Maffett ((r)
    Col. J. D. Nance (arrived late on July 3)
7th South Carolina: 408 / 28%: Col. D. Wyatt Aiken
8th South Carolina: 300 / 35%: Col. John W. Henagan
15th South Carolina: 449 / 32%: Col. William DeSaussure (k)
    Maj. William M. Gist
3rd South Carolina Battalion: 203 / 24%: Lt. Col. William G. Rice
Semmes's Brigade: Brig. Gen. Paul J. Semmes (mw)
    Col. Goode Bryan
10th Georgia: 303 / 33%: Col. John B. Weems (w)
50th Georgia: 303 / 32%: Col. William R. Manning
51st Georgia: 303 / 31%: Col. Edward Ball
53rd Georgia: 422 / 24%: Col. James P. Simms
Barksdale's Brigade: Brig. Gen. William Barksdale (mw)
    Col. Benjamin G. Humphreys
13th Mississippi: 481 / 51%: Col. John W. Carter (k)
    Lt. Col. Kennon McElroy (w)
17th Mississippi: 468 / 58%: Col. William D. Holder (w)
    Lt. Col. John C. Fiser
18th Mississippi: 242 / 57%: Col. Thomas M. Griffin (w)
    Lt. W. H. Luse
21st Mississippi: 424 / 33%: Col. Benjamin G. Humphreys
Wofford's Brigade: Brig. Gen. William T. Wofford
16th Georgia: 303 / 34%: Col. Goode Bryan (p) to Semmes's Brigade
18th Georgia: 302 / 12%: Lt. Col. Solon Z. Ruff
24th Georgia: 303 / 28%: Col. Robert McMillin
Cobb's (Georgia) Legion: 213 / 10%: Lt. Col. Luther J. Glenn
Phillips (Georgia) Legion: 273 / 24%: Lt. Col. Elihu S. Barclay Jr.
3rd Georgia Sharpshooters: 233 / 6%: Lt. Col. Nathan L. Hutchins Jr.
Artillery: Col. Henry G. Cabell
1st North Carolina, Battery A (2 Napoleons; 2 3-inch rifles): 131 / 10%: Capt.
  Basil C. Manly
Pulaski (Georgia) Artillery (2 3-inch rifles; 2 12-lb howitzers): 63 / 30%: Capt.
  John C. Fraser (mw)
    Lt. W. J. Furlong
1st Richmond Artillery (2 Napoleons; 2 3-inch rifles): 90 / 14%: Capt.
  Edwards McCarthy

Troup (Georgia) Artillery (2 12-lb howitzers; 2 10-lb Parrotts): 90 / 8%: Capt. Henry H. Carlton (w)

Pickett's Division: Maj. Gen. George E. Pickett
  Garnett's Brigade: Brig. Gen. Richard B. Garnett (k)
      Maj. Charles S. Peyton
    8th Virginia: 193 / 92%: Col. Eppa Hunton (w)
      Lt. Col. Norborne Berkeley (w,c)
      Maj. Edmund Berkeley (w)
    18th Virginia: 312 / 79%: Lt. Col. Henry A. Carrington (w,c)
    19th Virginia: 328 / 46%: Col. Henry Gantt (w)
      Lt. Col. John T. Ellis (k)
    28th Virginia: 333 / 55%: Col. Robert C. Allen (k)
      Lt. Col. William Watts (k)
    56th Virginia: 289 / 65%: Col. William D. Stewart (mw)
      Lt. Col. P. P. Slaughter
  Kemper's Brigade: Brig. Gen. James L. Kemper (w,c)
      Col. Joseph Mayo Jr.
    1st Virginia: 209 / 54%: Col. Lewis B. Williams Jr. (k)
      Maj. Francis H. Langley (w)
    3rd Virginia: 332 / 39%: Col. Joseph Mayo Jr. (p)
      Lt. Col. Alexander D. Callcote (k)
    7th Virginia: 335 / 45%: Col. Waller T. Patton (mw)
      Lt. Col. Charles C. Flowerree
    11th Virginia: 359 / 41%: Maj. Kirkwood Otey (w)
    24th Virginia: 395 / 41%: Col. William R. Terry
  Armistead's Brigade: Brig. Gen. Lewis A. Armistead (mw)
      Col. W. R. Aylett (w)
    9th Virginia: 257 / 69%: Col. Lewis B. Williams Jr. (k)
      Maj. Francis H. Langley (w)
    14th Virginia: 422 / 60%: Col. James G. Hodges (k)
      Lt. Col. William White (w)
      Maj. Robert H. Poore (mw)
    38th Virginia: 356 / 65%: Col. Edward C. Edmonds (k)
      Lt. Col. P. B. Whittle (mw)
    53rd Virginia: 435 / 49%: Lt. Col. William R. Aylett (p,w)
      Lt. Col. Rawley Martin (w,c)
    57th Virginia: 476 / 52%: Col. John Bowie Magruder (mw)

Lt. Col. Benjamin G. Wade (mw)

Maj. Clement R. Fontaine (w)

Artillery: Maj. James Dearing

Fauquier (VA) Artillery (4 Napoleons; 2 20-lb Parrotts): 135 / 4%: Capt. Robert M. Stribling

Hampden (VA) Artillery (2 Napoleons; 1 3-inch rifle; 1 10-lb Parrott): 90 / 4%: Capt. William H. Caskie

Richmond Fayette (VA) Artillery (2 Napoleons; 2 10-lb Parrotts): 90 / 6%: Capt. Miles C. Macon

Lynchburg (VA) Battery (4 Napoleons): 96 / 10%: Capt. Joseph G. Blount

Hood's Division: Maj. Gen. John B. Hood (w)

Brig. Gen. Evander M. Law

Law's Brigade: Brig. Gen. Evander M. Law (p)

Col. James L. Sheffield

4th Alabama: 346 / 27%: Col. Lawrence Scruggs

15th Alabama: 499 / 36%: Col. William C. Oates

Capt. Blanton A. Hill

44th Alabama: 363 / 24%: Col. William F. Perry

47th Alabama: 347 / 20%: Col. James W. Jackson (w)

Lt. Col. M. J. Bulger (w,c)

Maj. J. M. Campbell

48th Alabama: 374 / 28%: Col. James L. Sheffield (p)

Capt. T. J. Eubanks

Robertson's Brigade: Brig. Gen. Jerome B. Robertson (w)

3rd Arkansas: 479 / 38%: Col. Van H. Manning (w)

Lt. Col. R. S. Taylor

1st Texas: 426 / 23%: Col. Phillip A. Work

4th Texas: 415 / 27%: Col. John C. G. Key (w)

Maj. J. P. Bane

5th Texas: 409 / 52%: Col. Robert M. Powell (w,c)

Lt. Col. King Bryan (w)

Maj. J. C. Rogers

Anderson's Brigade: Brig. Gen. George T. Anderson (w)

Lt. Col. William Luffman (w)

7th Georgia: 377 / 6%: Col. William H. White

8th Georgia: 311 / 54%: Col. John R. Towers (w)

9th Georgia: 340 / 56%: Lt. Col. John C. Mounger (k)

Maj. W. M. Jones (w)

Capt. George Hillyer

11th Georgia: 309 / 65%: Col. Francis H. Little (w)

Lt. Col. William Luffman (p,w)

Maj. Henry D. McDaniel

Capt. William H. Mitchell

59th Georgia: 525 / 27%: Col. Jack Brown (w)

Lt. Col. J. D. Waddell

Benning's Brigade: Brig. Gen. Henry L. Benning

2nd Georgia: 348 / 29%: Lt. Col. William T. Harris (k)

Maj. W. S. Shepherd

15th Georgia: 368 / 47%: Col. M. Dudley Dubose

17th Georgia: 350 / 31%: Col. Wesley C. Hodges

20th Georgia: 350 / 39%: Col. John A. Jones (k)

Lt. Col. J. D. Waddell

Artillery: Maj. Mathis W. Henry

Bravely (NC) Artillery (1 6-lb. field gun; 1 12-lb howitzer; 3 Napoleons): 112 / 3%: Capt. Alexander C. Latham

German (SC) Artillery (4 Napoleons): 71 / 0%: Capt. William K. Bachman

Palmetto (SC) Light Artillery (2 Napoleons; 2 10-lb Parrotts): 63 / 11%: Capt. Hugh R. Garden

Rowan (NC) Artillery (2 Napoleons; 2 3-inch rifles; 2 10-lb. Parrotts): 148 / 4%: Capt. James Reilly

Artillery Reserve: Col. J. B. Walton

Alexander's Battalion: Col. E. P. Alexander

Ashland (VA) Artillery (2 Napoleons; 2 20-lb Parrotts): 103 / 27%: Capt. Pichegru Woolfolk Jr. (w)

Lt. James Woolfolk

Bedford (VA) Artillery (4 3-inch rifles): 78 / 12%: Capt. Tyler C. Jordan

Brooks (SC) Light Artillery (4 12-lb howitzers): 71 / 51%: Lt. S. C. Gilbert

Madison (LA) Light Artillery (4 24-lb howitzers): 135 / 24%: Capt. George V. Moody

Richmond (VA) Battery (3 3-inch rifles; 1 10-lb Parrott): 90 / 20%: Capt. William W. Parker

Bath (VA) Battery (4 Napoleons): 90 / 14%: Capt. Osmond B. Taylor

Washington (Louisiana) Artillery: Maj. Benjamin F. Eshleman

First Company (1 Napoleon): 77 / 5%: Capt. Charles W. Squires

Second Company (2 Napoleons; 1 12-lb howitzer): 80 / 8%: Capt. John B. Richardson

Third Company (3 Napoleons): 92 / 11%: Capt. Merritt B. Miller

Fourth Company (2 Napoleons; 1 12-lb howitzer): 80 / 13%: Capt. Joe Norcom (w)

    Lt. H. A. Battles

2nd Corps

Lt. Gen. Richard S. Ewell

Early's Division: Maj. Gen. Jubal A. Early

 Hays's Brigade: Brig. Gen. Harry T. Hays

  5th Louisiana: 196 / 34%: Maj. Alexander Hart (w)

    Capt. T. H. Biscoe

  6th Louisiana: 218 / 28%: Lt. Col. Joseph Hanlon

  7th Louisiana: 235 / 25%: Col. Davidson B. Penn

  8th Louisiana: 296 / 25%: Col. Trevanion D. Lewis (k)

    Lt. Col. A. de Blanc (w)

    Maj. G. A. Lester

  9th Louisiana: 347 / 21%: Col. Leroy A. Stafford

 Smith's Brigade: Brig. Gen. William Smith

  31st Virginia: 267 / 10%: Col. John s. Hoffman

  49th Virginia: 281 / 36%: Lt. Col. J. Catlett Gibson

  52nd Virginia: 254 / 21%: Lt. Col. James H. Skinner (w)

 Hoke's Brigade: Col. Isaac E. Avery (mw)

    Col. A. C. Godwin

  6th North Carolina: 509 / 41%: Maj. Samuel M. Tate

  21st North Carolina: 436 / 32%: Col. William Kirkland

  57th North Carolina: 297 / 22%: Col. Archibald C. Godwin

 Gordon's Brigade: Brig. Gen. John B. Gordon

  13th Georgia: 312 / 44%: Col. James L. Smith

  26th Georgia: 315 / 10%: Col. Edmund N. Atkinson

  31st Georgia: 252 / 26%: Col. Clement A. Evans

  38th Georgia: 341 / 39%: Capt. William L. McLeod

  60th Georgia: 299 / 20%: Capt. Walter B. Jones

  61st Georgia: 288 / 39%: Col. John H. Lamar

Artillery: Lt. Col. Hilary P. Jones

Charlottesville (VA) Artillery (4 Napoleons): 71 / 7%: Capt. James McD.
  Carrington
Courtney (VA) Artillery (4 3-inch rifles): 86 / 28%: Capt. William A. Tanner
Louisiana Guard Artillery (1 3-inch rifles; 1 10-lb Parrotts): 60 / 28%: Capt.
  Charles A. Green
Staunton (VA) Artillery (4 Napoleons): 60 / 7%: Capt. Asher W. Garber

Johnson's Division: Maj. Gen. Edward Johnson
  Steuart's Brigade: Brig. Gen. George H. Steuart
    1st Maryland Battalion: 400 / 47%: Lt. Col. James Herbert (w)
        Maj. W. W. Goldsborough (w)
        Capt. J. P. Crane
    1st North Carolina: 377 / 40%: Lt. Col. Hamilton Allen Brown
    3rd North Carolina: 548 / 40%: Maj. William M. Parsley
    10th Virginia: 276 / 28%: Capt. William B. Yancey
    23rd Virginia: 251 / 14%: Lt. Col. Simeon T. Walton
    37th Virginia: 264 / 37%: Maj. Henry C. Wood
  Nicholls's Brigade (Williams's Brigade): Col. J. M. Williams
    1st Louisiana: 172 / 23%: Col. Michael Nolan (k)
        Capt. E. D. Willet
    2nd Louisiana: 236 / 26%: Lt. Col. Ross E. Burke (w,c)
    10th Louisiana: 226 / 49%: Maj. Thomas N. Powell
    14th Louisiana: 281 / 23%: Lt. Col. David Zable
    15th Louisiana: 186 / 20%: Maj. Andrew Bradey
  Stonewall Brigade: Brig. Gen. James A. Walker
    2nd Virginia: 333 / 8%: Col. John Q. A. Nadenbousch
    4th Virginia: 257 / 53%: Maj. William Terry
    5th Virginia: 345 / 17%: Col. John H. S. Funk
    27th Virginia: 148 / 32%: Lt. Col. Daniel M. Shriver
    33rd Virginia: 236 / 30%: Capt. James B. Golladay
  Jones's Brigade: Brig. Gen. John M. Jones (w)
        Lt. Col. R. H. Duncan
    21st Virginia: 183 / 27%: Capt. William P. Moseley
    25th Virginia: 280 / 25%: Col. John C. Higginbotham (w)
        Lt. Col. J. A. Robinson
    42nd Virginia: 252 / 35%: Col. Robert Withers (w)
        Capt. S. H. Saunders
    44th Virginia: 252 / 26%: Maj. Norval Cobb (w)

Capt. T. R. Buckner
48th Virginia: 265 / 35%: Lt. Col. Robert H. Dungan
Maj. Oscar White
50th Virginia: 252 / 39%: Lt. Col. Logan H. N. Salyer
Artillery: Maj. J. W. Latimer (mw)
Capt. C. I. Raine
1st Maryland Battery (4 Napoleons): 90 / 6%: Capt. William F. Dement
Allegheny (VA) Artillery (2 Napoleons; 2 3-inch rifles): 91 / 26%: Capt. John
C. Carpenter
Chesapeake (MD) Artillery (4 10-lb Parrotts): 76 / 22%: Capt. William D.
Brown
Lynchburg Lee (VA) Battery (1 3-inch rifle; 1 10-lb Parrott; 2 20-lb Parrotts):
90 / 4%: Capt. Charles I. Raine (p)
Lt. William M. Hardwicke

Rodes's Division: Maj. Gen. Robert E. Rodes
Daniel's Brigade: Brig. Gen. Julius Daniel
32nd North Carolina: 465 / 39%: Col. Edmund C. Brabble
43rd North Carolina: 583 / 32%: Col. Thomas S. Kenan (w,c)
Lt. Col. William G. Lewis
45th North Carolina: 460 / 48%: Lt. Col. Samuel H. Boyd (w,c)
Maj. John R. Winston (w,c)
Capt. A. H. Gallaway (w)
Capt. J. A. Hopkins
53rd North Carolina: 409 / 52%: Col. Willaim A. Owens
2nd North Carolina Battalion: 240 / 83%: Lt. Col. Hezekiah L. Andrews (k)
Capt. Van Brown
Doles's Brigade: Brig. Gen. George Doles
4th Georgia: 341 / 16%: Lt. Col. David R. E. Winn (k)
Maj. M. H. Willis
12th Georgia: 327 / 16%: Col. Edward Willis
21st Georgia: 287 / 13%: Col. John T. Mercer
44th Georgia: 364 / 21%: Col. Samuel P. Lumkin (mw)
Maj. W. H. Peebles
Iverson's Brigade: Brig. Gen. Alfred Iverson
5th North Carolina: 473 / 61%: Capt. Speight B. West (w)
Capt. Benjamin Robinson (w)
12th North Carolina: 219 / 36%: Lt. Col. William C. Davis

20th North Carolina: 372 / 68%: Lt. Col. Nelson Slouh (w)
    Capt. Lewis T. Hicks
23rd North Carolina: 316 / 89%: Col. Daniel H. Christie (mw)
    Capt. William H. Johnston
Ramseur's Brigade: Brig. Gen. Stephen D. Ramseur
2nd North Carolina: 243 / 28%: Maj. Daniel W. Hurt (w)
    Capt. James T. Scales
12th North Carolina: 196 / 35%: Col. Bryan Grimes
20th North Carolina: 306 / 21%: Col. R. Tyler Bennett (w)
    Maj. Joseph H. Lambeth (w)
23rd North Carolina: 276 / 27%: Col. Francis M. Parker
    Maj. W. W. Sillers
O'Neal's Brigade: Col. Edward A. O'Neal
3rd Alabama: 350 / 26%: Col. Cullin A. Battle
5th Alabama: 317 / 66%: Col. Josephus M. Hall
6th Alabama: 382 / 43%: Col. James N. Lightfoot (w)
    Capt. M. L. Bowie
12th Alabama: 317 / 26%: Col. Samuel B. Pickens
26th Alabama: 319 / 41%: Lt. Col. John C. Goodgame
Artillery: Lt. Col. Thomas H. Carter
Jefferson Davis (AL) Artillery (4 3-inch rifles): 79 / 0%: Lt. Capt. William J. Reese
King William (VA) Artillery (2 Napoleons; 2 10-lb Parrots): 103 / 10%: Capt. William P. Carter
Morris (VA) Artillery (4 Napoleons): 114 / 21%: Capt. Richard C. M. Page (w)
Orange (VA) Artillery (2 3-inch rifles 2 10-lb Parrotts): 80 / 9%: Capt. Charles W. Fry

Artillery Reserve: Col. J. Thompson Brown
First Virginia Artillery: Capt. Willis J. Dance
2nd Richmond Howitzers (4 10-lb Parrotts): 64 / 5%: Capt. David Watson
3rd Richmond Howitzers (4 3-inch rifles): 62 / 7%: Capt. Benjamin H. Smith Jr.
Dance's Powhatan (VA) Artillery (4 20-lb Parrotts): 78 / 19%: Lt. John M. Cunningham
1st Rockbridge (VA) Artillery (4 3-inch rifles): 85 / 25%: Capt. Archibald Graham
Salem (VA) Artillery (2 Napoleons; 2 3-inch rifles): 69 / 10%: Lt. Charles B. Griffin

Nelson's Battalion: Lt. Col. William Nelson

Amherst (VA) Artillery (3 Napoleons; 1 3-inch rifle): 105 / 0%: Capt. Thomas J. Kirkpatrick

Fluvanna (VA) Artillery (3 Napoleons; 1 3-inch rifle): 90 / 1%: Capt. John L. Massie

Milledge's (GA) Battery (2 3-inch rifles; 1 10-lb Parrott): 73 / 0%: Capt. John Milledge Jr.

3rd Corps

Lt. Gen. Ambrose P. Hill

Anderson's Division: Maj. Gen. R. H. Anderson

  Wilcox's Brigade: Brig. Gen. Cadmus M. Wilcox

    8th Alabama: 477 / 56%: Lt. Col. Hilary A. Herbert

    9th Alabama: 306 / 38%: Capt. J. Horace King (w)

    10th Alabama: 311 / 33%: Col. William H. Forney (w,c)

        Lt. Col. James E. Shelley

    11th Alabama: 311 / 24%: Col. John C. C. Sanders (w)

        Lt. Col. George E. Taylor

    14th Alabama: 315 / 15%: Col. Locus Packard (w)

        Lt. Col. James A. Broome

  Wright's Brigade: Brig. Gen. Ambrose R. Wright

        Col. William Gibson

        Brig. Gen. Ambrose R. Wright

    3rd Georgia: 441 / 54%: Col. Edward Walker

    22nd Georgia: 400 / 43%: Col. Joseph A. Warden (k)

        Capt. B. C. McCarty

    48th Georgia: 395 / 57%: Col. William Gibson (w,c)

        Capt. M. R. Hall

    2nd Georgia Battalion: 173 / 47%: Maj. George W. Ross (mw)

        Capt. Charles J. Muffett

  Mahone's Brigade: Brig. Gen. William Mahone

    6th Virginia: 288 / 4%: Col. George T. Rogers

    12th Virginia: 348 / 6%: Col. David A. Weedier

    16th Virginia: 270 / 8%: Col. Joseph H. Ham

    41st Virginia: 276 / 8%: Col. William A. Parham

    61st Virginia: 356 / 7%: Co. Virginias D. Goner

  Perry's Brigade (Lang's Brigade): Col. David Lang

2nd Florida: 242 / 44%: Maj. Walter R. Moore (w,c)
    Capt. William D. Valentine (w,c)
    Capt. Alexander Mosley (c)
    Capt. C. Seton Fleming
5th Florida: 321 / 40%: Capt. Richmond N. Gardner (w)
    Capt. Council A. Bryan
8th Florida: 176 / 61%: Lt. Col. William Baya
Posey's Brigade: Brig. Gen. Carnot Posey
  12th Mississippi: 272 / 4%: Col. Walter H. Taylor
  16th Mississippi: 385 / 5%: Col. Samuel E. Baker
  19th Mississippi: 372 / 9%: Col. Nathaniel H. Harris
  48th Mississippi: 256 / 15%: Col. Joseph M. Jayne
Sumter Battalion Artillery: Maj. John Lane
  1st Company (Georgia) (1 12-lb howitzer, 1 Napoleon, 1 3-inch rifle, 3 10-lb Parrotts): 130 / 10%: Capt. Hugh M. Ross
  2nd Company (Georgia) (4 12-lb howitzers, 2 Napoleons): 124 / 7%: Capt George M. Patterson
  3rd Company (Georgia) (3 3-inch rifles, 2 10-lb Parrotts): 121 / 16%: Capt. John T. Wingfield (w)

Heth's Division: Maj. Gen. Henry Heth (w)
    Brig. Gen. J. Johnston Pettigrew
Pettigrew's Brigade: Brig. Gen. J. Johnston Pettigrew (p,w)
    Col. James K. Marshall
  11th North Carolina: 617 / 59%: Col. Collett Leventhorpe (w)
    Maj. Egbert A. Ross (k)
  26th North Carolina: 839 / 82%: Col. Henry K. Burgwyn Jr. (k)
    Lt. Col. John R. Lane (w)
    Capt. H. C. Albright
  47th North Carolina: 567 / 38%: Col. George H. Faribault (w)
    Lt. Col. John A Graves (c)
  52nd North Carolina: 553 / 63%: Col. James K. Marshall (p)
    Lt. Col. Marcus A. Parks (w,c)
    Maj. Q. A. Richardson (k)
Brockenbrough's Brigade: Col. John M. Brockenbrough
  40th Virginia: 254 / 26%: Capt. T. Edwin Betts
    Capt. R. B. Davis
  47th Virginia: 209 / 26%: Col. Robert M. Mayo

55th Virginia: 268 / 24%: Col. William S. Christian (c)

22nd Virginia Battalion: 237 / 13%: Maj. John S. Bowles

Archer's Brigade: Brig. Gen. James J. Archer (c)

        Col. Birkett D. Fry (w,c)

        Lt. Col. S. G. Shepard

13th Alabama: 308 / 69%: Col. Birkett D. Fry (p,w,c)

5th Alabama Battalion: 135 / 36%: Maj. Albert S. Van de Graaf

1st Tennessee (Provisional Army): 281 / 63%: Maj. Felix G. Buchanan (w)

7th Tennessee: 249 / 47%: Lt. Col. Samuel G. Shephard

14th Tennessee: 220 / 58%: Capt. Bruce L. Phillips

Davis's Brigade: Brig. Gen. Joseph R. Davis

2nd Mississippi: 492 / 47%: Col. John M. Stone (w)

        Lt. Col. David W. Humphreys (k)

        Maj. John A. Blair

11th Mississippi: 592 / 53%: Col. Francis M. Green

42nd Mississippi: 575 / 46%: Col. Hugh B. Miller (mw)

55th North Carolina: 640 / 65%: Col. John Kerr Connally (w)

        Maj. Alfred H. Belo

Artillery: Lt. Col. John J. Garnett

Donaldsonville (LA) Artillery (2 3-inch rifles, 1 10-lb Parrott): 114 / 5%: Capt. Victor Maurin

Moore's (VA) Artillery (2 Napoleons, 1 3-inch rifle, 1 10-1b Parrott): 77 / NR: Capt. Joseph D. Moore

Pittsylvania (VA) Artillery (2 Napoleons, 2 3-inch rifles): 90 / NR: Capt. John W. Lewis

Norfolk Light Artillery Blues (2 12-1b howitzers, 2 3-inch rifles): 106 / 2%: Capt. Charles R. Grandy

Pender's Division: Maj. Gen. William D. Pender (mw)

        Brig. Gen. James H. Lane (r)

        Maj. Gen. I. R. Trimble (w)

        Brig. Gen. James H. Lane

Perrin's Brigade: Col. Abner Perrin

1st South Carolina (Provisional Army): 328 / 35%: Maj. Charles W. McCreary

1st South Carolina Rifles: 366 / 2%: Capt. William M. Hadden

12th South Carolina: 366 / 35%: Col. John L. Miller

13th South Carolina: 390 / 37%: Lt. Col. Benjamin T. Brockman

14th South Carolina: 428 / 59%: Lt. Col. Joseph N. Brown (w)

Maj. Edward Croft (w)
Lane's Brigade: Brig. James H. Lane (p)
    Col. Clark M. Avery (r)
    Brig. James H. Lane
    Col. Clark M. Avery
  7th North Carolina: 291 / 55%: Capt. J. McLeod Turner (w,c)
    Capt. James G. Harris
  18th North Carolina: 346 / 25%: Col. John D. Barry
  28th North Carolina: 346 / 69%: Col. Samuel D. Lowe (w)
    Lt. Col. W. H. A. Speer
  33rd North Carolina: 368 / 36%: Col. Clark M. Avery
  37th North Carolina: 379 / 46%: Col. William M. Babour
Thomas's Brigade: Brig. Gen. Edward L. Thomas
  14th Georgia: 305 / 14%: Col. Robert W. Folson
  35th Georgia: 325 / 29%: Col. Bolling H. Holt
  45th Georgia: 325 / 15%: Col. Thomas J. Simmons
  49th Georgia: 329 / 26%: Col. Samuel T. Player
Scales's Brigade: Brig. Gen. Alfred M. Scales (w)
    Lt. Col. G. T. Gordon (w)
    Col. William L. J. Lowrance (w)
  13th North Carolina: 232 / 77%: Col. Joseph H. Hyman(w)
    Lt. Col. H. A. Rogers
  16th North Carolina: 321 / 38%: Capt. Leroy W. Stowe
  22nd North Carolina: 267 / 62%: Col. James Connor
  34th North Carolina: 311 / 33%: Col. William L. J. Lowrance (p,w)
    Lt. Col. G. T. Gordon
  38th North Carolina: 216 / 60%: Col. William J. Hoke (w)
    Lt. Col. John Ashford (w)
Artillery: Maj. William T. Poague
  Albemarle (VA) Artillery (1 12-lb howitzer, 2 3-inch rifles, 1 10-lb Parrott): 94 / 14%: Capt. James W. Wyatt
  Charlotte (NC) Artillery (2 12-lb howitzers, 2 Napoleons): 125 / 4%: Capt. Joseph Graham
  Madison Light (MS) Artillery (1 12-lb howitzer, 3 Napoleons): 91 / NR: Capt. George Ward
  Warrenton (VA) Battery (2 12-lb howitzers, 2 Napoleons): 58 / 9%: Capt. James V. Brooke

Artillery Reserve: Col. R. Lindsay Walker
  McIntosh's Battalion: Maj. D. G. McIntosh
    Danville (VA) Artillery (4 Napoleons): 114 / 3%: Capt. R. Sidney Rice
    Hardaway (AL) Artillery (2 3-inch rifles, 2 Whitworth rifles): 71 / 11%: Capt.
      William B. Hurt
    2nd Rockbridge (VA) Artillery (2 Napoleons, 2 3-inch rifles): 67 / 6%: Lt.
      Samuel Wallace
    Richmond (VA) Battery (4 3-inch rifles): 96 / 10%: Capt. Marmaduke Johnson
  Pegram's Battalion: Maj. W. J. Pegram
            Capt. E. B. Brunson
    Crenshaw's Virginia Battery (2 12-lb howitzers, 2 3-inch rifles): 76 / 20%:
      Capt. William Crenshaw
    Fredericksburg (VA) Artillery (2 Napoleons, 2 3-inch rifles): 71 / 3%: Capt.
      Edward A. Marye
    Letcher (VA) Artillery (2 Napoleons, 2 10-lb Parrotts): 65 / 26%: Capt.
      Thomas A Brander
    Pee Dee (SC) Artillery (4 3-inch rifles): 65 / 2%: Lt. William E. Zimmerman
    Purcell (VA) Artillery (4 Napoleons): 89 / 7%: Capt. Joseph McGraw

Cavalry

Maj. Gen. J. E. B. Stuart
Hampton's Brigade: Brig. Gen. Wade Hampton (w)
          Col. Laurence S. Baker
    1st North Carolina: 407 / 11%: Col. Laurence S. Baker
    1st South Carolina: 339 / 4%: Col. John L. Black
    2nd South Carolina: 186 / 4%: Col. Matthew C. Butler
    Cobb's (Georgia) Legion: 330 / 6%: Col. Pierce B. L. Young
    Jefferson Davis Legion: 246 / 6%: Col. Joseph F. Waring
    Phillips (Georgia) Legion: 238 / 4%: Lt. Col. Jefferson C. Phillips
Fitz Lee's Brigade: Brig. Gen. Fitzhugh Lee
    1st Maryland Battalion: 309 / 6%: Maj. Harry Gilmore
          Maj. Ridgely Brown
    1st Virginia: 310 / 7%: Col. James H. Drake
    2nd Virginia: 385 / 5%: Col. Thomas T. Munford
    3rd Virginia: 210 / 4%: Col. Thomas H. Owen
    4th Virginia: 544 / 6%: Col. William Carter Wickham
    5th Virginia: 150 / 0%: Col. Thomas Rosser

Jenkins's Brigade: Brig. Gen. Albert G. Jenkins (w)
  Col. Milton J. Ferguson
 14th Virginia: 265 / 2%: Maj. Benjamin F. Eakle (w)
 16th Virginia: 265 / 3%: Col. Milton J. Ferguson
 17th Virginia: 241 / 3%: Col. William H. French
 34th Virginia Battalion: 172 / NR: Lt. Col. Vincent A. Witcher
 36th Virginia Battalion: 125 / 1%: Capt. Cornelius T. Smith
W. H. F. Lee's Brigade: Col. John R. Chambliss Jr.
 2nd North Carolina: 145 / 6%: Lt. Col. William Payne
 9th Virginia: 490 / 4%: Col. Richard L. T. Beale
 10th Virginia: 236 / 5%: Col. Lucius Davis
 13th Virginia: 298 / 6%: Capt. Benjamin F. Winfield
Robertson's Brigade: Brig. Gen. Beverly H. Robertson
 4th North Carolina: not engaged
 5th North Carolina: not engaged
Jones's Brigade: Brig. Gen. William E. Jones
 6th Virginia: not engaged
 7th Virginia: not engaged
 11th Virginia: not engaged
Stuart Horse Artillery: Maj. R. F. Beckham
 Breathed's (VA) Battery (4 3-inch rifles): 106 / 1%: Capt. James Breathed
 Chew's (VA) Battery: not engaged: Capt. Preston Chew
 2nd Baltimore (MD) Battery (4 10-lb Parrotts): 103 / na: Capt. William H. Griffin
 Washington (SC) Battery (3 Blakely rifles): 79 / 1%: Capt. James F. Hart
 2nd Stuart Horse (VA) Battery (2 Napoleons, 2 3-inch rifles): 106 / 2%: Capt. William M. McGregor
 Moorman's (VA) Battery (1 Napoleon, 3 rifles): not engaged: Capt. Marcellus M. Moorman

Imboden's Command

Brig. Gen. John D. Imboden

18th Virginia: not engaged: Col. George W. Imboden
62nd Virginia Infantry, Mounted: not engaged: Col. George H. Smith
Virginia Partisan Rangers: not engaged: Capt. John H. McNeill
Staunton Horse (VA) Battery: not engaged: Capt. John H. McClanahan
Jackson's (VA) Battery: 107 / 1%: Capt. Thomas E. Jackson

Notes

Full bibliographical data can be found in the bibliography

Prologue

1. Reardon, *Pickett's Charge*, 51.
2. Haskell, letter, July 16, 1863.
3. Root and Stocker *"Isn't This Glorious!"* 42.
4. Sauers, *Fighting Them Over*, 334.
5. Harman, *Cemetery Hill*, 2
6. Sauers, *Fighting Them Over*, 334.
7. Haskell, letter, July 16, 1863.
8. Reardon, *Pickett's Charge*, 3.

Chapter 1: Gettysburg and Slavery

1. Bolin, "Slaveholders and Slaves in Adams County," 8.
2. Ibid.
3. Ibid., 33–35.
4. Creighton, *Colors of Courage*, 51.
5. Slade and Alexander, *Firestorm at Gettysburg*, 23.
6. Creighton, "Living on the Fault Line," 222–23.
7. *Historic People and Places of Gettysburg*, Mainstreet Gettysburg (n.d.), http://www.mainstreetgettysburg.org/images/Historic.pdf.
8. Smith, *Farms at Gettysburg*, 13.
9. Creighton, *Colors of Courage*, 60–61.
10. "The Brian Farm," Gettysburg National Military Park, Virtual Tour—Day Three, Ziegler's Grove, http://www.nps.gov/archive/gett/getttour/tstops/tstd3-21.htm.
11. Vermilyea, "Jack Hopkins' Civil War," 9–15.
12. Hofe, *That There Be No Stain Upon My Stones*, 38–40.
13. Ibid., 42.
14. Ibid., 43.

Chapter 2: George Sandoe

1. Pfanz, *Gettysburg—The First Day*, 53.
2. J. David Petruzzi, "Monuments of the 21st Pennsylvania Cavalry Company B

'Adams County Cavalry' and 'Bell's Cavalry,'" *Emmitsburg Area Historical Society,* http://www.emmitsburg.net/archive_list/articles/history/civil_war/21st_penn_cav .htm.

   3. Schildt, *Roads to Gettysburg*, 175; see also Gottfried, *Roads to Gettysburg*, 125.

Chapter 3: The Second Occupation of Gettysburg

   1. Faust, *Historical Times Illustrated Encyclopedia of the Civil War*, 677.
   2. T. F. Shuey, "From a Boy's Diary," in Sauers, *Fighting Them Over*, 27.
   3. *OR*, vol. 27, pt. 2, 465.
   4. Coddington, *Gettysburg Campaign*, 167.
   5. *OR*, vol. 27, pt. 2, 465.
   6. Slade and Alexander, *Firestorm at Gettysburg*, 25.
   7. Ibid., 29.
   8. Ibid.
   9. Schildt, *Roads to Gettysburg*, 235–37.
10. *OR*, vol. 27, pt. 2, 465–66.
11. Slade and Alexander, *Firestorm at Gettysburg*, 25.
12. Schildt, *Roads to Gettysburg*, 236.
13. Slade and Alexander, *Firestorm at Gettysburg*, 25.

Chapter 4: Lee and Ewell

   1. Freeman, *Lee's Lieutenants*, 1:347.
   2. Tagg, *The Generals of Gettysburg*, 251–52.
   3. Freeman, *Lee's Lieutenants*, 3:38.
   4. Pfanz, *Gettysburg—The First Day*, 344.
   5. "Famous Models: Situational Leadership," http://www.chimaeraconsulting .com/sitleader.htm.
   6. Ibid.
   7. Martin, *Gettysburg—July 1*, 559.
   8. Ibid., 557, 559–60.

Chapter 5: Words Between Lee and Stuart

   1. *OR*, vol. 27, pt. 2, 687–710.
   2. *OR*, vol. 27, pt. 2, 692.
   3. *OR*, vol. 27, pt. 2, 693.
   4. *OR*, vol. 27, pt. 3, 913.
   5. *OR*, vol. 27, pt. 3, 914–15.

6. Callihan, "Stuart's Fateful Ride," 8.
7. *OR*, vol. 27, pt. 2, 923.
8. Ibid.
9. Callihan, "Stuart's Fateful Ride," 10.
10. Wittenberg and Petruzzi, *Plenty of Blame to Go Around*, 9.
11. Ibid., 27.
12. Callihan, "Stuart's Fateful Ride," 12.
13. Wittenberg and Petruzzi, *Plenty of Blame to Go Around*, 209–61.
14. Ibid., 298.

Chapter 6: Harrison

1. Martin, *Gettysburg—July 1*, 9; see also Pfanz, *Gettysburg—The First Day*, 21.
2. Martin, *Gettysburg—July 1*, 19.
3. Trudeau, *Gettysburg*, 100; see also Coddington, *Gettysburg Campaign*, 181.
4. Becker, "A Man Called Harrison," 46–47.
5. Ibid., 48–50.

Chapter 7: The Shoes, Always the Shoes

1. Martin, *Gettysburg—July 1*, 29.
2. Thomas Flagel, interview with author, March 3, 2006.
3. McPherson, *Battle Cry of Freedom*, 646–47.
4. Gottfried, *Roads to Gettysburg*, 1–2.
5. Trudeau, *Gettysburg*, 3.
6. Ibid., 4–5.
7. McPherson, *Battle Cry of Freedom*, 646–47.
8. Ibid.
9. Gottfried, *Roads to Gettysburg*, 2.
10. Dowdey, *History of the Confederacy*, 269–70.

Chapter 8: What Is the Pipe Creek Line?

1. Trudeau, *Gettysburg*, 151.
2. Coddington, *Gettysburg Campaign*, 237–39.
3. Sears, *Gettysburg*, 150.
4. *OR*, ser. 1, vol. 27, pt. 3, 458.
5. *OR*, vol. 27, pt.3, 548.

Chapter 9: What Was Heth Thinking?

1. Tagg, *Generals of Gettysburg*, 340–41.
2. *OR*, vol. 27, pt. 2, 307.
3. Pfanz, *Gettysburg—The First Day*, 23.
4. Ibid., 25.
5. Henry Heth to Rev. J. William Jones, June 1877, Southern Historical Society, http://www.gdg.org/Research/Authored%20Items/shheth2.html; Wiley Sword, "We're Going 'To Get Those Shoes'" *Gettysburg Magazine*, January 2007, 123–24.
6. Coddington, *Gettysburg Campaign*, 264.
7. *OR*, vol. 27, pt. 2, 637.
8. Martin, *Gettysburg—July 1*, 60.
9. *OR*, vol. 27, pt. 2, 637.
10. Henry Heth to Rev. J. William Jones, June 1877, Southern Historical Society, http://www.gdg.org/Research/Authored%20Items/shheth2.html.
11. Walter Kempster, "The Cavalry at Gettysburg," *Gettysburg Papers* (Dayton, OH: Morningside Bookshop, 1986), 432.
12. Pfanz, *Gettysburg—The First Day*, 150, 275, 344; Gallagher, "Confederate Corps Leadership on the First Day at Gettysburg," 53.
13. Martin, *Gettysburg—July 1*, 340.
14. Coddington, *Gettysburg Campaign*, 273.
15. Tagg, *Generals of Gettysburg*, 342–43.

Chapter 10: John Reynolds

1. Ibid., 9; see also Pfanz, *Gettysburg—The First Day*, 48; Martin, *Gettysburg—July 1*, 35.
2. Coddington, *Gettysburg Campaign*, 307.
3. Riley, "For God's Sake Forward," 42.
4. Pfanz, *Gettysburg—The First Day*, 69–70. This was Johnston Pettigrew's brigade, which had ventured toward Gettysburg in search of supplies. Pettigrew was mindful of the general order not to bring on a general engagement, and he halted his troops at the Lutheran Seminary.
5. Pfanz, *Gettysburg—The First Day*, 72.
6. Ibid., 75.
7. Riley, "For God's Sake Forward," 51
8. Frassanito, *Early Photography*, 59–64.
9. Petruzzi, "Who Shot General Reynolds?"; see also Sanders, "Enduring Tales of Gettysburg: The Death of Reynolds," 34.

10. Petruzzi, "Who Shot General Reynolds?"

11. Sanders, "Enduring Tales of Gettysburg: The Death of Reynolds," 34–35.

12. Latimer, *Is She Kate?* 24–26.

13. Ibid., 21–23.

14. Ibid., 41.

Chapter 11: The World of John Burns

1. *OR*, vol. 27, pt. 1, 255.

2. Pfanz, *Gettysburg—The First Day*, 357.

3. Martin, *Gettysburg—July 1*, 373.

4. Pfanz, *Gettysburg—The First Day*, 357–58.

5. Martin, *Gettysburg—July 1*, 374

6. Pfanz, *Gettysburg—The First Day*, 358–59.

7. Martin, *Gettysburg—July 1*, 373–76.

8. Ibid., 374.

9. Smith, *John Burns*, 2.

10. Ibid., 28–31.

11. Ibid., 27.

12. Ibid., 99

13. Martin, *Gettysburg—July 1*, 376–77; Miller, "Emmitsburg and the Recoil of Gettysburg."

14. Smith, *John Burns*, 117.

15. Ibid., 11.

Chapter 12: The Long Shadow of Stonewall Jackson

1. "The Funeral of Stonewall Jackson," *Lexington Gazette*, May 20, 1863.

2. Robertson, *Stonewall Jackson*, 758–61.

3. Abram Fulkerson to his wife, Selina, May 18, 1863, Fulkerson Family Papers, Manuscript # 0363, Virginia Military Institute Archives, Lexington, VA, http://www.vmi.edu/archives/manuscripts/ms363009.html.

4. Freeman, *Lee's Lieutenants*, 2:690.

5. Jedediah Hotchkiss to Sara Hotchkiss, May 19, 1863, Reel 4, Jedediah Hotchkiss Papers, Library of Congress.

6. Freeman, *Lee's Lieutenants*, 2:712.

7. Taylor, *General Lee*, 190.

8. *OR*, vol. 27, pt. 2, 308.

9. Pfanz, *Gettysburg—The First Day*, 344.

10. Ibid., 346.

11. Coddington, *Gettysburg Campaign*, 319; Pfanz, *Gettysburg—The First Day*, 346.

12. Coddington, *Gettysburg Campaign*, 318–19.

13. Pfanz, *Gettysburg—The First Day*, 346.

14. Ibid., 349.

Chapter 13: Getting Slocum to Move

1. Tagg, *Generals of Gettysburg*, 143–44.

2. Martin, *Gettysburg—July 1*, 524; see also *OR*, vol. 27, pt. 2, 825.

3. *OR*, vol. 27, pt. 2, 758–869.

4. *OR*, vol. 27, pt. 2, 816, 790.

5. Martin, *Gettysburg—July 1*, 525.

6. Pfanz, *Gettysburg—The First Day*, 142–43.

7. Ibid., 143.

8. *OR*, vol. 27, pt. 2, 758–59.

9. *OR*, vol. 27, pt. 2, 763–65.

10. Pfanz, *Gettysburg—Culp's Hill and Cemetery Hill*, 98.

11. Ibid.

12. Ibid., 83.

13. Martin, *Gettysburg—July 1*, 535.

Chapter 14: In a Pigsty

1. Gottfried, *Brigades of Gettysburg*, 301.

2. Ibid., 304.

3. Tagg, *Generals of Gettysburg*, 126.

4. Martin, *Gettysburg—July 1*, 331.

5. Ibid., 332.

Chapter 15: Someone Blundered

1. Longstreet, *From Manassas to Appomattox*, 403.

2. An example of this can be found in a letter sent to Gettysburg's first historian, John Bachelder, by Isaac Trimble, who offered to send Bachelder a list of "some facts of great interest to communicate showing why the battles were lost to us." Trimble's offer did not include reasons of why the North won. Trimble to Bachelder, June 11, 1881, in *The Bachelder Papers*, ed. David Ladd and Audrey Ladd (Dayton, OH: Morningside House, 1994), 2:756.

3. Wert, *Longstreet*, 14; see also Gallagher. "If the Enemy Is There We Must Attack Him," 6.

4. Wert, *Longstreet*, 422–23.

5. Hall, *Stand of the U.S. Army at Gettysburg*, 90; see also Piston, "Cross Purposes," 47; Tucker, *Lee and Longstreet at Gettysburg*, 1–35; Pfanz, *Gettysburg—The Second Day*, 28.

6. Wert, *Longstreet*, 97.

7. Coddington, *Gettysburg Campaign*, 360–61; see also Martin, *Gettysburg—July 1*, 505–6.

8. Wert, *Longstreet*, 259.

9. Coddington, *Gettysburg Campaign*, 371; see also Trudeau, *Gettysburg*, 279.

10. Pfanz, *Gettysburg—The Second Day*, 110–11.

11. Coddington, *Gettysburg Campaign*, 375.

12. Wert, *Longstreet*, 268.

13. Pfanz, *Gettysburg—The Second Day*, 112–13.

14. Wert, *Longstreet*, 268.

15. Pfanz, *Gettysburg—The Second Day*, 119–21.

16. Luvaas and Nelson, *U.S. Army War College Guide to the Battle of Gettysburg*, 59–60.

17. Coddington, *Gettysburg Campaign*, 382.

18. Hess, *Pickett's Charge*, 12.

19. Ibid., 29.

20. Faust, *Historical Times Illustrated Encyclopedia of the Civil War*, 6.

21. Hess, *Pickett's Charge*, 159–61.

22. Ibid., 161.

23. Wert, *Longstreet*, 410–17.

24. Longstreet, *From Manassas to Appomattox*, 385.

25. Ibid., 404–5.

Chapter 16: Sickles

1. Quoted in Swanberg, *Sickles the Incredible*, vii.

2. Tagg, *Generals of Gettysburg*, 61–62; see also Sauers, *A Caspian Sea of Ink*, 5.

3. Tagg, *Generals of Gettysburg*, 62.

4. The order to Sickles from Meade was part of the famous Pipe Creek circular that later was used by Sickles to prove that he had initiated the battle while Meade wanted to retire.

5. Sauers, *A Caspian Sea of Ink*, 19–21.

6. Pfanz, *Gettysburg—The Second Day*, 46.

7. Ibid., 93.

8. Ibid., 94.

9. Ibid., 97.

10. Ibid., 102.

11. Sauers, *A Caspian Sea of Ink*, 36–38.

12. Pfanz, *Gettysburg—The Second Day*, 420–33.

Chapter 17: Mahone and Anderson

1. Coddington, *Gettysburg Campaign*, 384.

2. Pfanz, *Gettysburg—Culp's Hill and Cemetery Hill*, 205; see also *OR*, vol. 27, pt. 2, 318–19.

3. Tagg, *Generals of Gettysburg*, 306–7.

4. Imhof, *A Study in Maps*, 32–33.

5. Coddington, *Gettysburg Campaign*, 405–7, 417.

6. Pfanz, *Gettysburg—The Second Day*, 379–80.

7. Ibid., 386.

8. *OR*, vol. 27, pt. 2, 621.

9. Busey and Martin, *Regimental Strengths and Losses*, 309, 589.

10. *OR*, vol. 27, pt. 2, 614.

11. Hess, *Pickett's Charge*, 28.

12. *OR*, vol. 27, pt. 2, 319.

13. *OR*, vol. 27, pt. 2, 320.

14. Hall, *Stand of the U.S. Army at Gettysburg*, 148.

Chapter 18: What's in a Name?

1. *OR*, vol. 27 pt. 2, 367–70.

2. Ladd and Sauers, *Bachelder Papers*, 1:456–57.

Chapter 19: The Savior of Little Round Top

1. Tagg, *Generals of Gettysburg*, 89–90.

2. LaFantasie, *Twilight at Little Round Top*, 111.

3. Tagg, *Generals of Gettysburg*, 96

4. Pfanz, *Gettysburg—The Second Day*, 229–30.

5. The eight Union regiments, from left to right flank, were the 20th Maine, 83rd Pennsylvania, 44th New York, 16th Michigan, 140th New York, 91st Pennsylvania, 146th Pennsylvania, and 155th Pennsylvania.

6. LaFantasie, *Twilight at Little Round Top*, 141–43.

7. Downey, *Guns of Gettysburg*, 92–94.

8. Trulock, *In the Hands of Providence*, 8–12.

9. Ibid., 110–12.

10. Flagel and Allers, *History Buff's Guide to Gettysburg*, 133–34.

Chapter 20: The Broken 11th Corps

1. Faust, *Historical Times Illustrated Encyclopedia of the Civil War*, 177–78.

2. Ferguson, *Chancellorsville*, 336–37.

3. Tagg, *Generals of Gettysburg*, 125–26.

4. Martin, *Gettysburg—July 1*, 199.

5. Ibid., 199–200.

6. Coddington, *Gettysburg Campaign*, 282.

7. Bennett, *Days of Uncertainty and Dread*, 28.

8. Pfanz, *Gettysburg—Culp's Hill and Cemetery Hill*, 127–28.

9. Lash, *Gibraltar Brigade*, 84; see also Pfanz, *Gettysburg—Culp's Hill and Cemetery Hill*, 259–62.

10. Lash, *Gibraltar Brigade*, 96.

11. Pfanz, *Gettysburg—Culp's Hill and Cemetery Hill*, 214.

12. Paul F. Rohrbacker, address at dedication of the 74th Pennsylvania monument, July 2, 1888, in Nicholson, *Pennsylvania at Gettysburg*, 1:433–34.

Chapter 21: It Wasn't That Close

1. Gallagher. "If the Enemy Is There We Must Attack Him," 25.

2. Pfanz, *Gettysburg—Culp's Hill and Cemetery Hill*, 211.

3. Hall, *Stand of the U.S. Army at Gettysburg*, 153.

4. Pfanz, *Gettysburg—Culp's Hill and Cemetery Hill*, 218.

5. Ibid., 223.

6. Coddington, *Gettysburg Campaign*, 432–33.

Chapter 22: The Essential Business Meeting

1. Trudeau, *Gettysburg*, 415.

2. Ibid.

3. Coddington, *Gettysburg Campaign*, 449–51.

4. Tagg, *Generals of Gettysburg*, 65–67.

5. Hyde, *Union Generals Speak*, 155–56.

6. Ibid., 148.

7. Ibid.

8. Tagg, *Generals of Gettysburg*, 67.

9. Hyde, *Union Generals Speak*, 33–35.

10. Faust, *Historical Times Illustrated Encyclopedia of the Civil War*, 100–101; see also Hyde, *Union Generals Speak*, 239.

11. Hyde, *Union Generals Speak*, 238–39.

12. Trudeau, *Gettysburg*, 415.

13. Coddington, *Gettysburg Campaign*, 338–39; see also Trudeau, *Gettysburg*, 292.

14. Hyde, *Union Generals Speak*, 257.

Chapter 23: Prelude to Pickett's Charge

1. Reardon, *Pickett's Charge*, 6.

2. Longstreet, *From Manassas to Appomattox*, 386. Longstreet gave no basis for his statement of fifteen thousand men.

3. Reardon, *Pickett's Charge*, 6.

Chapter 24: The Absent A. P. Hill

1. Tagg, *Generals of Gettysburg*, 302.

2. Gallagher, "Confederate Corps Leadership on the First Day at Gettysburg," 40.

3. Tagg, *Generals of Gettysburg*, 302–3.

4. Gottfried, *Roads to Gettysburg*, 203–4.

5. Hassler, *Crisis at the Crossroads*, 16.

6. Pfanz, *Gettysburg—The First Day*, 27–28.

7. Ibid., 28.

8. *OR*, ser. 1, vol. 27, pt. 2, 607.

9. *OR*, ser. 1, vol. 27, pt. 2, 637

10. Gallagher, "Confederate Corps Leadership on the First Day at Gettysburg," 32.

11. Martin, *Gettysburg—July 1*, 340.

12. Ibid., 340–41.

13. Martin, *Gettysburg—July 1*, 503–4; see also Pfanz, *Gettysburg—The First Day*, 319–320.

14. *OR*, ser. 1, vol. 27, pt. 2, 607.

15. En echelon is defined as parallel or subparallel, closely spaced, overlapping, or steplike.

16. Pfanz, *Gettysburg—The Second Day*, 113.

17. Imhof, *A Study in Maps*, 171. Imhof's book is an invaluable aid in the study of the en echelon attack on July 2.

18. Pfanz, *Gettysburg—The Second Day*, 386.

19. Ibid.

20. *OR*, ser. 1, vol. 27, pt. 2, 607–8.

21. Gottfried, *Brigades of Gettysburg*, 583.

22. *OR*, ser. 1, vol. 27, pt. 2, 621.

23. *OR*, ser. 1, vol. 27, pt. 2, 614.

24. Hess, *Pickett's Charge*, 387.

25. Ibid., 306.

26. Ibid., 327.

Chapter 25: Fog or Smoke?

1. Downey, *Guns of Gettysburg*, 118.

2. Hess, *Pickett's Charge*, 133.

3. Cleaves, *Meade of Gettysburg*, 160.

4. Coddington, *Gettysburg Campaign*, 496.

5. Cleaves, *Meade of Gettysburg*, 160; see also Hess, *Pickett's Charge*, 134.

6. Hess, *Pickett's Charge*, 135.

7. Ibid., 136.

8. Coddington, *Gettysburg Campaign*, 498.

9. Downey, *Guns of Gettysburg*, 133

10. Hall, *Stand of the U.S. Army at Gettysburg*, 190–92.

11. Hess, *Pickett's Charge*, 299.

12. Ibid., 141.

13. Ibid., 141–42.

14. Downey, *Guns of Gettysburg*, 135.

15. Coddington, *Gettysburg Campaign*, 497.

Chapter 26: Pickett and Who?

1. Reardon, *Pickett's Charge*, 49, 453.

2. Ibid., 2.

Chapter 27: North Carolina vs. Virginia

1. Bond, *Pickett or Pettigrew?* title page.

2. Martin, *Confederate Monuments at Gettysburg*, 148. The Armistead monument is an area marker because the exact site of Armistead's wounding is not known.

3. Rollins, *Pickett's Charge!* 257; see also Rollins, *Damned Red Flags of the Rebellion*, 188.

4. Rollins, *Pickett's Charge!* 255.

5. Reardon, *Pickett's Charge*, 55.

6. Hess, *Pickett's Charge*, 183.

7. Rollins, *Pickett's Charge!* 235.

8. Reardon, *Pickett's Charge*, 197; see also Hess, *Pickett's Charge*, 178.

Chapter 28: Where Is Pickett? Where Is Pickett's Report?

1. Selcer, "Faithfully and Forever Your Soldier," 7–8.

2. Ibid., 13–17

3. Ibid., 10–18.

4. Georg and Busey, *Nothing But Glory*, 4.

5. Ibid.

6. Ibid., 186.

7. Reardon, *Pickett's Charge*, 156.

8. Georg and Busey, *Nothing But Glory*, 194.

9. Reardon, *Pickett's Charge*, 157.

10. Ibid., 158.

11. Georg and Busey, *Nothing But Glory*, 204.

12. *OR*, vol. 27, pt. 3, 1075.

13. Ibid.

14. Wert, *Gettysburg: Day Three*, 297.

15. Ibid.

16. Foote, *The Civil War: A Narrative—Red River to Appomattox*, 930.

17. Selcer, "Faithfully and Forever Your Soldier," 53.

Chapter 29: The Ignored and Neglected Child

1. Wittenberg, *Protecting the Flank*, 22.

2. Wert, *Gettysburg: Day Three*, 263.

3. Longacre, *Cavalry at Gettysburg*, 212.

4. Wittenberg, *Gettysburg's Forgotten Cavalry Charges*, 40.

5. Ibid., 47.

6. See Riggs, *East of Gettysburg* (1970) and Walker, *Cavalry Battle That Saved the Union* (2002). My criticism of the titles should not be interpreted as criticism of the contents or reflect on the veracity of either book.

7. Wert, *Gettysburg: Day Three*, 263.

8. Ibid., 266–67.

9. Wittenberg, *Protecting the Flank*, 118–19.

10. Wert, *Gettysburg: Day Three*, 271.

11. Tagg, *Generals of Gettysburg*, 179–81.

12. Wittenberg, *Gettysburg's Forgotten Cavalry Charges*, 44.

13. Ibid., 45–52.

14. Ibid., 87–88.

Chapter 30: One More Needless Death

1. Robert A. Welch, "The Ballad of Jennie Wade," Snow Flakes in June Publishing ASCAP. Words and music Copyright © 2004.

2. Jennie's full name was Mary Virginia Wade. Although Ginny was her nickname, after the war, the name Jennie became widely used and has persisted.

3. Small, *Jennie Wade Story*, 13.

4. Ibid., 62.

5. Slade and Alexander, *Firestorm at Gettysburg*, 114.

6. Pfanz, *Gettysburg—Culp's Hill and Cemetery Hill*, 328.

7. Small, *Jennie Wade Story*, 14–15.

8. Ibid., 16–17.

9. Ibid., 18–20.

10. Ibid., 29–30.

11. Ibid., 32–34.

12. Busey and Martin, *Regimental Strengths and Losses*, 281.

13. Robert A. Welch, "The Ballad of Jennie Wade," Snow Flakes in June Publishing ASCAP. Words and music Copyright © 2004.

14. Small, *Jennie Wade Story*, 62.

15. Prowell, *History of the 87th Pennsylvania Volunteers*, 84.

16. Ibid., 72.

17. Small, *Jennie Wade Story*, 64–65

18. Pfanz, *Gettysburg—Culp's Hill and Cemetery Hill*, 465.

19. Kennel, *Beyond the Gatehouse*, 55.

20. Ibid., 55.

21. Ibid., 52.

22. Robert A. Welch, "The Ballad of Jennie Wade," Snow Flakes in June Publishing ASCAP. Words and music Copyright © 2004.

Chapter 31: The Attack of July 4

1. Schildt, *Roads from Gettysburg*, 22–23.

2. Green, "From Gettysburg to Falling Waters," 165.

3. For further information on losses, see Flagel and Allers, *History Buff's Guide to Gettysburg*, 135–46.

4. Green, "From Gettysburg to Falling Waters," 165.

5. Ibid., 164.

6. Ibid., 164; see also an excellent map in Brown, *Retreat from Gettysburg*, 104.

7. Wright, *Oxford Dictionary of Civil War Quotations*, 253.

8. Ibid., 254.

9. Hyde, *Union Generals Speak*, 4–5.

10. Ibid., 55.

11. Ibid., 33.

12. Brown, *Retreat from Gettysburg*, 259.

13. Ibid., 322.

14. Ibid., 326.

15. Green, "From Gettysburg to Falling Waters," 171–72.

Chapter 32: In Harm's Way

1. Coco, *Strange and Blighted Land*, 363.

2. Slade and Alexander, *Firestorm at Gettysburg*, 107.

3. Ibid., 87.

4. Coco, *Strange and Blighted Land*, 361.

5. Ibid., 363.

6. Coco, *Vast Sea of Misery*, 61.

7. Slade and Alexander, *Firestorm at Gettysburg*, 101.

8. Coco, *Strange and Blighted Land*, 338.

9. Coco, *Vast Sea of Misery*, 37–38.

10. Bennett, *Days of Uncertainty and Dread*, 29.

11. Coco, *Vast Sea of Misery*, 37–38.

12. Slade and Alexander, *Firestorm at Gettysburg*, 107.

13. Coco, *Strange and Blighted Land*, 257.

14. Ibid., 337–44.

Chapter 33: Who Lived? Who Died?

1. Reardon, *Pickett's Charge*, 42.

2. *OR*, vol. 27, pt. 1, 113.

3. *OR*, vol. 27, pt. 2, 346.

4. *OR*, vol. 27, pt. 2, 346.

5. *OR*, vol. 27, pt. 2, 344.

6. *OR*, vol. 27, pt. 2, 667.

7. Busey and Martin, *Regimental Strengths and Losses*, 301.

8. Ibid., 307.

9. David Lang to Annie Eliza Atkinson, July 9, 1963, David and Alma Lang Collection, Tallahassee, Florida.

10. Busey and Martin, *Regimental Strengths and Losses*, 4–5.

11. Ibid., 385.

12. Ibid., 259.

13. Krick and Ferguson, *Gettysburg Death Roster: Confederate*, 1, 17.

14. Ibid., 5.

15. Busey and Martin, *Regimental Strengths and Losses*, 125.

16. Howard, *Gettysburg Death Roster: Union*, 7.

Chapter 34: The Photographs Lie

1. Frassanito, *Journey in Time*.

2. Ibid., 198–215.

3. Ibid., 21–22.

4. Frassanito, *Early Photography at Gettysburg*, 26–53.

Chapter 35: Ectoplasm or Imagination?

1. Mark Nesbitt has written six books on the ghosts of Gettysburg, all of which were published by Thomas Publications of Gettysburg.

2. Nesbitt, *Ghosts of Gettysburg IV*, 30.

3. Ibid., 22.

Chapter 36: Under the Spreading Chestnut Tree

1. National Park Service, *General Management Plan*.

2. Smith, *Farms at Gettysburg*, 8.

Chapter 37: Was the War Fought West of Gettysburg?

1. McPherson, *Battle Cry of Freedom*, 638.

2. Ward, *Civil War*, xix.

3. Leech, *Reveille in Washington*, 257.

4. McPherson, *Battle Cry of Freedom*, 665–65.

5. Leech, *Reveille in Washington*, 255–57.

6. McPherson, *Battle Cry of Freedom*, 638.

7. Wright, *Oxford Dictionary of Civil War Quotations*, 254.

8. Ibid., 253.
9. Ibid., 254.
10. Eaton, *Jefferson Davis*, 183.
11. Ibid., 184.
12. Hendrick, *Statesmen of the Lost Cause*, 230.

Appendix: The Fog of Order

1. Flagel, *History Buff's Guide to the Civil War*, 117–24.
2. Gottfried, *Brigades of Gettysburg*, 584.
3. Moe, *Last Full Measure*, 267.
4. Ibid., 281.
5. Coffin, *Nine Months to Gettysburg*, 169–70.
6. Busey and Martin, *Regimental Strengths and Losses*, 345.

Bibliography

Adelman, Gary. *The Early Gettysburg Battlefield: Selected Photographs from the Gettysburg National Military Park Commission Reports, 1895–1904.* Gettysburg: Thomas Publications, 2001.

———. *Little Round Top: A Detailed Tour Guide.* Gettysburg: Thomas Publications, 2000.

———. *The Myth of Little Round Top.* Gettysburg: Thomas Publications, 2003.

———, and Timothy Smith. *Devil's Den: A History and Guide.* Gettysburg: Thomas Publications, 1997.

Alleman, Tillie. *At Gettysburg, or What a Girl Saw and Heard of the Battle.* 1889. Reprint, Baltimore, MD: Butternut and Blue, 1987.

Andrews, Mary Raymond Shipman. *The Perfect Tribute.* New York: Scribner, 1906.

Archer, John. *The Hour Was One of Horror: East Cemetery Hill at Gettysburg.* Gettysburg: Thomas Publications, 1997.

Arrington, B. T. *The Medal of Honor at Gettysburg.* Gettysburg: Thomas Publications, 1996.

Bandy, Ken, and Florence Freeland, comp. *The Gettysburg Papers.* 2 vols. Dayton, OH: Morningside Bookshop, 1986.

Basler, J. H. *The Color Episode of the One Hundred and Forty-ninth Regiment Pennsylvania Volunteers in the First Day's Fight at Gettysburg, July 1st, 1863.* Baltimore, MD: Butternut and Blue, 1983.

Baumgartner, Richard. *Buckeye Blood: Ohio at Gettysburg.* Huntington, WV: Blue Acorn Press, 2003.

Becker, Bernie. "A Man Called Harrison." *America's Civil War* (November 2004): 46–50.

Beitler, Lewis Eugene, ed. *Fiftieth Anniversary of the Battle of Gettysburg.* Rev. ed. Harrisburg, PA: W. S. Ray, 1915.

Bennett, Gerald. *Days of Uncertainty and Dread: The Ordeal Endured by the Citizens at Gettysburg.* Camp Hill, PA: Gerald Bennett, 1994.

Bertera, Martin, and Ken Oberholtzer. *The 4th Michigan Volunteer Infantry at Gettysburg: The Battle for the Wheatfield*. Dayton, OH: Morningside House, 1997.

Bigelow, John. *The Peach Orchard: Gettysburg, July 2, 1863*. 1910. Reprint, Baltimore, MD: Butternut and Blue, 1984.

Bloom, Richard. *"We Never Expected a Battle": The Civilians at Gettysburg, 1863*. Gettysburg: Adams County Historical Society, 1988.

Bolin, Larry. "Slaveholders and Slaves in Adams County." *Adams County History* 9 (2003): 8–35.

Bond, W. R. *Pickett or Pettigrew? An Historical Essay*. 1888. Reprint, Gaithersburg, MD: Butternut Press, 1984.

Boritt, Gabor. *The Gettysburg Gospel: The Lincoln Speech That Nobody Knows*. New York: Simon & Schuster, 2006.

———, ed. *The Gettysburg Nobody Knows*. New York: Oxford University Press, 1997.

Bowden, Scott, and Bill Ward. *Last Chance for Victory: Robert E. Lee and the Gettysburg Campaign*. Cambridge, MA: Da Capo Press, 2001.

Broadhead, Sarah. *The Diary of a Lady of Gettysburg, Pennsylvania from June 15 to July 15, 1863*. Hershey, PA: Gary T. Hawbaker, 1990.

Brooke-Rawle, William. *The Right Flank at Gettysburg*. Philadelphia: Philadelphia Weekly Times, 1878.

Brown, Herbert, and Dwight Nitz. *Fields of Glory: The Facts Book of the Battle of Gettysburg*. Gettysburg: Thomas Publications 1990.

Brown, Kent Masterson. *Cushing of Gettysburg: The Story of Union Artillery Commander*. Lexington: University of Kentucky Press, 1993.

———. *Retreat from Gettysburg: Lee, Logistics and the Pennsylvania Campaign*. Chapel Hill: University of North Carolina Press, 2005.

Busey, John W. *The Last Full Measure: Burials in the Soldiers' National Cemetery at Gettysburg*. Hightstown, NJ: Longstreet House, 1988.

———. *These Honored Dead: The Union Casualties at Gettysburg*. Hightstown, NJ: Longstreet House, 1988.

———, and David Martin. *Regimental Strengths at Gettysburg*. Baltimore, MD: Gateway Press, 1982.

———, and David Martin. *Regimental Strengths and Losses at Gettysburg*. Hightstown, NJ: Longstreet House 1986.

————, and David Martin. *Regimental Strengths and Losses at Gettysburg*. 4th ed. Hightstown, NJ: Longstreet House, 2005.

Caba, G. Craig, ed. *Episodes of Gettysburg and the Underground Railroad as Witnessed by Prof. Howard J. Wert*. Gettysburg: C. Craig Caba Antiques, 1998.

Callihan, David. "JEB Stuart's Fateful Ride." *Gettysburg Magazine* 24 (January 2001): 8–10.

Carper, Denise, and Renae Hardoby. *The Gettysburg Battlefield Farmstead Guide*. Gettysburg: Friends of the National Park, 2000.

Catton, Bruce. *Gettysburg: The Final Fury*. Garden City, NY: Doubleday Press, 1974.

Chamberlain, Joshua. *Through Blood and Fire: Gettysburg*. Gettysburg: Stan Clark Military Books, 1994.

Christ, Elwood. *The Struggle of the Bliss Farm at Gettysburg: July 2nd and 3rd 1863*. Baltimore, MD: Butternut and Blue, 1992.

Clark, Champ, ed. *Gettysburg: The Confederate High Tide*. Alexandria, VA: Time-Life Books, 1985.

Cleaves, Freeman. *Meade of Gettysburg*. Dayton, OH: Morningside, 1980.

Coco, Gregory. *Confederates Killed in Action at Gettysburg*. Gettysburg: Thomas Publications, 2001.

————. *A Concise Guide to the Artillery at Gettysburg*. Gettysburg: Thomas Publications, 1998.

————. *Gettysburg's Confederate Dead*. Gettysburg: Thomas Publications, 2003.

————. *Killed in Action: Eyewitness Accounts of the Last Moments of 100 Union Soldiers Who Died at Gettysburg*. Gettysburg: Thomas Publications, 1992.

————. *On the Bloodstained Field*. Gettysburg: Thomas Publications, 1987.

————. *On the Bloodstained Field II*. Gettysburg: Thomas Publications, 1989.

————. *Recollections of a Texas Colonel at Gettysburg*. Gettysburg: Thomas Publications, 1990.

————. *A Strange and Blighted Land—Gettysburg: The Aftermath of Battle*. Gettysburg: Thomas Publications, 1995.

————. *A Vast Sea of Misery: A History and Guide to the Union and Confed-*

erate Field Hospitals at Gettysburg, July1—November 20, 1863. Gettysburg: Thomas Publications, 1988.

————. *War Stories: A Collection of 150 Little Known Human Interest Accounts of the Campaign and Battle of Gettysburg.* Gettysburg: Thomas Publications, 1992.

————. *Waster Valor: The Confederate Dead at Gettysburg.* Gettysburg: Thomas Publications, 1990.

Coddington, Edwin. *The Gettysburg Campaign: A Study in Command.* 1968. Reprint, Dayton, OH: Morningside Press, 1979.

Coffin, Howard. *Nine Months to Gettysburg: Stannard's Vermonters and the Repulse of Pickett's Charge.* Woodstock, VT: Countryman Press, 1997.

Cohen, Stanley. *Hands Across the Wall: The 50th and 75th Reunions of the Gettysburg Battle.* Charleston, WV: Pictorial Histories Publishing, 1997.

Cole, James, and Roy Frampton. *Lincoln and the Human Interest Stories of the Gettysburg National Cemetery.* Hanover, PA: Sheridan Press, 1995.

Comte de Paris. *The Battle of Gettysburg.* Baltimore, MD: Butternut and Blue, 1987.

Cox, John D. *Culp's Hill: The Attack and Defense of the Union Flank, July 2, 1863.* Cambridge, MA: Da Capo Press, 2003.

Creighton, Margaret S. *The Colors of Courage: Gettysburg's Forgotten History.* New York: Basic Books, 2005.

————. "Living on the Fault Line: African American Civilians and the Gettysburg Campaign." In *The War That Was You and Me: Civilians in the American Civil War,* edited by Joan E. Cashin, 209–36. Princeton: Princeton University Press, 2002.

Crumb, Herb, ed. *The Eleventh Corps Artillery at Gettysburg: The Papers of Major Thomas Ward Osborn, Chief of Artillery.* Hamilton, NY: Edmonston Publishing, 1991.

Custer, Andie. *Commanders at Gettysburg.* Gettysburg: Friends of the National Parks, 2001.

————. *The States at Gettysburg.* Gettysburg: Friends of the National Parks, 2002.

Dalton, Pete, and Cyndi Dalton. *Into the Valley of Death: The Story of the 4th Maine Volunteer Infantry at the Battle of Gettysburg July 2, 1863.* Union, ME: Union Publishing Co., 1994.

Desjardin, Thomas. *These Honored Dead: How the Story of Gettysburg Shaped American Memory*. Cambridge, MA: Da Capo Press, 2003.

Discorfano, Ken. *They Save the Union at Little Round Top*. Gettysburg: Thomas Publications, 2002.

Doubleday, Abner. *Gettysburg Made Plain*. New York: Century Co., 1909.

Dougherty, James. *Stones' Brigade and the Fight for McPherson Farm: Battle of Gettysburg, July 1, 1863*. Conshohocken, PA: Combined Publishing, 2001.

Dowdey, Clifford. *Death of a Nation: The Story of Lee and His Men at Gettysburg*. Baltimore, MD: Butternut and Blue, 1988.

————. *The History of the Confederacy 1832–1865*. New York: Marlboro Press, 1992.

Downey, Fairfax. *The Guns of Gettysburg*. 1958. Reprint, Gaithersburg, MD: Butternut Press, 1985.

Dreese, Michael. *The Hospital on Seminary Ridge at the Battle of Gettysburg*. Jefferson, NC: McFarland & Company, 2002.

————. *Never Desert the Old Flag: 50 Stories of Union Battle Flags and Color-Bearers at Gettysburg*. Gettysburg: Thomas Publications, 2002.

————. *This Flag Never Goes Down: 40 Stories of Confederate Battle Flags and Color-Bearers at Gettysburg*. Gettysburg: Thomas Publications, 2004.

Dudley, William W. *The Iron Brigade at Gettysburg: Official Report of the Part Borne by the 1st Brigade, 1st Division, 1st Army Crops, Army of the Potomac in Action at Gettysburg, Pennsylvania, July 1st, 2nd, and 3rd, 1863*. 1879. Reprint, Baltimore, MD: Butternut and Blue, 2001.

Dunkelman, Mark. *The Coster Ave. Mural in Gettysburg*. Providence, RI: Mark Dunkelman, 1989.

Eaton, Clement. *Jefferson Davis*. New York: Free Press, 1977.

Eckenrode, H. J., and Bryan Conrad. *James Longstreet: Lee's War Horse*. Chapel Hill: University of North Carolina Press, 1986,

Editors of Time-Life Books. *Gettysburg*. Voices of the Civil War. Alexandria, VA: Time-Life Books, 1995.

Eicher, David. *Gettysburg Battlefield: The Definitive Illustrated History*. San Francisco, CA: Chronicle Books, 2003.

Fahle, Michael. *The Best the Union Could Muster: The True Story of Berdan's U.S. Sharpshooters at the Battle of Gettysburg*. Lindsey, OH: Greencoat Productions, 1998.

Faust, Patricia L., ed. *Historical Times Illustrated Encyclopedia of the Civil War*. New York: Harper Collins, 1986.

Fennel, Charles. *Battle for the Barb: the Attack and Defense of Culp's Hill on July 2, 1863*. Gettysburg: Friends of the National Parks of Gettysburg, 2001.

Ferguson, Ernest. *Chancellorsville 1863*. New York: Knopf, 1992.

Fiebeger, Gustav J. *The Campaign and Battle of Gettysburg*. New Oxford, PA: Bloodstone Press, 1984.

Flagel, Thomas R. *The History Buff's Guide to the Civil War*. Nashville: Cumberland House, 2003.

———, and Ken Allers Jr. *The History Buff's Guide to Gettysburg*. Nashville: Cumberland House, 2006.

Foote, Shelby. *The Civil War: A Narrative—Red River to Appomattox*. New York: Random House, 1974.

———. *Stars in Their Courses: The Gettysburg Campaign*. New York: Modern Library Edition, 1994.

Fox, William F. *Regimental Losses in the American Civil War, 1861–1865*. Albany: Albany Publishing Co., 1889.

Frassanito, William. *Early Photography at Gettysburg*. Gettysburg: Thomas Publications, 1995.

———. *Gettysburg: A Journey in Time*. New York: Scribner, 1975.

———. *Gettysburg: Then and Now—Touring the Battlefield with Old Photos, 1863–1889*. Gettysburg: Thomas Publications, 1996.

———. *The Gettysburg: Then and Now Companion*. Gettysburg: Thomas Publications, 1997.

———. *The Gettysburg Bicentennial Album*. Gettysburg: Gettysburg Bicentennial Committee, 1987.

Freeman, Douglas Southall. *Lee's Lieutenants*. 3 vols. New York: Scribner, 1972.

Frinfrock, Barbara, ed. *Mr. Lincoln's Army: The Army of the Potomac in the Gettysburg Campaign*. Programs of the Sixth Annual Gettysburg Seminar. Gettysburg: Gettysburg National Military Park, 1997.

———, ed. *Unsung Heroes of Gettysburg*. Programs of the Fifth Annual Gettysburg Seminar. Gettysburg: Gettysburg National Military Park, 1996.

Gallagher, Gary W. "Confederate Corps Leadership on the First Day at Gettysburg: A. P. Hill and Richard S. Ewell in a Difficult Debut." In *The First Day at Gettysburg: Essays on Confederate and Union Leadership*, ed. Gary W. Gallagher, 30–56. Kent, OH: Kent State University Press, 1992.

―――, ed. *The First Day at Gettysburg: Essays on Confederate and Union Leadership*. Kent, OH: Kent State University Press, 1992.

―――. "If the Enemy Is There We Must Attack Him: R. E. Lee and the Second Day at Gettysburg." In *The Second Day at Gettysburg: Essays on Confederate and Union Leadership*, edited by Gary W. Gallagher, 1–32. Kent, OH: Kent State University Press, 1993.

―――. *Lee and His Army in Confederate History*. Chapel Hill: University of North Carolina Press, 2001.

―――, ed. *The Second Day at Gettysburg: Essays on Confederate and Union Leadership*. Kent, OH: Kent State University Press, 1993.

―――, ed. *The Third Day at Gettysburg and Beyond*. Chapel Hill: University of North Carolina Press, 1994.

Gambone, A. M. *Hancock at Gettysburg and Beyond*. Baltimore, MD: Butternut and Blue, 1997.

Georg, Kathleen, and John Busey. *Nothing But Glory: Pickett's Division at Gettysburg*. Hightstown, NJ: Longstreet Press, 1987.

Gettysburg National Military Park. *The Gettysburg Campaign and the First Day of Battle: Papers of the Tenth Gettysburg National Military Park Seminar*. Gettysburg: Gettysburg National Military Park, 2005.

Gottfried, Bradley. *Brigades at Gettysburg: The Union and Confederate Brigades at the Battle of Gettysburg*. Cambridge, MA: Da Capo Press, 2002.

―――. *Roads to Gettysburg: Lee's Invasion of the North, 1863*. Shippensburg, PA: White Mane Books, 2001.

Gragg, Rod. *Covered with Glory: The 26th North Carolina Infantry at the Battle of Gettysburg*. New York: HarperCollins, 2000.

Green, A. Wilson. "From Gettysburg to Falling Waters." In *The Third Day at Gettysburg and Beyond*, edited by Gary W. Gallagher, 161–202. Chapel Hill: University of North Carolina Press, 1994.

Grimm, Herbert, and Paul Roy. *Human Interest Stories of the Three Days Battles at Gettysburg*. Gettysburg: Times and News Publishing, 1927.

Hall, Jeffrey. *The Stand of the U.S. Army at Gettysburg*. Bloomington: University of Indiana Press, 2003.

Harman, Troy. *Cemetery Hill: "The General Plan Was Unchanged."* Baltimore, MD: Butternut & Blue, 2001.

Harrison, Kathy Georg. *The Location of the Monuments, Markers, and Tablet on Gettysburg Battlefield*. Gettysburg: Thomas Publications, 1993.

Hartwig, D. Scott, and Ann Marie Hartwig. *Gettysburg: The Complete Pictorial of Battlefields Monuments*. Gettysburg: Thomas Publications, 1995.

Hassler, Warren. *Crisis at the Crossroads: The First Day at Gettysburg*. Gaithersburg, MD, Butternut Press, 1986.

Hassler, William. *A. P. Hill: Lee's Forgotten General*. Chapel Hill: University of North Carolina Press, 1962.

Hawthorne, Frederick. *Gettysburg: Stories of Men and Monuments as Told by Battlefield Guides*. Hanover, PA: Sheridan Press, 1988.

Hendrick, Burton. *Statesmen of the Lost Cause: Jefferson Davis and His Cabinet*. New York: Literary Guild of America, 1939.

Herdegen, Lance, and William Beaudot. *In the Bloody Railroad Cut at Gettysburg*. Dayton, OH: Morningside Bookshop, 1990.

Hess, Earl. *Pickett's Charge: The Last Attack at Gettysburg*. Chapel Hill: University of North Carolina Press, 2001.

Hillyer, George. *My Gettysburg Battle Experiences*. Gettysburg: Thomas Publications, 2005.

History Gettysburg–Adams County and the Hospital and Healthsystem Association of Pennsylvania. *Gettysburg Civil War Field Hospital Tour*. Gettysburg: History Gettysburg–Adams County and the Hospital and Healthsystem Association of Pennsylvania, 2001.

Hofe, Michael. *That There Be No Stain Upon My Stones: Lt. Col. William L. McLeod, 38th Georgia Regiment, 1843–1863*. Gettysburg: Thomas Publications, 1995.

Hoisington, Daniel. *Gettysburg and the Christian Commission*. Roseville, MN: Edinborough Press, 2002.

Howard, William. *The Gettysburg Death Roster: The Federal Dead at Gettysburg*. Dayton, OH: Morningside Bookshop, 1990.

Hunt, Henry. *Three Days at Gettysburg: July 1, 2, & 3, 1863*. Golden, CO: Outbooks, 1981.

Hyde, Bill, ed. *The Union Generals Speak: The Meade Hearings on the Battle of Gettysburg.* Baton Rouge: Louisiana State University Press, 2003.

Imhof, John D. *Gettysburg: Day Two: A Study in Maps.* Baltimore, MD: Butternut and Blue, 1999.

Joint Committee, Report. *Positions Occupied by the 1st and 2nd Delaware Regiments at the Battle of Gettysburg, July 2nd and 3rd, 1863.* Hightstown, NJ: Longstreet House, 1998.

Jones, Terry L. *Cemetery Hill: The Struggle For the High Ground, July 1–2, 1963.* Cambridge, MA: Da Capo Press, 2003.

Jorgensen, Jay. *Gettysburg's Bloody Wheatfield.* Shippensburg, PA: White Mane Books, 2002.

———. *The Wheatfield at Gettysburg: A Walking Tour.* Gettysburg: Thomas Publications, 2002.

Judson, Amos. *History of the Eighty-third Regiment Pennsylvania Volunteers.* Alexandria, VA: Stonewall House, 1985.

Kegel, James. *North with Lee and Jackson: The Lost Story of Gettysburg.* Mechanicsburg, PA: Stackpole Books, 1996.

Kelly, Michael. *"I Will Have Justice Done": Gen. Gouverneur K. Warren, USA.* Gettysburg: Farnsworth Military Impressions, 1997.

Kennell, Brian. *Beyond the Gatehouse: Gettysburg's Evergreen Cemetery.* Gettysburg: Evergreen Cemetery Association, 2000

Kowalis, Jeffrey, and Loree Kowalis. *Died at Gettysburg! "No Prouder Epitaph Need Any Man Covet."* Hightstown, NJ: Longstreet House, 1998.

Krick, Robert. *The Gettysburg Death Roster: The Confederate Dead at Gettysburg.* Dayton, OH: Morningside Bookshop, 1981.

Krick, Robert K., and Chris L. Ferguson. *The Gettysburg Death Roster: The Confederate Dead at Gettysburg.* 4th ed. Dayton, OH: Morningside Bookshop Press, 2004.

Krumweide, John F. *"Old Waddy's Coming": The Military Career of Brigadier General James Wadsworth.* Baltimore, MD: Butternut and Blue Press, 2002.

Ladd, David, and Audrey Ladd, eds. *John Bachelder's History of the Battle of Gettysburg.* Dayton, OH: Morningside Bookshop, 1997.

Ladd, David, and Audrey Sauers, eds. *The Bachelder Papers: Gettysburg in Their Own Words.* Vol. 1: January 5, 1863 to July 27, 1880. Dayton, OH: Morningside Bookshop, 1994.

————, eds. *The Bachelder Papers: Gettysburg in Their Own Words*. Vol. 2: September 6, 1880 to April 12, 1886. Dayton, OH: Morningside Bookshop, 1994.

————, eds. *The Bachelder Papers: Gettysburg in Their Own Words*. Vol. 3: April 12, 1886 to December 22, 1894. Dayton, OH: Morningside Bookshop, 1995.

LaFantasie, Glenn. *Twilight at Little Round Top: July 2 1863—The Tide Turns at Gettysburg*. Hoboken, NJ: Wiley, 2005.

————, ed. *Lt. Frank Haskell, U.S.A., and Col. William C. Oates, C.S.A.: Gettysburg*. New York: Bantam Books, 1992.

Lash, Gary. *The Gibraltar Brigade on East Cemetery Hill*. Baltimore, MD: Butternut and Blue, 1995.

Latimer, Marian. *"Is She Kate?" The Woman Major General John Fulton Reynolds Left Behind*. Gettysburg: Farnsworth Military Impressions, 2005.

Lee, Alfred E. *The Battle of Gettysburg*. Ohio Memorials at Gettysburg. 1888. Reprint, Baltimore, MD: Butternut and Blue, 1998.

Leech, Margaret. *Reveille in Washington*. New York: Harper and Brothers, 1942.

Livermore, Thomas L. *Number and Losses in the Civil War in America, 1861–65*. Boston: Houghton Mifflin, 1901.

Longacre, Edward. *The Cavalry at Gettysburg*. Cranbury, NJ: Associated University Press, 1986.

————. *General John Buford: A Military Biography*. Cambridge, MA: Da Capo Press, 1985.

Longstreet, James. *From Manassas to Appomattox*. New York: Mallard Press, 1991.

Loski, Diana. *Gettysburg Experience: A Biographical Collection*. Gettysburg: Princess Publications, 2002.

Luvas, Jay, and Harold W. Nelson, eds. *The U.S. Army War College Guide to the Battle of Gettysburg*. Carlisle, PA: South Mountain Press, 1986.

MacLachlan, Renae. *Our Bravest and Best: The Iron Brigade at Gettysburg*. Gettysburg: Friends of the National Park, 2001.

Magner, Blake A. *Traveller and Company: The Horses of Gettysburg*. Gettysburg: Farnsworth Military Impressions. 1995

Maine, Gettysburg Commission. *Maine at Gettysburg: Report of the Maine Commissioners Prepared by the Executive Committee*. 1898. Reprint, Gettysburg: Stan Clark Military Books, 1994.

Martin, David G. *Confederate Monuments at Gettysburg: The Gettysburg Battle Monuments*. Hightstown, NJ: Longstreet House, 1986.

———. *Gettysburg, July 1*. Conshohocken, PA: Combined Books, 1996.

Marvel, William. *The First New Hampshire Battery, 1861–1865*. Conway, NH: Minuteman Press, 1985.

Maust, Roland. *Grappling with Death: The Union Second Corps Hospital at Gettysburg*. Dayton, OH: Morningside Bookshop, 2001.

McDonald, JoAnna. *The Faces of Gettysburg: Photographs from the Gettysburg National Military Park Library*. Redondo Beach, CA: Rank and File Publications, 1997.

McIntosh, Davie Gregg. *Review of the Gettysburg Campaign*. Falls Church, VA: Confederate Printers, 1984.

McLaughlin, Jack. *Gettysburg, The Long Encampment*. New York: Appleton-Century, 1963.

McLean, James, and Judy McLean, eds. *Gettysburg Sources Volume I*. Baltimore, MD: Butternut and Blue, 1986.

———, eds. *Gettysburg Sources Volume II*. Baltimore, MD: Butternut and Blue, 1987.

———, eds. *Gettysburg Sources Volume III*. Baltimore, MD: Butternut and Blue, 1990.

McLean, James, Jr. *Cutler's Brigade at Gettysburg*. Baltimore, MD: Butternut and Blue, 1987.

McNeily, J. S. *Barksdale's Mississippi Brigade at Gettysburg*. Gaithersburg, MD: Olde Soldier Books, 1987.

McPherson, James. *Battle Cry of Freedom: The Civil War Era*. New York: Oxford University Press, 1988.

Meligakes, Nicholas A. *Gettysburg: The National Shrine*. Gettysburg: N. A. Meligakes, 1948.

———. *The Story of Gettysburg in Pictures*. Gettysburg: N. A. Meligakes, n.d.

Michigan, Gettysburg Battle Field Commission. *Michigan at Gettysburg: Proceedings Incident to the Dedication of the Michigan Monuments upon the Battlefield of Gettysburg, June 12th, 1889*. Detroit: Winn & Hammond, 1889.

Moe, Richard. *The Last Full Measure: The Life and Death of the First Minnesota Volunteers*. New York: Henry Holt, 1993.

Motts, Wayne. *"Trust in God and Fear Nothing": Gen. Lewis Armistead, CSA*. Gettysburg: Farnsworth House Military Impressions, 1994.

Murray, R. L. *E. P. Alexander and the Artillery Action in the Peach Orchard*. Wolcott, NY: Benedum Books, 2000.

———. *"Nothing Could Exceed Their Bravery": New Yorkers in Defense of Little Round Top*. Wolcott, NY: Benedum Books, 1999.

———. *A Perfect Storm of Lead: George Sears Greene's New York in Defense of Culp's Hill*. Wolcott, NY: Benedum Books, 20002.

———. *The Redemption of the "Harper's Ferry Cowards": The 111th and 126th New York State Volunteers at Gettysburg*. Wolcott, NY: Benedum Books, 1994.

National Park Service. *General Management Plan and Environment Impact Statement*. Gettysburg: Gettysburg National Military Park, 1998.

Nesbitt, Mark. *35 Days to Gettysburg: The Campaign Diaries of Two American Enemies*. Harrisburg, PA: Stackpole Books, 1992.

Nesbitt, Mark. *Ghosts of Gettysburg IV: Spirits, Apparitions, ad Haunted Places of the Battlefield*. Gettysburg: Thomas Publications, 1998.

New York Monuments Commission for the Battlefields of Gettysburg and Chattanooga. *Final Report of the Battlefield of Gettysburg*. 3 vols. Albany: J. B. Lyon, 1900.

Newton, Steven. *McPherson's Ridge: The First Battle for the High Ground*. Cambridge, MA: Da Capo Press, 2002.

Nicholson, John P., et al., eds. *Pennsylvania at Gettysburg*. 2 vols. Harrisburg, PA: E. K. Meyers, 1893.

Nicholson, John P., et al., eds. *Pennsylvania at Gettysburg*. 4 vols. Harrisburg, PA: William Stanley Ray, State Printer, 1914.

Nofi, Albert. *The Gettysburg Campaign: June and July 1863*. New York: Gallery Books, 1986.

Norton, Oliver. *The Attack and Defense of Little Round Top, Gettysburg, July 2, 1863*. Dayton, OH: Morningside Bookshop, 1978.

Osborne, Charles C. *Jubal: The Life and Times of General Jubal A. Early,*

CSA—Defender of the Lost Cause. Baton Rouge: Louisiana State University Press, 1994.

Osborne, Seward. *Holding the Left at Gettysburg: The 20th New York State Militia on July 1, 1863*. Hightstown, NJ: Longstreet House, 1990.

Paradis, James M. *African Americans and the Gettysburg Campaign*. Lanham, MD: Scarecrow Press, 2005.

Patterson, Gerald. *Debris of Battle: The Wounded of Gettysburg*. Mechanicsburg, PA: Stackpole Books, 1997.

Penny, Morris, and J. Gary Lane. *Struggle for the Round Tops: Law's Alabama Brigade at the Battle of Gettysburg*. Shippensburg, PA: Burd Street Press, 1999.

Perisco, Joseph. *My Enemy, My Brother: Men and Days of Gettysburg*. Cambridge, MA: Da Capo Press, 1996.

Perry, Mark. *Conceived in Liberty: Joshua Chamberlain, William Oates, and the American Civil War*. New York: Viking Press, 1997.

Pfanz, Harry. *Gettysburg—Culp's Hill and Cemetery Hill*. Chapel Hill: University of North Carolina Press, 1993.

———. *Gettysburg—The First Day*. Chapel Hill: University of North Carolina Press, 2001.

———. *Gettysburg—The Second Day*. Chapel Hill: University of North Carolina Press, 1987.

Phipps, Michael, and John S. Peters. *"The Devil's to Pay": Gen. John Buford, USA*. Gettysburg: Farnsworth House Military Impressions, 1995.

Pinchon, Edgcumb. *Dan Sickles: Hero of Gettysburg and "Yankee King of Spain."* Garden City, NY: Doubleday, Doran and Company, 1945.

Piston, William G. "Cross Purposes: Longstreet, Lee, and the Confederate Attack Plans for July 3 at Gettysburg." In *The Third Day at Gettysburg and Beyond*, edited by Gary W. Gallagher, 31–55. Chapel Hill: University of North Carolina Press, 1994.

Pitts, Calista. *Gettysburg Addresses*. Gettysburg, PA. Calista Pitts, 1987.

Platt, Barbara. *"This is Holy Ground": A History of the Gettysburg Battlefield*. Harrisburg, PA: Huggins Printing, 2001.

Powell, Walter, ed. *Connecticut Yankees at Gettysburg by Charles P. Hamblen*. Kent, OH: Kent State University Press, 1993.

Priest, John. *Into the Fight: Pickett's Charge at Gettysburg*. Shippensburg, PA: White Mane Books, 1998.

Prowell, George R. *History of the 87th Pennsylvania Volunteers*. York, PA: Press of the York Daily, 1901.

Raus, Edmund, Jr. *A Generation on the March: The Union Army at Gettysburg*. Gettysburg: Thomas Publications, 1996.

Reardon, Carol. *Pickett's Charge in History and Memory*. Chapel Hill: University of North Carolina Press, 1997.

Riggs, David F. *East of Gettysburg: Custer vs. Stuart*. Fort Collins, CO: Old Army Press, 1970.

Riley, Michael A. *"For God's Sake Forward!" Gen. John F. Reynolds, USA*. Gettysburg: Farnsworth Military Impressions, 1995.

Robertson, James I., Jr. *General A. P. Hill The Story of a Confederate Warrior*. New York: Vintage Civil War Books, 1992.

———. *The Stonewall Brigade*. Baton Rouge: Louisiana State University Press, 1985.

———. *Stonewall Jackson: The Man, the Soldier, the Legend*. New York: Macmillan, 1997.

Rollins, Richard. *The Damned Red Flags of the Rebellion: The Confederate Battle Flag at Gettysburg*. Redondo Beach, CA: Rank and File Publications, 1997.

———, ed. *Pickett's Charge! Eyewitness Account*. Redondo Beach, CA: Rank and File, 1994.

———, and David Shultz. *Guide to Pennsylvania Troops at Gettysburg*. Redondo Beach, CA: Rank and File Publications, 1998.

Root, Edwin R., and Jeffrey Stocker. *"Isn't This Glorious!" The 15th, 19th, and 20th Massachusetts Volunteer Infantry Regiments at Gettysburg's Copse of Trees*. Bethlehem, PA: Moon Trail Books, 2006.

Roy, Paul, comp. *Pennsylvania at Gettysburg: The Seventy-fifth Anniversary of the Battle of Gettysburg, Report of the Pennsylvania Commission*. Vol. 4. Gettysburg: Times and News Publishing Co., 1939.

Sauers, Richard. *A Caspian Sea of Ink: The Meade-Sickles Controversy*. Baltimore, MD: Butternut and Blue, 1989.

———, ed. *Fighting Them Over: How the Veterans Remembered Gettysburg in the Pages of the National Tribune*. Baltimore, MD: Butternut and Blue, 1998.

———. *The Gettysburg Campaign: June 3—August 1, 1863: A Comprehen-*

sive Selectively Annotated Bibliography. Baltimore, MD: Butternut and Blue Books, 2004.

———, and Peter Tomasak. *Ricketts' Battery: A History of Battery F, 1st Pennsylvania Light Artillery*. Luzerne, PA: Luzerne National Bank, 2001.

Schildt, John. *Roads from Gettysburg*. Chewsville, MD: John Schildt, 1979.

———. *Roads to Gettysburg*. Parsons, WV: McClain Printing Co., 1978.

Schultz, David. "Double Canister at Ten Yards": The Federal Artillery and The Repulse of Pickett's Charge. Redondo Beach, CA: Rank and File Publications: 1995.

———, and David Wieck. *The Battle Between the Farm Lanes*. Columbus, OH: Ironclad Publishing, 2006.

Scott, James P. K. *The Story of the Battles at Gettysburg*. Harrisburg, PA: Telegraph Press, 1927.

Sears, Stephen W. *Gettysburg*. New York: Houghton Mifflin, 2003.

Selcer, Richard. *"Faithfully and Forever Your Soldier": Gen. George E. Pickett, CSA*. Gettysburg: Farnsworth House Military Impressions, 1995.

Select Committee Relative to the Soldiers' National Cemetery. *Soldiers' National Cemetery—Gettysburg*. 1865. Reprint, Gettysburg: Thomas Publications, 1988.

Sessarego, Alan. *Letters Home V: Gettysburg!* Gettysburg: Americana Gifts & Souvenirs, 2003.

Shue, Richard S. *Morning at Willoughby Run: July 1, 1863*. Gettysburg: Thomas Publications, 1995.

Skelly, Daniel Alexander. *A Boy's Experiences During the Battles of Gettysburg*. Hershey, PA: Gary T. Hawbaker, n.d.

Slade, Jim, and John Alexander. *Firestorm at Gettysburg: Civilian Voices, June–November 1863*. Atglen, PA: Schiffer Publishing, 1998.

Small, Cindy L. *The Jennie Wade Story*. Gettysburg: Thomas Publications, 1991.

Smith, Timothy. *Farms at Gettysburg: The Fields of Gettysburg*. Gettysburg: Thomas Publications, 2007.

———. *Gettysburg's Battlefield Photographer: William H. Tipton*. Gettysburg: Thomas Publications, 2005.

———. *John Burns: The Hero of Gettysburg*. Gettysburg: Thomas Publications, 2000.

————. *The Story of Lee's Headquarters: Gettysburg Pennsylvania*. Gettysburg: Thomas Publications, 1995.

Storrick, W. C. *The Battle of Gettysburg*. Harrisburg, PA: J. Horace McDonald, 1953.

————. *Gettysburg: The Places, the Battles, the Outcome*. Harrisburg, PA: J. Horace McFarland, 1932.

Stouffer, Cindy, and Shirley Cubbison. *A Colonel, a Flag, and a Dog*. Gettysburg: Thomas Publications, 1998.

Swanberg, W. A. *Sickles the Incredible*. New York: Scribner, 1956.

Swinton, Wilton. *Campaigns of the Army of the Potomac*. New York: Charles B. Richardson, 1866.

Symonds, Craig. *Gettysburg: A Battlefield Atlas*. Baltimore, MD: Nautical and Aviation Publishing, 1992.

Tagg, Larry. *The Generals of Gettysburg*. Campbell, CA: Savas Publishing, 1998.

Taylor, Walter H. *General Lee, His Campaigns in Virginia, 1861–1865*. Brooklyn, NY: Braunworth & Co., 1906.

Teague, Charles. *Gettysburg by the Numbers*. Gettysburg: Adams County Historical Society, 2006.

Thomas, James E. *The First Day at Gettysburg: Walking Tour*. Gettysburg: Thomas Publications, 2005.

Tilberg, Frederick. *Gettysburg National Military Park Pennsylvania*. Washington DC: National Park Service Historical Handbook Series, 1954.

Toney, B. Keith. *Gettysburg: Tours and Tales with a Battlefield Guide*. Shepherdsville, KY: Publishers Press, 1994.

Toombs, Samuel. *New Jersey Troops in the Gettysburg Campaign*. Hightstown, NJ: Longstreet Press, 1988.

Toomey, Daniel. *Marylanders at Gettysburg*. Baltimore, MD: Toomey Press, 1994.

Trudeau, Noah. *Gettysburg: A Testing of Courage*. New York: HarperCollins, 2002.

Trulock, Alice Rains. *In the Hands of Providence: Joshua L. Chamberlain and the American Civil War*. Chapel Hill: University of North Carolina Press, 1992.

Tucker, Glenn. *High Tide at Gettysburg: The Campaign in Pennsylvania*. Dayton, OH: Morningside Bookshop, 1973.

————. *Lee and Longstreet at Gettysburg*. Indianapolis: Bobbs-Merrill, 1968.

Tucker, Phillip. *Storming Little Round Top*. Cambridge, MA: Da Capo Press, 2002.

Valuska, David, and Christian Keller. *Damn Dutch: Pennsylvania Germans at Gettysburg*. Mechanicsburg, PA: Stackpole Books, 2004.

Vanderslice, John. *Gettysburg: Then and Now*. Dayton, OH: Morningside Bookshop, 1983.

Venner, William. *Hoosier's Honor Roster: The Iron Brigade's 19th Indiana Regiment*. Shippensburg, PA: Burd Street Press, 1998.

————. *The 19th Indiana Infantry at Gettysburg: Hoosiers' Courage*. Shippensburg, PA: Burd Street Press, 1998.

Vermilyea, Peter C. "Jack Hopkins' Civil War." *Adams County History* 11 (2005): 9–15.

Walker, Paul D. *The Cavalry Battle That Saved the Union: Custer vs. Stuart at Gettysburg*. Gretna, LA: Pelican, 2002.

Ward, Geoffrey. *The Civil War*. New York: Knopf, 1990.

Wasel, Bob, and Mimi Johnson-Bosler. *A Soldier's Grave: Original Burial Sites on the Gettysburg Battlefield*. N.p.p.: Quick and Dirty Publications, 2000.

————, and Sarah Richardson. *The Gettysburg You Never Knew*. Gettysburg: Wasel/Richardson, 1996.

————, and Sarah Richardson. *More Gettysburg You Never Knew*. Gettysburg: Wasel/Richardson, 1997.

Wert, Jeffrey. *General James Longstreet: The Confederacy's Most Controversial Soldier*. New York: Simon and Schuster, 1993.

————. *Gettysburg: Day Three*. New York: Simon and Schuster, 2001.

Wheeler, Richard. *Witness to Gettysburg*. New York: Harper & Row, 1987.

Wilkinson, Warren, and Steven Woodworth. *A Scythe of Fire: A Civil War Story of the Eighth Georgia Infantry Regiment*. New York: HarperCollins, 2002.

Willis, Garry. *Lincoln at Gettysburg: The Words That Remade America*. New York: Touchstone, 1992.

Wittenberg, Eric. *Gettysburg's Forgotten Cavalry Actions*. Gettysburg: Thomas Publications, 1998.

————. *Protecting the Flank: The Battles of Brinkerhoff's Ridge and East*

Cavalry Field, Battle of Gettysburg, July 2–3, 1863. Celina, OH: Ironclad Publishing, 2002.

———, and J. David Petruzzi. *Plenty of Blame to Go Around: Jeb Stuart's Controversial Ride to Gettysburg.* New York: Savas Beattie, 2006.

Wright, John D. *The Oxford Dictionary of the Civil War Quotations.* New York: Oxford University Press, 2006.

Young, Emma. *They Will Remember: The Rupp Family, House and Tannery.* Gettysburg: Friends of the National Parks at Gettysburg, 2004.

Young, Jesse Bowman. *The Battle of Gettysburg.* Dayton, OH: Morningside Bookshop, 1976.

Other Sources: Periodicals

Adams County History, vols. 1–12. Gettysburg: Adams County Historical Society, 1995–2006.

The Gettysburg Magazine. vols. 1–38. Dayton, OH: Morningside Bookshop, 1989–2008.

Sanders, Steve. "Enduring Tales of Gettysburg: The Death of Reynolds." *Gettysburg Magazine* 14 (1996): 27–36.

Newspapers

Lexington (VA) Gazette
National Tribune

Maps

Desjardin, Thomas A. *Field Maps: Battle of Gettysburg, July 1, 2, 3 1863.* Friends of the National Parks at Gettysburg, Gettysburg, 1998.

The Batchelder Maps. Dayton, OH: Morningside Books, n.d.

Web Sites

Draw the Sword, http://www.drawthesword.goellnitz.org
Main Street Gettysburg, http://www.mainstreetgettysburg.org

The Civil War Home, http://www.civilwarhome.com/custerbi.htm

Miller, John Allen. "Emmitsburg and the Recoil of Gettysburg." http://www.emmitsburg.net/archive_list/articles/history/civil_war /emmitsburg_%20recoil_gettysburg.htm.

The New Jersey Civil War History Page. http://www.newjersey1861.com/

Petruzzi, J. David. "Who Shot General Reynolds?" *The Battle of Gettysburg Resource Center*, October 3, 2004, http://gburginfo.brinkster.net /reynolds.htm.

Virginia Military Institute Archives, http://www.vmi.edu/archives

Collections

Letters from the David and Alma Lang collection

Fulkerson Family Papers, Virginia Military Institute Archives

Jedediah Hotchkiss Papers, Winchester–Frederick County Historical Society, Winchester, VA

Index